CYBER 2019

The Fourth International Conference on Cyber-Technologies and Cyber-Systems

September 22 - 26, 2019

Porto, Portugal

CYBER 2019 Editors

Anne Coull, University of New South Wales, Information and Engineering, Australia

Steve Chan, Decision Engineering Analysis Laboratory, USA

Rainer Falk, Siemens AG, Corporate Technology, Germany

Printed from e-media with permission by:

Curran Associates, Inc.
57 Morehouse Lane
Red Hook, NY 12571

Printed with permission by Curran Associates, Inc. (2020)

International Academy, Research, and Industry Association (IARIA)
412 Derby Way
Wilmington, DE 19810

Phone: (408) 893-6407
Fax: (408) 527-6351

petre@iaria.org

Additional copies of this publication are available from:

Curran Associates, Inc.
57 Morehouse Lane
Red Hook, NY 12571 USA
Phone: 845-758-0400
Fax: 845-758-2633
Email: curran@proceedings.com
Web: www.proceedings.com

Table of Contents

CYBER 2019

Forward

The Fourth International Conference on Cyber-Technologies and Cyber-Systems (CYBER 2019), held between September 22-26, 2019 in Porto, Portugal, continued the inaugural event covering many aspects related to cyber-systems and cyber-technologies considering the issues mentioned above and potential solutions. It is also intended to illustrate appropriate current academic and industry cyber-system projects, prototypes, and deployed products and services.

The increased size and complexity of the communications and the networking infrastructures are making it difficult the investigation of the resiliency, security assessment, safety and crimes. Mobility, anonymity, counterfeiting, are characteristics that add more complexity in Internet of Things and Cloud-based solutions. Cyber-physical systems exhibit a strong link between the computational and physical elements. Techniques for cyber resilience, cyber security, protecting the cyber infrastructure, cyber forensic and cyber crimes have been developed and deployed. Some of new solutions are nature-inspired and social-inspired leading to self-secure and self-defending systems. Despite the achievements, security and privacy, disaster management, social forensics, and anomalies/crimes detection are challenges within cyber-systems.

The conference had the following tracks:

- Cyber security
- Cyber infrastructure
- Cyber Attack Surfaces and the Interoperability of Architectural Application Domain Resiliency
- Embedded Systems for the Internet of Things
- Cyber resilience

We take here the opportunity to warmly thank all the members of the CYBER 2019 technical program committee, as well as all the reviewers. The creation of such a high quality conference program would not have been possible without their involvement. We also kindly thank all the authors that dedicated much of their time and effort to contribute to CYBER 2018. We truly believe that, thanks to all these efforts, the final conference program consisted of top quality contributions.

We also gratefully thank the members of the CYBER 2019 organizing committee for their help in handling the logistics and for their work that made this professional meeting a success.

We hope that CYBER 2019 was a successful international forum for the exchange of ideas and results between academia and industry and to promote further progress in the domain cyber technologies and cyber systems. We also hope that Porto provided a pleasant environment during the conference and everyone saved some time to enjoy the historic charm of the city.

CYBER 2019 Chairs

CYBER Steering Committee

Carla Merkle Westphall, Federal University of Santa Catarina (UFSC), Brazil
Cong-Cong Xing, Nicholls State University, USA
Jean-Marc Robert, Polytechnique Montréal, Canada
Steve Chan, Decision Engineering Analysis Laboratory, USA
Jan Richling, South Westphalia University of Applied Sciences, Germany
Duminda Wijesekera , George Mason University, USA
Francesco Buccafurri, University Mediterranea of Reggio Calabria, Italy
Syed Naqvi, Birmingham City University, UK

CYBER Industry/Research Advisory Committee

Rainer Falk, Siemens AG, Corporate Technology, Germany
Cristina Serban, AT&T Security Research Center, Middletown, USA
Juan-Carlos Bennett, SSC Pacific, USA
Barbara Re, University of Camerino, Italy
Daniel Kaestner, AbsInt GmbH, Germany
George Yee, Carleton University / Aptusinnova Inc., Canada
Yao Yiping, National University of Defence Technology - Hunan, China
Thomas Klemas, SimSpace Corporation, USA

CYBER 2019

COMMITTEE

CYBER Steering Committee

Carla Merkle Westphall, Federal University of Santa Catarina (UFSC), Brazil
Cong-Cong Xing, Nicholls State University, USA
Jean-Marc Robert, Polytechnique Montréal, Canada
Steve Chan, Decision Engineering Analysis Laboratory, USA
Jan Richling, South Westphalia University of Applied Sciences, Germany
Duminda Wijesekera , George Mason University, USA
Francesco Buccafurri, University Mediterranea of Reggio Calabria, Italy
Syed Naqvi, Birmingham City University, UK

CYBER Industry/Research Advisory Committee

Rainer Falk, Siemens AG, Corporate Technology, Germany
Cristina Serban, AT&T Security Research Center, Middletown, USA
Juan-Carlos Bennett, SSC Pacific, USA
Barbara Re, University of Camerino, Italy
Daniel Kaestner, AbsInt GmbH, Germany
George Yee, Carleton University / Aptusinnova Inc., Canada
Yao Yiping, National University of Defence Technology - Hunan, China
Thomas Klemas, SimSpace Corporation, USA

CYBER 2019 Technical Program Committee

Abdulghani Ali Ahmed, Universiti Malaysia Pahang (UMP), Kuantan, Malaysia
Irfan Ahmed, University of New Orleans, USA
Hamzah Al-Najada, Florida Atlantic University, Boca Raton, USA
Khalid Alemerien, Tafila Technical University, Jordan
Abdullahi Arabo, Centre for Complex and Cooperative Systems - CSCT, UWE Bristol, UK
A. Taufiq Asyhari, Coventry University, UK
Hannan Azhar, Canterbury Christ Church University, UK
Liz Bacon, University of Greenwich, Old Royal Naval College, UK
Pooneh Bagheri Zadeh, Leeds Beckett University, UK
Hayretdin Bahşi, Tallinn University of Technology, Estonia
Morgan Barbier, GREYC - ENSICAEN, France
Najoua Essoukri Ben Amara, National Engineering School of Sousse | University of Sousse, Tunisia
Juan-Carlos Bennett, SSC Pacific, USA
Davidson Boccardo, Clavis Information Security, Brazil
Paul Bogdan, University of Southern California, USA
David Brosset, Naval Academy Research Institute, France
Francesco Buccafurri, University Mediterranea of Reggio Calabria, Italy
Steve Chan, Decision Engineering Analysis Laboratory, USA
Steve Chan, University of Colorado, Boulder, USA

Hossain Shahriar, College of Computing and Software Engineering - Kennesaw State University, USA
Thar Baker Shamsa, Liverpool John Moores University, UK
Zhihao Shang, Free University of Berlin, Germany
Sandeep Shukla, Virginia Tech, USA
Kristina Soukupova, I3CAS Ltd., Czech Republic
Angelo Spognardi, Sapienza University of Rome, Italy
Kuo-Feng Ssu, National Cheng Kung University, Taiwan
Marco Steger, Virtual Vehicle research center, Graz, Austria
Kazuo Takaragi, National Institute of Advanced Industrial Science and Technology (AIST), Japan
Eniye Tebekaemi, George Mason University, USA
Aderonke F. Thompson, Federal University of Technology, Akure, Nigeria
Panagiotis Trimintzios, EU Agency for Cybersecurity, Greece
Elochukwu Anthony Ukwandu, Edinburgh Napier University, Scotland
Timothy Vidas, Dell Secureworks, USA
Stefanos Vrochidis, Information Technologies Institute - Centre for Research and Technology Hellas, Greece
Khan Ferdous Wahid, Airbus, Munich, Germany
Peipei Wang, North Carolina State University, USA
Ruoyu (Fish) Wang, Arizona State University, USA
Duminda Wijesekera , George Mason University, USA
Zhen Xie, Paypal Inc, USA
Cong-Cong Xing, Nicholls State University, USA
Wuu Yang, National Chiao-Tung University, HsinChu, Taiwan
Mao Ye, University of Central Florida, USA
George Yee, Carleton University / Aptusinnova Inc., Canada
Yao Yiping, National University of Defence Technology - Hunan, China
Xiao Zhang, Palo Alto Networks, USA
Piotr Zwierzykowski, Poznan University of Technology, Poland

Copyright Information

Towards Secure Robot Process Automation Environments

Petri Jurmu
Connectivity Research Area
Technical Research Centre of Finland VTT
Oulu, Finland
email: Petri.Jurmu@vtt.fi

Abstract— **Information security is a part of the cyber security, but the information security will increasingly play a key role in securing and implementing cyber security operations in the future. A big challenge in deployment of robot process automation RPA is that organisations have to give an access to information for software robots like for authorised personnel. People have to take into account the information security and data protection as a basis for a risk assessment, when planning the processing of personal data. This report considers threats and vulnerabilities related to the RPA and examines the opportunities to improve security level in environments of the robot process automation. Observations of security risks are investigated in the case study part, where RPA is deployed in a public service system. Future work of a security assurance in RPA deployment is also described in this paper.**

Keywords-robot process automation; RPA; cyber security; mobiilimittari.

I. INTRODUCTION

Cyber security thinking combines the perspective of information security, continuity management and crisis management in today's society. Cyber security guarantees a rolling of wheels in our society and securing of critical functions in all circumstances. Information security is a part of the cyber security, but the information security will increasingly play a key role in securing and implementing cyber security operations in the future. People have to take the information security and data protection into account as a basis for a risk assessment, when planning a processing of personal data.

Robot process automation RPA develop an action list by repeating a user's performance for a workflow in an application's graphical user interface GUI. RPA is built with a trust on cornerstones of the information security, confidentiality, integrity and availability [1]. Undisputed and traceability of events are important aspects of protecting personal data. In the implementation of the RPA, routine tasks, that do not require a special discretion, are naturally fruitful from a viewpoint of an automation [2].

From an angle of cyber security, a big challenge of RPA deployment is that organisations have to give an access to information to software robots like to authorised personnel. Similarly, organisations have to give an access to a processing service to certain persons or software robots. It is important and in an interest of various parties to find ways to separate parts of the information or activities, which are necessary to be automated.

This paper gives practical information for a deployment of the RPA. We investigated which kind of new surface an adversarial actor can get, if we utilise RPA in maintenance operations of Mobiilimittari service [3]. Mobiilimittari service offers iOS and Android applications for end-users to test their mobile connection quality and speed. With this kind of survey, we can get additional information about safety of our Mobiilimittari service system and make certain actions for the production environment, if needed. This paper presents briefly a case study of Mobiilimittari service, where we started to deploy RPA and made observations. Some useful ideas of the security assurance were proposed as well.

The structure of this paper is as follows. Section 2 presents related work. Section 3 includes description of threats and vulnerabilities related to the RPA. Section 4 presents the overview of security assurance in the robot process automation. Section 5 describes our case study environment and security specific observations in the case study. Section 6 presents lessons learned and Section 7 concludes the paper and gives briefly ideas about the future work.

II. RELATED WORK

To be an RPA pioneer, you will need to take some risks [4]. Authors in [4] proved in a trial the effectiveness of RPA, which produced alarms in the company's IT Security system. It was stated in [4] that IT team had a mature Business Process Management System (BPMS) in-house and questioned why additional automation software was needed. Of course, a risk means more work for IT team.

Security requirements for a global RPA platform are considered in Deckard's article [5], which gives technical security guidelines for deployment of RPA. Much of the responsibility for this security lies with RPA vendors, who incorporate certain security measures into their software products. The vendor takes care of RPA tool, not whole target environment. Therefore, not all of security concerns could be pushed to vendor side.

Authors in [6] propose a new method that analyses business processes and identifies the most suitable for RPA.

That method has measurable parameters for the evaluation of processes. Security aspect is not especially considered in the method, however.

RPA can improve quality and efficiency of manual operations and decrease a mistake probability that would cause problems in production [7]. RPA can reduce costs of production, but handling of data is constituent operation in image recognition systems and security requirements has to be taken tightly into account in the environment as well.

In [8] RPA is mentioned to be next generation testing. From that perspective, it is an excellent way to improve security level of the software and systems.

In our earlier research, we have examined the applying of RPA and artificial intelligence AI in the public sector [1]. In addition to that, we investigated how information security and data protection should be taken into account in the application of RPA and AI in the public sector.

Our approach in this paper is to apply results of earlier research to real service environment, which has been used already several years. In addition, it has been investigated, if there is any sense to start wider deployment of RPA. From that viewpoint security level of existing service and opportunities to improve it are considered.

III. THREATS AGAINST ROBOT PROCESS AUTOMATION

A security threat poses a threat to some of security's components, such as confidentiality, integrity, or availability. Threats against processing and using of the information are a phenomenon of recent years and it will continue to strengthen [9]. It is a consequence of a growth of microservices and an increase of the number of interfaces visible to a network [9]. The development of the prevalence of security threats is from malware to code hijacking and data phishing. The most common threats are still injections, such as SQL injection, which is a database intrusion technology. Threats to an identification and a session management have been intense at the beginning of this millennium.

Privacy is always a challenge in systems that work with machines [10]. A misuse of confidential information is the most important security threat in development and application of the robot process automation [1]. An external hostile actor can hijack codes and control a computer or software. Figure 1 describes a adversarial actor in the RPA environment exploiting observed vulnerabilities in software and systems and causes various disturbing features such as Denial of Service (DoS) to paralyse an ability of system to work or Man-In-the-Middle MItM to listen or disturb a communication path between two messengers by modifying or deleting messages and hacking encryption keys or other information. Additionally, the hostile actor can use Structured Query Language SQL injection to penetrate into a database-based applications and systems. Viruses, worms, Trojan horses and other programs are used to sniff or otherwise fill objectives of the hostile actor. Network security assurance software might also be used for hostile purposes.

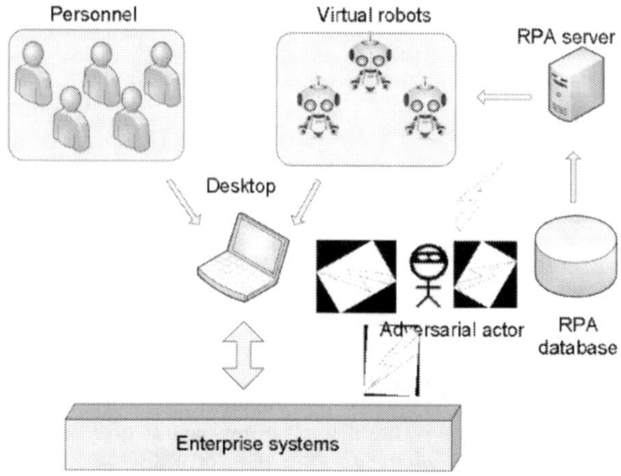

Figure 1. An adversarial actor in the RPA environment.

Robot techniques themselves are generally safer than human-oriented processes from the security point of view [10]. Robots work strictly within regulations and safety parameters of people they replace. Robots follow an accurately programmed and automated event sequence. For example robots do not respond to new arriving emails or leave a screen containing sensitive information unlocked.

One of the threats to deployment of the robot process automation and AI systems is an obsolescence of back-end systems. In a fast-paced business, organisation does not remember to modernise underlying systems, because processes are handled by robotics. In this case, a next security update may possibly break the system. A hacker can find this vulnerability and access data in corporate databases, web servers or employee computers by violating system features and functionality.

RPA and AI are conceptually separated, but it seems that in practical solutions they will be integrated [1]. Today an application of AI is mainly implemented by machine learning ML, which algorithms are tools to help AI to show smarter behavior. Algorithms need information to work correctly and accurately. More information used for learning means more accurate algorithms. The primary threat to the machine learning is through data processing [1]. Classification-based ML algorithms work by finding patterns in a data source. Identifying a source or training method for an algorithm is a valuable tool for hackers. Suitably formatted and injected malicious or incorrect inputs into a system may cause the system to produce erroneous results. Deliberate manipulation of a data source used in a teaching phase can cause bias in decisions of the AI system and even produce inaccurate results. A malicious actor may also attempt to steal algorithms or teaching resources for AI models to produce copies of models for illegal use.

IV. ENSURING SECURITY OF ROBOT PROCESS AUTOMATION

Modernisation of information and communication technologies by the RPA and deployment of new tools and methods always require a management and consideration of new type of risks. The risk-based approach to protect personal data is highlighted, among others, in the new EU Data Protection Regulation [11]. Changes give people better control of their personal data and make it easier for them to access their personal information. It also guarantees protection of the information in all situations, where data is transmitted, processed or stored.

Different security standards define tasks of security risk assessment. For example, the International Organization for Standardization (ISO) has defined the ISO/IEC 27001 standard, which defines the general requirements for creation, implementation and use of a system of information security management. The most important security aspect of RPA is how the robots are managed, how processes are automated and how they are maintained and developed. Security and availability must be a goal in every level of software and systems. Physical level sets own requirements to the information security as well as a level of networking, application and human interaction.

In environments of the robot process automation, it is important to take the access and data security seriously into consideration. Responsibilities and obligations have to be defined accurately for a controller of register and who is dealing with data. Role-based access management has to be a built-in authentication system, in which an access to RPA can be restricted to authorised users and tasks to be automated can be separated [5]. Using of encryption mechanisms, anonymisation or pseudonymisation of personal data have an essential role to protect sensitive data. These mechanisms wholly or partially hide an original content of the information. To achieve a stable state in every phase of automation, it is wise to automate a piece at a time. RPA tools based on TLS (Transport Layer Security) best protect the privacy of data transmitted over a network [5]. Storing logs and operations of robots and users gives traceability in problem situations.

If learning algorithms are supporting RPA functionality, a quality assurance of a system must focus more on a testing of borders and balance [12]. For example in deployment phase a corresponding output of a chatbot feed is known, but after learning, an output has become something different. In a test system, a test case corresponding to this feed is not working similarly as before. When you use the chatbot, you must also test the entire package during use. Testing during operations defines tests to check if the system is working as expected or the system has learned right things. It is also particularly useful to monitor the functionality of the system during operation. Based on the monitoring data effects of the changes can be analysed and noticed if the system has remained within specified limits and tolerances.

Traditional testing methods of software-based systems are still in strong role in a quality assurance of the RPA systems. Source code analyser of software finds the most obvious errors in a program code and errors can be removed before executing the program. Vulnerability scanning searches for commonly known security issues in the target system. Fuzz testing is a form of random testing, where random inputs are generated to a program and program outputs are monitored. Penetration testing evaluates a level of system or network security by attacking a software or system. At the same time, potential vulnerabilities in the system are monitored and analysed.

Ensuring security of a learning system requires, in addition to traditional methods, a special effort in testing design. It is important to strive to ensure strict security already in development phase of software and systems. The learning system does not necessarily have a predetermined activity that can be tested with certain inputs. Testing is done for a specific configuration and predefined functionality, but through the learning, the operation of the software or system changes. That is why a comprehensive set of historical information is needed to test the design to ensure that the right things in the system are learned and that the system does not learn harmful things.

V. CASE STUDY

A. *Overview of Mobiilimittari service*

Mobiilimittari service developed in Technical Research Centre of Finland VTT offers iOS and Android applications made publicly available for end-users in Finland to test their mobile connection quality and speed as presented in Figure 2. It measures downlink/uplink speed, delay and forms an overall connection quality metric (0-10). In addition, it has own tabs for measurement, representing results on a map (own/all), settings and detailed information about the latest measurement.

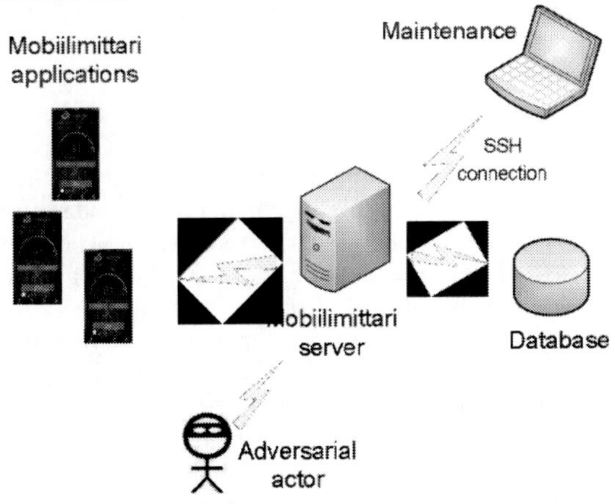

Figure 2 . A fictional adversarial actor in Mobiilimittari service.

This service has been created during the year 2015 without any support of a robot process automation. Security requirements are properly fulfilled and things are in sufficient level from that viewpoint. Security protocols are used behind port configurations, accesses for user applications are delivered via special security mechanisms. Secured connections are used for remote connections and for a handling of SQL database. In this study our aim was to investigate, how certain routines like weekly reporting to maintenance team could be performed with the RPA and which kind of security requirements this kind of deployment sets. In the maintenance team, we make a secure remote connection to move measurement results or get periodical reports about the state of the service. All of these actions have been built and is performed under tight security control.

We use Uipath free trial licence for our case study [13]. UiPath is a RPA vendor providing a complete software platform to help organisation to automate business processes. A software robot aims to manipulate the presentation layer of application software in the same manner a human does. UiPath platform includes the security and audit capabilities related to the target system as well.

In this study, we reflect findings from our earlier research to our real service environment. We used RPA in development environment with a test data, not in production environment with real personal data. In this study, we made observations of a practical RPA deployment from security perspective for example how some kind adversarial actor could have possibility to try something unexpected.

B. Observations

Earlier automated routines in Mobiilimittari service are more like solutions of Business Process Management BPM, which have built deeper to the server code. If there is need for an updating, larger coding and compiling operation is required. Robot process automation gives possibility to build certain routine without any coding skills, but you have to know details about underlying service system or other back-end systems, when building robot process automation however.

A lot of access rights have to be created and given to robots for opening remote connections and logging to databases. Remarkable amount of sensitive data could be in robot hands, which means that it has to be encrypted. In SSH connection user names and passwords may be open for the misuse if the work station is not locked during the break or some one is behind you. Robots don't leave work station unlocked and they are not doing other things same time.

It was observed, that quite a lot of malicious traffic is knocking towards server interface, which is wasting processor capacity of the server. If the RPA is used, robot does not recognize the traffic as human can see from a real time traces on the screen in other words robot's eyes are limited. It means that we have to build separate functionality for a monitoring this kind of traffic.

The utilization of RPA in a wider scale needs quite a lot of modifications to the existing service system. It could be easier to start RPA development in parallel with a product development to get best results. If we need heavy and deep analysis for example of the measurement results, learning algorithms are worth thinking to support the RPA functionality.

VI. LESSONS LEARNED

With this way, we can get additional information about safety of our service system and make certain actions for the production environment. We can watch carefully our server system and keep eye on things, what adversarial actor can do. Robot techniques themselves are generally safer than human-oriented processes, but a challenge of the RPA deployment are accesses to use services and accesses to information.

The tool used in the case study seemed to be suitable to support our requirements, but this may not be the case with all tools on the market. Special attention should be paid on selection of the robot process automation tools, how it fulfills special requirements of certain organisation and user.

Although the first look to the case study seems quite promising, it should be noted that the case study was not executed with real RPA tools yet. Full service development with early phase support of the RPA would be needed to gather metrics and information about the real benefits of the RPA from the security point of view.

VII. CONCLUSIONS AND FUTURE WORK

In this paper, we described observations, how routines like weekly report delivering to maintenance team could be performed with the RPA and which kind of security requirements this kind of service development sets. Robot process automation was applied to VTT's Mobiilimittari service, which has been made publicly available for end-users in Finland to test their mobile connection quality and speed. We observed that there is a lot of new surface for adversial actors, which requires taking tightly care of accesses to be created and given to robots. It was noted that robots should move a remarkable amount of sensitive data between separate servers.

Our case study continues with a real integration of RPA and possibly AI features to the maintenance processes of Mobiilimittari. In addition, we will investigate how we can test the system from the angle of cyber security by applying the RPA. AI comes to performing of security testing as well. AI can determine which test cases or values of parameters are best to use to detect errors. Test tools are able to do certain things in a certain phase. Based on the test results, smart test tools can further modify the tests and try new things to find bugs and bottlenecks of the target system.

In future RPA solutions will increasingly integrate with artificial intelligence solutions. This means increasing of security challenges in the RPA environments as well. Another noteworthy issue is the explosive growth of the application of RPA, which means the level of security has also to be kept up.

ACKNOWLEDGMENT

This research is a part of the research project cluster of Technical Research Centre of Finland VTT in the field of robot process automation. The author wish to thank project members and project partners involved in the projects.

REFERENCES

[1] J. Kääriäinen et al., "Robotic process automation and artificial intelligence – application roadmap". Publications of Government's analysis, assessment and research activities 65/2018.

[2] Quora, "What are the Feasibility parameters in robotic process automation?" https://www.quora.com/What-are-the-Feasibility-parameters-in-robotic-process-automation 2019.08.06.

[3] Mobiilimittari https:/www.mobiilimittari.fi 2019.08.06.

[4] L. Willcocks, M. Lacity, and A. Craig, "Robotic Process Automation at Telefónica O2 (Paper 15/02)," The Outsourcing Unit Working Reasearch Paper Series, 2015.

[5] M. Deckard, https://www.uipath.com/blog/the-security-requirements-for-a-global-rpa-platform 2019.08.06.

[6] A. Bourgouin, A. Leshob, and L. Renard, "Towards a Process Analysis Approach to Adopt Robotic Process Automation", 2018 IEEE 15th International Conference on e-Business Engineering (ICEBE), page 46-53.

[7] S. C. Lin, L. H. Shih, D. Yang, J. Lin, J. F. Kung, "Apply RPA (Robotic Process Automation) in Semiconductor Smart Manufacturing", e-Manufacturing & Design Collaboration Symposium 2018.

[8] S. Bhukan, "Robot Process Automation and the Testing future", https://www.testingbits.com/robotic-process-automation-and-the-testing-future/ 2019.08.06.

[9] OWASP Foundation, The Open Web Application Security Project, https://owasp.org 2019.08.06.

[10] The Shared Services and Outsourcing Network SSON, "How to Manage Risk and Ensure Control – What to Look Out for in Robotic Process Implementation", https://www.ssonetwork.com/robotic-process-automation/articles/how-to-manage-risk-and-ensure-control-what-to 2019.08.06.

[11] EU 2016/679, Regulation of the European Parliament and the Council, https://eur-lex.europa.eu/legal-content/EN/TXT/PDF/?uri=CELEX:32016R0679&from=FI 2019.08.06.

[12] H. Shaukat, T. Gansel, R. Marselis, "Testing of Artificial Intelligence, AI Quality Engineering Skills - An Introduction", https://www.sogeti.com/globalassets/global/downloads/reports/testing-of-artificial-intelligence_sogeti-report_11_12_2017-.pdf 2019.08.06.

[13] Uipath Platform, Robot Process Automation RPA tool, https://www.uipath.com/product/platform 2019.08.06.

Enhancing Attack Resilience by Protecting the Physical-World Interface of Cyber-Physical Systems

Rainer Falk, Steffen Fries
Corporate Technology
Siemens AG
Munich, Germany
e-mail: {rainer.falk|steffen.fries}@siemens.com

***Abstract*—Cyber physical systems operate and supervise physical, technical systems using information and communication technology, also called Operation Technology (OT). Cyber security solutions focus on the OT part, i.e., on the information and communication technology. The focus of cyber security is protection, detection, and respondence to cyber attacks. Cyber resilience aims at delivering an intended outcome despite attacks and adverse cyber events and even failures not directly related to attacks. Protecting the link between the control systems and the physical world, has been addressed only in some very specific cases, e.g., charging of electric vehicles. We propose a physical-world firewall that limits the impact on the physical world of a successful attack of automation systems, thereby enhancing the resilience of cyber-physical system against successful attacks against its OT systems.**

Keywords–cyber security; cyber resilience; system integrity; cyber physical systems; industrial automation and control system; Internet of Things.

I. INTRODUCTION

The traditional focus of IT security relates to IT-based control equipment and data communication (Ethernet, IP). In addition to this, in OT systems also the field level has to be considered down to the interface between the control system and the physical world via sensors and actuators.

Traditionally, IT security has been focusing on information security, protecting confidentiality, integrity, and availability of data at rest and data in transit. In Cyber-Physical Systems (CPS), major protection goals are availability, meaning that automation systems stay productive, and system integrity, ensuring that it is operating as intended. Typical application domains are factory automation, process automation, building automation, railway signaling systems, and energy management. Cyber security is covering phases protect, detect, and react: Protecting against threats, detecting when an attack has occurred, and recovering from attacks.

We see resilience of cyber-physical systems as an important protection goal, limiting the effect of potential successful attacks on a cyber-physical system in the physical world. It can be rather seen as a strategy than a specific technology. Our objective is to increase the robustness with respect to intentional attacks, although resilience in general would consider also accidental failures.

After giving an overview on cyber physical systems and on industrial cyber security in Sections II and III, a new approach on protecting the interface of a CPS between the cyber-world and the physical world is described in Section IV. It is a concept to increase the resilience of a CPS when being under attack. Aspects to evaluate the new approach are discussed in Section V. Section VI concludes the paper.

II. CYBER PHYSICAL SYSTEMS

A cyber-physical system, e.g., an industrial automation and control system, monitors and controls a technical system. Examples are process automation, machine control energy automation, and cloud robotics. Automation control equipment is connected with sensors (S) and actuators (A), connected directly with automation components, or via remote input/output modules. The technical process is controlled by measuring its current state using the sensors, and be determining the corresponding actuator signals to influence the technical process.

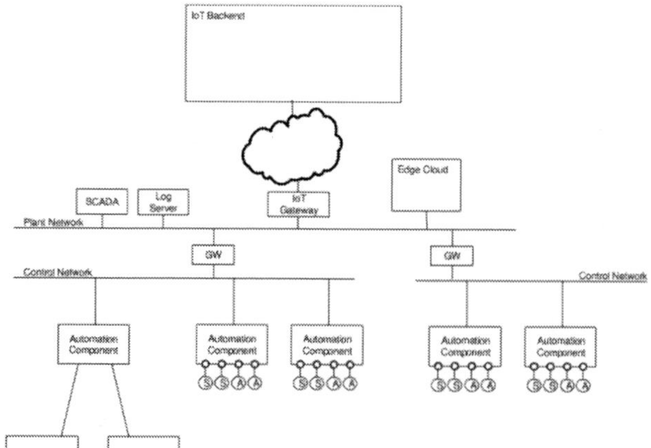

Figure 1. Example CPS System

Figure 1 shows an example of an industrial automation and control system, comprising different control networks connected to a plant network and a cloud backend system. Separation of the network is typically used to realize distinct control networks with strict real-time requirements for the interaction between sensors and actuators of a production cell, or to enforce a specific security policy within a production cell. Such an industrial automation and control system is an example of a cyber-physical system.

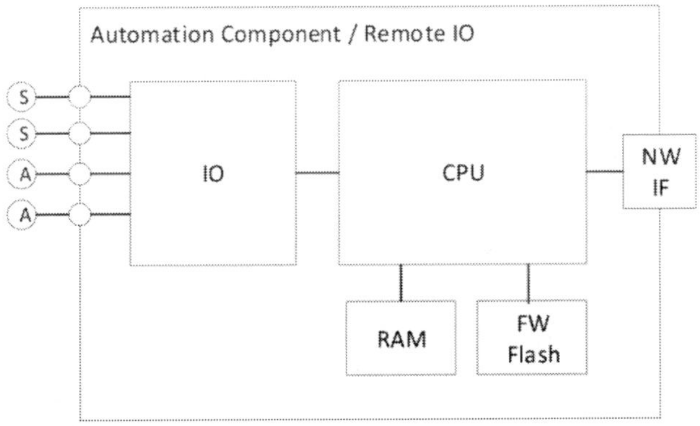

Figure 2. Automation Component

Figure 2 shows the typical structure of automation components. The functionality realized by an automation component is largely defined by the firmware/software and the configuration data stored in its flash memory. In practice, it has to be assumed that each software component may comprises vulnerabilities, independent of the effort spend to ensure high software quality. The impact of a vulnerability in automation equipment does not affect only data on the automation component, but the effect it has on the physical world.

III. Industrial Cyber Security

Protecting industrial automation control systems against intentional attacks is increasingly demanded by operators to ensure a reliable operation, and also by regulation. This section gives an overview on industrial security, and on the main relevant industrial security standard IEC 62443 [8] and integrity security requirements.

A. *Industrial CPS Security Requirements*

Industrial security is called also Operation Technology security (OT security), to distinguish it from general Information Technology (IT) security. Industrial systems have not only different security requirements compared to general IT systems, but come also with specific side conditions that prevent that security concepts established in the IT domain can be applied directly in an OT environment. For example, availability and integrity of an automation system often have a higher priority than confidentiality. As an example, high availability requirements, different organization processes (e.g., yearly maintenance windows), and required certifications may prevent the immediate installations of updates.

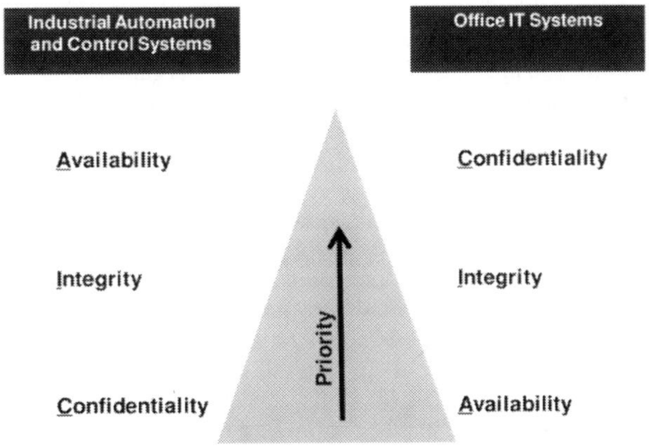

Figure 3. The CIA Pyramid [6]

The three basic security requirements are confidentiality, integrity, and availability. They are also named "CIA" requirements. Figure 3 shows that in common IT systems, the priority is "CIA". However, in automation systems or industrial IT, the priorities are commonly just the other way round: Availability has typically the highest priority, followed by integrity. Confidentiality is often no strong requirement for control communication, but may be needed to protect critical business know-how. Shown graphically, the CIA pyramid is inverted (turned upside down) in many automation systems.

Specific requirements and side conditions of industrial automation systems like high availability, planned configuration (engineering info), long life cycles, unattended operation, real-time operation, and communication, as well as safety requirements have to be considered when designing a security solution. Depending on the considered industry (vertical), they may also be part of the critical infrastructure domain, for which security requirements are also imposed for instance by the European Network and Information Systems (NIS) directive [7] or country specific realizations of the directive. Further security requirements are provided by applying standards defining functional requirements, for instance defined in IEC 62443. The defined security requirements can be mapped to different automation domains, including energy automation, railway automation, building automation, process automation.

Security measures to address these requirements range from security processes, personal and physical security, device security, network security, and application security. No single security technology alone is adequate, but a combination of security measures addressing prevention, detection, and reaction to incidents is required ("defense in depth").

B. *Overview IEC 62443 Industrial Security Standard*

The international industrial security standard IEC 62443 [8] is a security requirements framework defined by the International Electrotechnical Commission (IEC). It addresses the need to design cybersecurity robustness and resilience into industrial automation and control systems, covering both organizational and technical aspects of security over the life cycle. It is applied successfully in different automation domains, including factory and process automation, railway automation, energy automation, and building automation. The standard specifies security for industrial automation and control systems (IACS) and covers both, organizational and technical aspects of security. Specifically addressed is the setup of a security organization and the definition of security processes as part of an information security management system (ISMS) based on already existing standards like ISO 27002. Furthermore, technical security requirements are specified distinguishing different security levels for industrial automation and control systems, and also for the used components. The standard has been created to address the specific requirements of industrial automation and control systems. In the set of corresponding documents, security requirements are defined, which target the solution operator and the integrator but also the product manufacturer.

Part 3-3 of IEC 62443 [10] defines seven foundational requirements group specific requirements of a certain category:

- FR 1 Identification and authentication control
- FR 2 Use control
- FR 3 System integrity
- FR 4 Data confidentiality
- FR 5 Restricted data flow
- FR 6 Timely response to events
- FR 7 Resource availability

For each of the foundational requirements there exist several concrete technical security requirements (SR) and requirement enhancements (RE) to address a specific security level. In the context of communication security, these security levels are specifically interesting for the conduits connecting different zones.

Four Security Levels (SL1, SL2, SL3, SL4) are defined that correlate with the strength of a potential attacker as shown in Figure 4. The targeted security level of a zone of the industrial automation and control system is determined based on the identified risk.

4 Security Level (SL)	
SL 1	Protection against **casual or coincidental** violation
SL 2	Protection against **intentional violation** using **simple means** with low resources, generic skills and low motivation
SL 3	Protection against intentional violation using **sophisticated means** with **moderate resources**, IACS specific skills and moderate motivation
SL 4	Protection against intentional violation using sophisticated means with **extended resources**, IACS specific skills and high motivation

Figure 4. IEC 62443 defined Security Level [6]

To reach a dedicated security level, the System Requirements (SR) and potential Requirement Enhancements (RE) defined for that security level have to be fulfilled. The standard foresees that a security requirement can be addressed either directly, or by a compensating countermeasure. The concept of compensating countermeasures allows to reach a certain security level even if some requirements cannot be implemented directly, e.g., as some components do not support the required technical features. This approach is in particular important for existing industrial automation and control systems, so called "brown-field installations", as existing equipment can be continued to be used.

C. *Resilience*

Being resilient means to be able to withstand or recover quickly from difficult conditions [1]. It shifts the focus of "classical" IT/OT security, that puts the focus on preventing, detecting, and reacting on cyber-security attacks, to the aspect to continue to deliver an intended outcome despite an adverse cyber attack is taking place. More specifically, resilience of a system is the property to be resistant to a range of threats and withstand the effects of a partial loss of capability, and to recover and resume its provision of service with the minimum reasonable loss of performance [2]. It has been addressed in telecommunications, ensuring that subscribers can continue to be served even when one line is out of service. Bodeau and Graubart [5] define resilience guidelines for providers of critical national telecommunications infrastructure in the UK.

In a cyber-physical environment, a main objective is to ensure that the CPS stays operational and that its integrity is ensured. In the context of an industrial automation and control system, that means in particular that (only) intended actions in the physical world continue to take place even when the automation and control system of the CPS should be attacked.

IV. Protecting the CPS Physical World Interface

Well-known IT security technologies like encryption and access control, protecting data at rest, in transit, and partly even data in use. In cyber-physical systems, this is not enough. Also, the interface between the OT part (automation systems) and the physical world has to be protected, limiting the potential danger that an automation system can have on the physical world when it is attacked. A successful attack on the automation system or control network can have an impact on the physical world [3].

This section describes the concept of a "physical world firewall" that limits the access to the physical world from OT automation systems. The objective is to increase the resilience of cyber-physical systems, by limiting the impact of an attacked automation system on the physical world.

A. *Physical-World Firewall*

The main idea is to filter the communication between sensors and actuators on one side, and the control equipment on the other side. This can be called physical-world firewall. It limits in which way a control system, which might be under attack, can impact a physical system in the real world. The filtering takes place directly at the input/output interface, so that it is independent from the software-based functionality of the automation component.

Similar as a communication firewall for data traffic that analyzes and filters data packets (IP packets and IP-based communication), here the actuator and sensor signals are filtered. The allowed signal ranges and dynamic parameters are monitored and limited.

If the signal filtering policy is violated, the signal cannot be simply dropped like an IP packet. Instead, a replacement signal is provided. The replacement signal may be a fixed default value, or a clipped maximum/minimum value that is within the allowed value range, or it may be an out-of-range signal that will be detected by an actuator as failure signal).

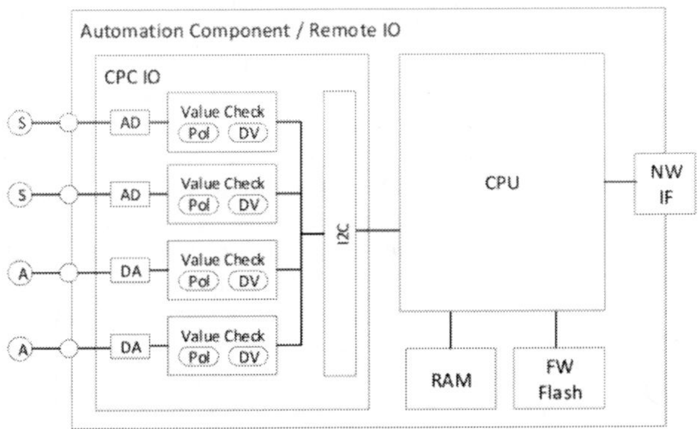

Figure 5. Automation Component with Integrated Physical World Firewall

Figure 5 shows an automation component with an integrated Cyber Physical Controlled IO Interface (CPC IO). The CPU can authenticate towards its CPC IO after a successful self-integrity check. Each input/output channel is monitored separately by the "Value Check" component: It verifies whether the sensor input value or the actuator output value is in the given allowed corridor and thus is compliant with the policy Pol. Besides value range, also statistical parameters and dynamic parameters can be checked. If the policy is met, the value is allowed, otherwise, the configured default value (DV) of provided to ensure the system stays operational. It is possible to lock the input/output interface in the case of a policy violation. The lock may be permanent, or it can be reset at a reboot of by manual user interaction.

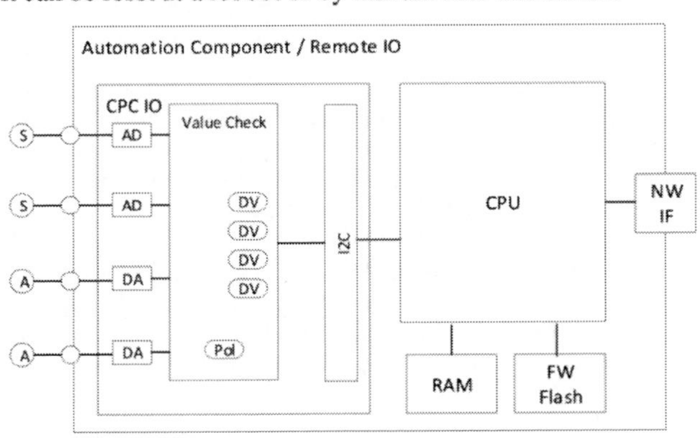

Figure 6. Automation Component with Integrated Physical World Firewall

A different variant is shown in Figure 6, where the signals of multiple input/output channels are checked in combination. This allows to perform cross-checks between sensor and actuator signals. Moreover, if this approach is applied in a distributed system, it allows to take certain properties of potentially different sensors/actuators into account. Specifically, if the sensors/actuators used are a mixture of standard (legacy) and specifically hardened, trusted sensors, a potential security assertion can be used in the evaluation of the signals giving the trusted sensor a higher weight in the evaluation. This is especially advantageous if a larger number of legacy sensors/actuators is already deployed and secure siblings are installed as add-on in a stepwise manner. More information on the basic concept of trusted sensors is described in [6].

B. Dynamic Resilience Management

The policy of the physical-world firewall can be adapted dynamically, depending on the current operating state of the CPS. This allows to restrict the possibility to influence the physical world even more strictly, as the current state of the production system and the currently performed production step, e.g., cooling or filtering a fluid, can be reflected in the current configuration of the physical-world firewalls.

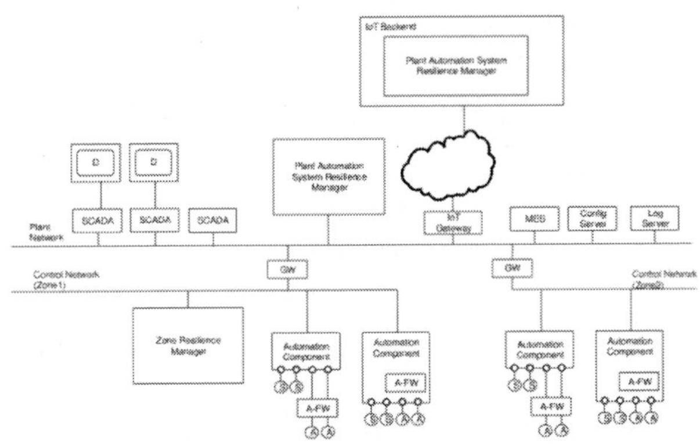

Figure 7. Dynamic Resilience Management

Resilience managers determine the physical-world firewall policy dynamically, depending on the current state and context of the CPS, see Figure 7. They adapt during operation the current policy configuration of the physical-world firewalls.

The policy adaptation performed by resilience managers can use in particular the following information:

- The current state of the physical world, as obtained by trusted sensor nodes [6].
- The current production batch, the current production step, operating state (e.g., standby, preparation, active, service, alarm). In real-world deployments, the information may be obtained from a Manufacturing Execution System (MES).
- Cyber attacks detected by an integrity monitoring system or an intrusion detection system, supervising the CPS.

C. *Authenticating Physical Signals*

In data communication, the sender of a data packet can be identified by an identifier, e.g., an internet protocol (IP) address or a media access control (MAC) address. The sender may be authenticated cryptographically. A data firewall can filter data packets depending on address information and content.

In a physical world, the source of a signal can in general not be identified by an explicit identifier, included in the data communication. However, it is usually possible to identify the source implicitly based on the cabling.

A higher level of confidence can be achieved by performing signal authentication. The sender of a signal can be identified by a sender-specific fingerprint information, e.g., a noise signal. Furthermore, it is possible to actively add a signal marker (signal watermarking), e.g., a coded spread-spectrum signal [14][15][16]. This allows to identify the source of a signal by evaluation properties of the signal.

V. EVALUATION

The security of a cyber system can be evaluated in practice in various approaches and stages of the system's lifecycle:

- Threat and Risk Analysis (TRA or TARA) of a cyber physical system (for a system being under design or in operation). In a TRA, possible attacks (threats) on the system are identified. The possible impact and probability are evaluated to determine the risk of the identified threats.
- Security checks can be performed during operation or during maintenance windows to determine key performance indicators (e.g., check for compliance of device configurations).
- Security testing (penetration testing) can be performed for a system that has been built, but that is currently not in operation. The system is attacked by "white hat" hackers to identify vulnerabilities that need to be addressed.
- Security testing can be performed also on a digital representation of a target system, e.g., a simulation in the easiest case. This allows to perform pentesting for systems that are not existing yet physically (design phase), or to perform pentesting of operational systems without the risk of disturbing the regular operation of the real-world system.

A holistic protection concept has to address measures for protect, detect, and react. No single measure or security technology alone can result in an adequate security level. It is always a set of measures that, when used in combination, can bring down the risk to an acceptable level.

The security measures presented in this paper, acting on the interface between the cyber world and the physical world, provide an additional security measure that can be used as part of a defense-in-depth security concept. It is complementary to well-known security measures that focus on the IT/cyber part. The protection is complementary, as it operates directly at the interface towards the physical world, not on computer-based control functions as conventional IT security technologies. Even if all security measures in the pure IT/cyber world fail, still the impact on the physical world can be controlled. It can serve as "last line of defense", allowing to connect cyber systems from the physical world in a tightly controlled way, or even disconnecting some automation systems from the physical world when needed.

As long as the proposed technology has not been proven in real-world operational setting, it can be evaluated conceptually by analyzing the impact the additional measure has on the identified residual risks of a TRA. A TRA identifies threats against a system, and determines the risk depending on probability and impact. The general effect of the presented security measure is that the impact of a threat on the physical world is reduced. Whatever attack is ongoing on the automation and control system, still the possible impact on the real, physical world is limited. So, the measure helps to reduce the risk of threats having an impact on the physical world. However, TRAs for real-world CPS are not available publicly. Nevertheless, an illustrative example may be given by a chemical production plant performing a specific process like refinery, or a factory producing glue or cement. If the plant is attacked, the attack may target to destroy the production equipment by immediately stopping the process leading to physical hardening and thus to a permanent unavailability of the production equipment. In this case, trusted sensors could be used to detect a falsified sensor signal, and the physical-world firewall can be used to limit actions in the physical world. Thereby, a physical damage of the production equipment can be avoided. If needed, a controlled shutdown of the production site can be performed.

A major advantage of the physical-world firewall is the property that it can be added to existing brownfield deployments. Legacy equipment, may be 10 or even 20 years old, not even been designed with security in mind, and without getting patches. In such cases, the physical-world firewall can be used as an "add-on" security measure for an existing CPS. It can be used as compensating countermeasure to address security requirements defined by industrial security standards like IEC62443-3.3 [10], where conventional cyber security measures cannot be deployed. However, it can be used also as additional layer of defense in CPS having state-of-the-art security measures integrated, thereby increasing the level of protection even further.

VI. CONCLUSION

A CPS comprises cyber-technology and the physical world. Both parts have to be covered by a security concept and solution. Traditional cyber security puts the focus on the cyber-part, i.e., automation and control systems. The security of the physical part, like machinery, is protected often by physical and organizational security measures, only. This paper presented the concept for a new approach that enhances the achieved level of security by protecting the interface between the cyber-part and the physical world, thereby enhancing the resilience of a CPS being under attack.

REFERENCES

[1] P. England, R. Aigner, A. Marochko, D. Mattoon, R. Spiger, S. Thom, "Cyber resilient platforms", Microsoft Technical Report MSR-TR-2017-40, Sep. 2017, available from: https://www.microsoft.com/en-us/research/publication/cyber-resilient-platforms-overview/ 2019.07.19

[2] Electronic Communications Resilience&Response Group, "EC-RRG resilience guidelines for providers of critical national telecommunications infrastructure", version 0.7, March 2008, available from: https://assets.publishing.service.gov.uk/government/uploads/system/uploads/attachment_data/file/62281/telecoms-ecrrg-resilience-guidelines.pdf 2019.07.19

[3] D. Urbina, J. Giraldo, N. O. Tippenhauer, A. Cardenas, "Attacking fieldbus communications in ICS: applications to the SWaT testbed", Singapore Cyber-Security Conference (SG-CRC), IOS press, pp. 75–89, 2016, available from: http://ebooks.iospress.nl/volumearticle/42054 2019.07.19

[4] C. C. Davidson, T. R. Andel, M. Yampolskiy, J. T. McDonald, W. B. Glisson, T. Thomas, "On SCADA PLC and fieldbus cyber security", 13th International Conference on Cyber Warfare and Security, National Defense University, Washington, DC, pp. 140–148, 2018

[5] D. Bodeau and R. Graubart, "Cyber resiliency design principles", MITRE Technical Report, January 2017, available from: https://www.mitre.org/sites/default/files/publications/PR%2017-0103%20Cyber%20Resiliency%20Design%20Principles%20MTR17001.pdf 2019.07.19

[6] R. Falk and S. Fries, "Enhancing integrity protection for industrial cyber physical systems", The Second International Conference on Cyber-Technologies and Cyber-Systems, CYBER 2017, pp. 35–40, November 12 - 16, 2017, Barcelona, Spain, available from: http://www.thinkmind.org/index.php?view=article&articleid=cyber_2017_3_30_80031 2019.07.19

[7] European Commission, "The directive on security of network and information systems (NIS Directive)", available from: https://ec.europa.eu/digital-single-market/en/network-and-information-security-nis-directive 2019.07.19

[8] IEC 62443, "Industrial automation and control system security" (formerly ISA99), available from: http://isa99.isa.org/Documents/Forms/AllItems.aspx 2019.07.19

[9] ISO/IEC 27001, "Information technology – security techniques – Information security management systems – requirements", October 2013, available from: https://www.iso.org/standard/54534.html 2019.07.19

[10] IEC 62443-3-3:2013, "Industrial communication networks – network and system security – Part 3-3: System security requirements and security levels", Edition 1.0, August 2013

[11] IEC 62554-4.2, "Industrial communication networks - security for industrial automation and control systems - Part 4-2: technical security requirements for IACS components", CDV:2017-05, May 2017

[12] P. Bock, J.-P. Hauet, R. Françoise, R. Foley, "Ukrainian power grids cyberattack - A forensic analysis based on ISA/IEC 62443", ISA InTech magazine, 2017, https://www.isa.org/templates/news-detail.aspx?id=152995 2019.07.19

[13] ZVEI, „Orientation guideline for manufacturers on IEC 62443", "Orientierungsleitfaden für Hersteller zur IEC 62443" [German], ZVEI Whitepaper, 2017, https://www.zvei.org/presse-medien/publikationen/orientierungsleitfaden-fuer-hersteller-zur-iec-62443/ 2019.07.19

[14] T. Hupperich, H. Hosseini, T. Holz, "Leveraging sensor fingerprinting for mobile device authentication", International Conference on Detection of Intrusions and Malware, and Vulnerability Assessment, LNCS 9721, Springer, pp. 377–396, 2016, available from: https://www.syssec.ruhr-uni-bochum.de/media/emma/veroeffentlichungen/2016/09/28/paper.pdf 2019.07.19

[15] H. Bojinov, D. Boneh, Y. Michalevsky, G. Nakibly, "Mobile device identification via sensor fingerprinting", arXiv:1408.1416, 2016, available from: https://arxiv.org/abs/1408.1416 2019.07.19

[16] P. Hao, "Wireless device authentication techniques using physical-layer device fingerprint", PhD thesis, University of Western Ontario, Electronic Thesis and Dissertation Repository, 3440, 2015, available from: https://ir.lib.uwo.ca/etd/3440 2019.07.19

A Fraud Detection Framework Using Machine Learning Approach

Aderonke Thompson
Department of Cybersecurity
Federal University of Technology
Akure, Nigeria
afthompson@futa.edu.ng

Oghenerukvwe Oyinloye
Department of Computer Science
Ekiti State University of Technology
Ado Ekiti, Nigeria
oeoyinloye@eksu.edu.ng

Leon Aborisade
Department of Computer Science
Federal University of Technology
Akure, Nigeria
aborisadelo@futa.edu.ng

Esther Odeniyi
Department of Computer Science
Federal University of Technology
Akure, Nigeria
eaodeniyi@futa.edu.ng

Abstract— **Credit card fraud describes cases in which a threat actor gains unauthorized access in order to obtain money or property. The importance of machine learning and Data Science cannot be over emphasized. This work develops an efficient fraud detection framework using non-rule-based approach of Multi-layer perceptron. It correctly predicts and detects frauds on a given financial transaction dataset. The algorithm on the datasets evaluates its effectiveness vis-à-vis frauds detection in bank transactions. The results are compared and evaluated using various evaluation metrics.**

Keywords- fraud; credit cards; Multi-layer perceptron;

I. INTRODUCTION

Recent information technology (IT) proliferation deployed in major financial services by Nigerian banking institutions has led to an increase in threats posed to these systems. Debit/Credit cards are one of the most common payment methods used over the Internet. It was asserted that financial fraud can be viewed as an act intended for deception involving financial transactions for personal gain purpose [1]. Fraudsters have it easier as most transactions do not require the presence of a bank account/ card holder; stealing relevant customers details or perform identity theft by posing as the customer at point of payments is all that is vital to perpetrating their acts, including phishing and unsuspecting customers to redirection to malicious websites in with a hidden act of harvesting customer banking details and information. Credit card fraud is equally viewed as a type of theft and fraud done using a payment card, as a fraudulent funds source in a transaction. Some security issues are mostly faced by banks everywhere, but the prevention of card fraud attracts high priority, and this is set to grow with the exponential rate of Internet awareness and transactions. Increase in online purchases has made criminals take advantage of various weak authentication checks to commit credit card fraud [2].

Models provide a way to mitigate these occurrences, protect clients' transactions and play an essential role in payment service providers' profitability and sustainability. This can be achieved using a fraud detection system (FDS). FDS is computational analysis fraud detection techniques via fraud identification or anomaly transactions in a swift a proven technique is adopting machine learning as presented in [3]. Modeling of past credit card transactions has to do with detecting via the knowledge of the ones that turned out to be fraud. This model is then used to identify whether a new transaction is fraudulent or not in the two major existing fraud methods of physical and virtual frauds. Physical fraud is done by stealing a card and using it for the payment or purchasing while virtual fraud is committed by using someone's card details through the internet for transactions. Further classification of credit card fraud is given in Figure.1. Section I deals with the introduction of various acts of fraud. A guide to available credit card fraud is presented in Section II, while Section III gives a detail of related study in the fraud detection domain. In Section IV, multilayer perceptron methodology approach to fraud detection is extensively discussed. Implementation of a feed forward Artificial Neural Network for the machine learning approach is presented in Section V in addition to Section VI which further shows the implementation with various parameters. Observations from the proposed model and evaluation id given in Section VII with the performance of the Logistic regression study based on the same dataset.

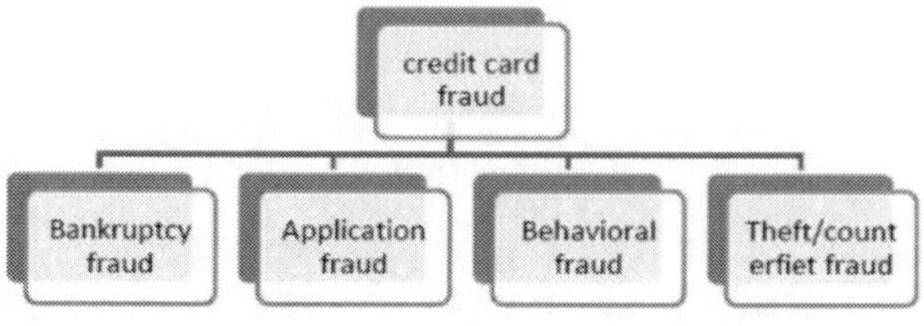

Figure 1. Classification of Credit Card Fraud

II. MAJOR METHODS USED TO MITIGATE CREDIT CARD

There are basically two major forms of mitigating credit car fraud. it could be in the preventive or detective mode. The preventive mode involves blocking fraudulent transaction at the point of transaction. Such as passwords, pin and blocked cards; while the detective mode identifies successful fraud transaction through predictive models with machine learning approach.

Traditionally Fraud resolution process usually involves: fraud detection, investigation, confirmation, and prevention. Therefore, a self-learning computer program automates the above processes using various methods. Signature based detection method detects fraud traces through the signature technology using known patterns or byte sequence, it is efficient for known frauds. However, fraudsters have continued to manipulate the system by finding creative ways to beat signature strings. The anomaly detection method comes with the ability to detect both known and novel frauds; although, this method is limited by false positive error, that is, previously unknown legitimate transactions. This paper exploits machine learning to detect fraudulent activities as well as measuring its performance.

III. LITERATURE REVIEW

Financial fraud had been a major challenge for corporate organizations, government and mostly specifically businesses that utilize information technology. Financial fraud is defined as an intentional act of deception involving financial transactions for purpose of personal gain. Another definition for financial fraud is "to take advantage over another by false representations" which include "surprise, trickery, cunning and unfair ways by which another is cheated" [1]. Fraud costs some financial industry approximately $80 billion annually where the United States' credit and debit card issuers alone lost $2.4 billion.

The occurrence of financial fraud in any organization undermines both the effort and prospects. Financial fraud brings about losses owing to theft, distrust in transaction, and litigation. These losses owing to fraud are grossly detrimental to institutions where they occur. As advances in cloud technology plums and cyber-security measures declines, there exists high possibility of financial fraud bound to threaten businesses worldwide. Detection of financial fraud had not come so easy, mostly at a high cost and time. The cost of financial fraud reported to cost about $1 million per incident, occupational fraud costs $150 to $200k per incident while losses due to fraud costs an average of 5% of gross profit and take around 24 to 36 months to discover - usually via a tip (40%), by accident (20%), or during an audit (10%).

Some motivations for committing financial fraud has been reported and identified by senior management to be most responsible for most fraud [4]. They argued that meeting external forecasts emerged as the primary motivation and it was conceptualized that three elements common among all fraud is called the fraud triangle. These elements include a perceived pressure, a perceived opportunity, and a rationalization of the fraud act as the three main areas of pressure that motivate individuals who commit fraud. He stated that motivation for need, greed and addictions (or vices). He asserted the motivation for greed which in turn feeds the motivation for vices. These motivators become a vicious cycle leading to fraud. Financial fraud is categorized mainly into three areas, bank fraud, corporate fraud and insurance fraud. Bank fraud is subdivided into credit card fraud, mortgage fraud and money laundering fraud [5].

Fraud modelling is one important tool in addressing financial fraud. It expands in importance as corporate organizations and government determine which type of models to use and continuous update in order to protect against evolving threats. In the past, traditional fraud models are used to automatically detect unauthorized transactions such as determining when a card has been used without the owner's consent. Most card issuers use fraud models to identify fraudulent card usage in order to maintain the integrity and security of their network as it is core to earning trust in online business world. However, diverse range of payment services offered by organizations and businesses to clients also presents higher opportunities for fraud occurrence. Consequently, fraud models provide a way to mitigate these occurrences, protect clients' transactions and play an essential role in payment service providers' profitability and sustainability with attributes of a given transaction as variables used in fraud models. Thereafter, it classifies or attempts to label the transaction fraudulent or legitimate. Some extensive models label the type or category of fraud. Some of the common attributes used by fraud models include: Merchant (the business charging the transaction), transaction location, amount, type (online or offline), volume, account history, transaction history, and so on, depending on the amount of attribute information captured in a transaction. The five basic fields, which describe type, time (hours, minutes), location, amount, and date (week days) of a transaction were used in the fraud model. While 16 significant ratios out of 29 financial ratios were used in detection of fraud in the financial statements of banks which were categorized into asset quality ratios, earnings & profitability ratios, liquidity/solvency ratios, long term solvency/leverage ratio, capital adequacy ratio, cash flow analysis and trends. These fraud models utilized 29 variables of which 24 are financial variables while 5 are non-financial variables as it proved that model tools based on financial numbers, linguistic behaviour, and non-verbal vocal cues have each demonstrated the potential for detecting financial fraud. Fifty-one (51) financial ratios were utilized in detecting fraud in financial statements by means of financial ratios [6].

Notable fraud detection models are mainly categorized as rule-based models and algorithmic (or machine learning) models. Rule-based models are collection of rules used to detect fraudulent transactions with a single rule containing as a set of conditions that, when present, labels a transaction either as fraudulent or not. Rule-based models are made up of an expert knowledge base. In addition, new rules evolve from time to time because of inference action on streams of time changing data. However, one major limitation of rule-based fraud models is time complexity in handling big data. Algorithmic models make use of machine-learning methods to classify a transaction as either fraudulent or legitimate. Algorithmic models are more complex than rule-based models; this is dependent on the type of algorithm used. These models are computationally complex than rule-based models but achieve high performance. They are far better at detecting complex relationships between variables than the rule-based models. Machine-learning methods also require a pre-requisite of having many variables to implement and ensure learning. Therefore, when there is limited number of variables usage, the benefit of algorithmic methods over rule-based models is diminished.

The presentation of a review on financial accounting fraud detection based on data mining techniques was motivated by the idea that the failure of internal auditing system of the organization in identifying the accounting frauds has led to the use of specialized procedures to detect financial accounting fraud. The findings of this review showed that data mining techniques such as logistic models, neural networks, Bayesian belief network, and decision trees have been applied most extensively to provide primary solutions to the problems inherent in the detection and classification of fraudulent data.

In [6], financial fraud detection using vocal, linguistic and financial cues is presented and observed that these methods for automating financial fraud detection (FFD) have mainly relied on financial statistics, although some recent research has suggested that linguistic or vocal cues may also be useful indicators of deception. The hypothesis investigated in the study is that an improved tool (based on financial numbers, linguistic behaviour, and non-verbal vocal cues) could be developed if specific attributes from these feature categories were analyzed concurrently. A set of 1,572 public company quarterly earnings conference call audio file samples was used as their sample in the study. The authors re-affirmed that earnings from conference calls are ideal for our investigation because they involve corporate executives publicly discussing financial information, thereby simultaneously providing financial, linguistic and vocal cues. The research proved that tools based on financial numbers, linguistic behaviour, and non-verbal vocal cues have each demonstrated the potential for detecting financial fraud. However, it is quite tasking (and computationally intensive) to source and compute concurrently large amount of vocal and linguistic data [7].

In another presentation, a difference between precision-recall and ROC curves for evaluating the performance of credit card fraud detection models was motivated by the need to solve the problem of fraudulent transactions detection with use of machine learning for legitimate or fraudulent the credit card transactions classification. In order to solve this problem, the precision-recall curves are described as an approach. Weighted logistic regression is used as an algorithm level technique and random under-sampling is proposed as data-level technique to build credit card fraud classifier. Performance evaluation of these approaches adopted the Receiver Operator Characteristic (ROC) curves, which showed the variance of the number of correctly classified positive examples with the number of incorrectly classified negative examples. However, ROC curves present an overly optimistic view of an algorithm's performance. It established that precision-recall curves have more advantages than ROC curves in dealing with credit card fraud detection. The study was limited by inability to find the best solution to the problem of imbalanced data in the dataset [8].

A study on "Combatting Financial Fraud: A Co-evolutionary Anomaly Detection Approach" evolved around the motivation as a result of the major difficulty in anomaly detection which lies in discovering boundaries between normal and anomalous behaviour. The objective was to present a co-evolutionary algorithm which tackles the anomaly detection problem and discover the boundary between normal and abnormal behaviour. The co-evolutionary algorithm was used to provide a competitive interaction between different populations which minimize detection errors and the adaptive evolutionary environment accelerated by the process of finding good solution. The authors implemented the algorithm using anonymized transactional data from a real financial institution. The data set contains two-year ABM (Automated Bank Machine) and POS (Point Of Sale) fraud-free transaction history. The research has contributed to knowledge by using concept of evolution to detect anomalies in fraudulent transactions only it was not applied to realistic data [9].

IV. METHODOLOGY

The study deploys multilayer perceptron approach to detect fraud using financial datasets. Each transaction by a customer on card contains the transaction API, which is stripped into attributes. The attributes (model variables) from the API include; Source IP address, Destination IP address, Card pan, Location of transaction, Item bought, Unit of items bought, Amount of transaction and the Date and Time of transaction. The model architectural design is depicted in Figure. 2.

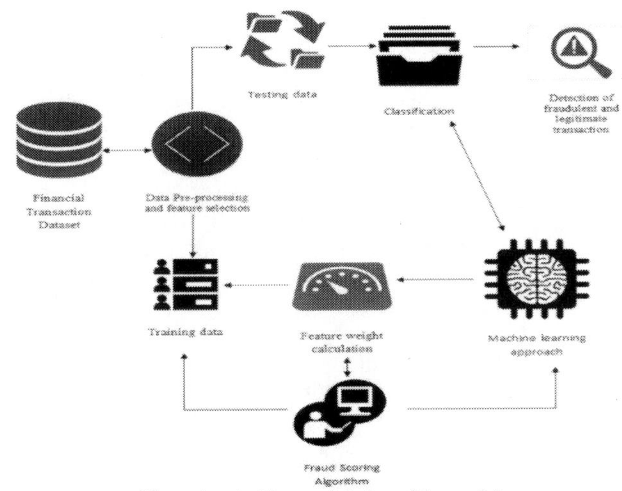

Figure 2. Architectural design of the model

The Architecture is divided into 3 major parts, namely:

i. Data preprocessing & Feature Selection
ii. Data Training & Learning
iii. Classification

Financial credit card datasets were selected (Dataset 1 and Dataset 2) were obtained from "Kaggle Data Repository" which are publicly available containing anonymized real-life credit card transactions with an evident presence of fraudulent cases. Dataset 1 was obtained from Kaggle Data Repository, and contains anonymized data to protect user's vital information. Data was from Credit Card Transactions for users in Europe in 2013. It has 284,808 entries. It has 31 attributes with class labels The Dataset 1 sample is shown in Table 1.

TABLE I. SAMPLE OF DATASET I

1	Time	V1	V2	V3	V4	V5	V6	V7	V8
2	0	-1.35981	-0.07278	2.536347	1.378155	-0.33832	0.462388	0.239599	0.098698
3	0	1.191857	0.266151	0.16648	0.448154	0.060018	-0.08236	-0.0788	0.085102
4	1	-1.35835	-1.34016	1.773209	0.37978	-0.5032	1.800499	0.791461	0.247676
5	1	-0.96627	-0.18523	1.792993	-0.86329	-0.01031	1.247203	0.237609	0.377436
6	2	-1.15823	0.877737	1.548718	0.403034	-0.40719	0.095921	0.592941	-0.27053
7	2	-0.42597	0.960523	1.141109	-0.16825	0.420987	-0.02973	0.476201	0.260314
8	4	1.229658	0.141004	0.045371	1.202613	0.191881	0.272708	-0.00516	0.081213
9	7	-0.64427	1.417964	1.07438	-0.4922	0.948934	0.428118	1.120631	-3.80786
10	7	-0.89429	0.286157	-0.11319	-0.27153	2.669599	3.721818	0.370145	0.851084
11	9	-0.33826	1.119593	1.044367	-0.22219	0.499361	-0.24676	0.651583	0.069539
12	10	1.449044	-1.17634	0.91386	-1.37567	-1.97138	-0.62915	-1.42324	0.048456
13	10	0.384978	0.616109	-0.8743	-0.09402	2.924584	3.317027	0.470455	0.538247
14	10	1.249999	-1.22164	0.38393	-1.2349	-1.48542	-0.75323	-0.6894	-0.22749
15	11	1.069374	0.287722	0.828613	2.71252	-0.1784	0.337544	-0.09672	0.115982
16	12	-2.79185	-0.32777	1.64175	1.767473	-0.13659	0.807596	-0.42291	-1.90711
17	12	-0.75242	0.345485	2.057323	-1.46864	-1.15839	-0.07785	-0.60858	0.003603
18	12	1.103215	-0.0403	1.267332	1.289091	-0.736	0.288069	-0.58606	0.18938
19	13	-0.43691	0.918966	0.924591	-0.72722	0.915679	-0.12787	0.707642	0.087962
20	14	-5.40126	-5.45015	1.186305	1.736239	3.049106	-1.76341	-1.55974	0.160842

creditcard

Dataset 2 contains anonymized data to protect user's vital information, Data contains Credit Card Transactions. It has 151,113 entries. It has 11 attributes with class labels, partitioned into testing set and training set. Training set contained 105,778 records and testing set had 453,347 records. Sample records of the Dataset 2 are shown in Table II

The data pre-processing and preparation was carried out on the raw financial dataset to remove outliers using max-min normalization technique. As shown in equation (1)

$$Normalized\_Value = \frac{(f_{value} - f_{\min})}{(f_{\max} - f_{\min})} \quad (1)$$

where f_{value}, is the feature value to be normalized, f_{min} is the minimum feature value and
f_{max} is the maximum feature value respectively.

Feature selection was performed by computing feature importance. This is done using Information gain calculation. Thus, given a set of financial transaction dataset S_c

$$E(F) = \sum_{j=1}^{c} \frac{S1_j + ... + Sc_j}{S} * I(si_j, ..., sc_j) \quad (2)$$

where (I = information, S = total number of financial transaction data instances, c = total classes (i.e. fraudulent and legitimate classes, F = Features)
The information gain, G(F) is defined as:

$$G(F) = I(s_1, s_2, ..., s_c) - E(F) \quad (3)$$

Features with high information gain are selected for model development while the others are removed.

TABLE II: SAMPLE OF DATASET II

user_id	signup_time	purchase_time	purchase_	device_id	source	browser	sex	age	ip_address	class
22058	2/24/2015 22:55	4/18/2015 2:47	34	QVPSPJUC	SEO	Chrome	M	39	732758368.8	0
333320	6/7/2015 20:39	6/8/2015 1:38	16	EOGFQPIZ	Ads	Chrome	F	53	350311387.9	0
1359	1/1/2015 18:52	1/1/2015 18:52	15	YSSKYOSJI	SEO	Opera	M	53	2621473820	1
150084	4/28/2015 21:13	5/4/2015 13:54	44	ATGTXKYK	SEO	Safari	M	41	3840542444	0
221365	7/21/2015 7:09	9/9/2015 18:40	39	NAUITBZF	Ads	Safari	M	45	415583117.5	0
159135	5/21/2015 6:03	7/9/2015 8:05	42	ALEYXFXIN	Ads	Chrome	M	18	2809315200	0
50116	8/1/2015 22:40	8/27/2015 3:37	11	IWKVZHJC	Ads	Chrome	F	19	3987484329	0
360585	4/6/2015 7:35	5/25/2015 17:21	27	HPUCUYLI	Ads	Opera	M	34	1692458728	0
159045	4/21/2015 23:38	6/2/2015 14:01	30	ILXYDOZIH	SEO	IE	F	43	3719094257	0
182338	1/25/2015 17:49	3/23/2015 23:05	62	NRFFPPHZ	Ads	IE	M	31	341674739.6	0
199700	7/11/2015 18:26	10/28/2015 21:59	13	TEPSJVVX(	Ads	Safari	F	35	1819008578	0
73884	5/29/2015 16:22	6/16/2015 5:45	58	ZTZZJUCRI	Direct	Chrome	M	32	4038284553	0
79203	6/16/2015 21:19	6/21/2015 3:29	18	IBPNKSMC	SEO	Safari	M	33	4161540927	0
299320	3/3/2015 19:17	4/5/2015 12:32	50	RMKQNVE	Direct	Safari	M	38	3178510015	0
82931	2/16/2015 2:50	4/16/2015 0:56	15	XKIFNYUZI	SEO	IE	M	24	4203487754	0
31383	2/1/2015 1:06	3/24/2015 10:17	58	UNUAVQX	SEO	Safari	F	24	995732779	0
78986	5/15/2015 3:52	8/11/2015 2:29	57	TGHVAWE	SEO	FireFox	M	23	3503883392	0
119824	3/20/2015 0:31	4/5/2015 7:31	55	WFIIFCPIC	Ads	Safari	M	38	131423.789	0
357386	2/3/2015 0:48	3/24/2015 18:27	40	NWSVDOI	Ads	FireFox	M	24	3037372279	0
289172	7/17/2015 5:48	11/12/2015 22:08	46	KFZGQIWI	Direct	FireFox	F	53	1044590098	0

V. MULTI LAYER PERCEPTRON (MLP)

The implementation is a feed-forward artificial neural networks; MLP consists of the input layer, output layer, and one or more hidden layers. Each layer of MLP includes one or more neurons directionally linked with the neurons from the previous and the next layer. Figure 3 represents a 3-layer perceptron having three inputs, two outputs, and the hidden layer including five neurons

The values retrieved from the previous layer are summed up with certain weights, individual for each neuron, plus the bias term [10]. The sum is transformed using the activation function.

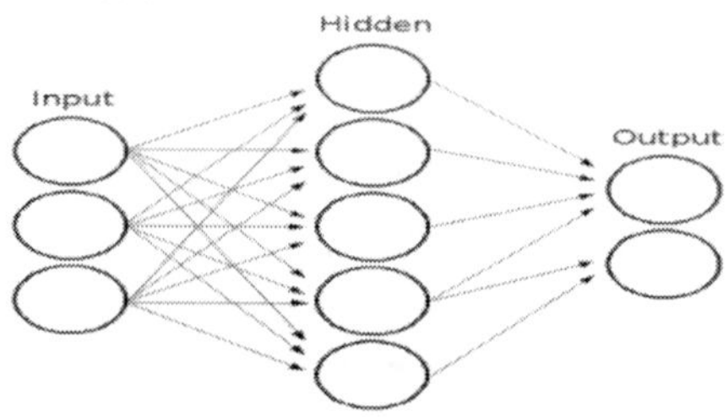

Figure 3. A Multi-Layer perceptron

The perceptron computes a single output from multiple real-valued inputs by forming a linear combination according to its input weights and then putting the output through some nonlinear activation function:

Given output (u_i)

$$u_i = \sum_{j=1}^{n} (w_{i,j}\, x_j + b_i) \tag{4}$$

With the activation function (φ) applied, mathematically the MLP can be written as:

$$y_i = \varphi\left(\sum_{j=1}^{n} (w_{i,j}\, x_j + b_i)\right) \tag{5}$$

where w = weight going to the hidden unit layer
x= Input to hidden unit
b= bias input
φ= Activation function

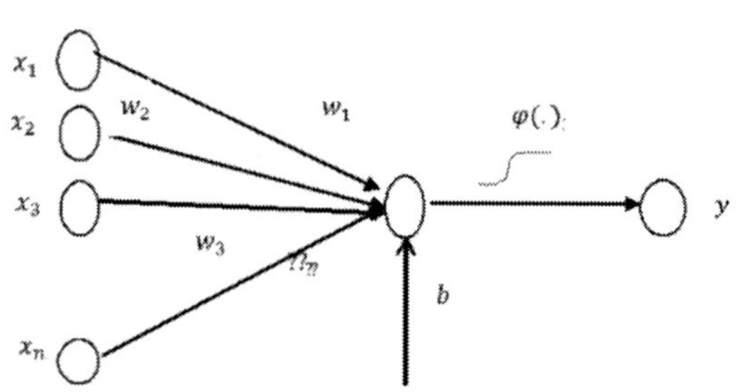

Figure 4. Representation of the MLP equation

A. *Learning Algorithm*

The MLP uses a backpropagation algorithm to learn and train from the dataset

The back-propagation algorithm is in 2 phases:

- The forward pass phase- computes 'functional signal', feed forward propagation of input pattern signals through network.
- Backward pass phase- computes 'error signal', *propagates* the error *backwards* through network starting at output units (where the error is the difference between actual and desired output values).

Forward pass Algorithm

- Step 1: Initialize weights at random, choose a learning rate η
- Until network is trained:
- For each training example i.e. input pattern and target output(s):
- Step 2: Do forward pass through net (with fixed weights) to produce output(s)
  - i.e., in Forward Direction, layer by layer:
    - Inputs applied
    - Multiplied by weights
    - Summed
    - 'Squashed' by sigmoid activation function
    - Output passed to each neuron in next layer
  - Repeat above until network output(s) produced

Backward pass /Back propagation of error

- Compute error (delta or local gradient) for each
- output unit δ *k*
- Layer-by-layer, compute error (delta or local
- gradient) for each hidden unit δ *j* by backpropagating
- errors (as shown previously)
- Next, update all the weights Δ*wij*
- By gradient descent, and go back to Step 2

The overall MLP learning algorithm, involving forward pass and backpropagation of error (until the network training completion), is known as the Generalized Delta Rule (GDR), or more commonly, the Back Propagation (BP) algorithm

VI. MLP IMPLEMENTATION

The multi-layer perceptron model was implemented on a Personal Computer with 2.30 GHz and 8GB of RAM in Microsoft Windows 10 Operating system platform and Microsoft Excel 2013 with Python Programing Language. The MLP training was defined with parameters epochs = 20, dim_size = 15, num_seq = 30, batch_size = 200, activation function = Sigmoid

Due to the high imbalance in the datasets, the data were synthetically balanced using the smote method, The datasets 1 and dataset 2 stored in csv format were loaded into python 3.6 IDLE via a read_csv() command . The datasets were divided into two parts (Input and Output). The input data are those with the attributes while the output data contain the target class ('Fraudulent' and 'Normal').

A. *Evaluation Metrics*

The evaluation of the model was carried out using the various evaluation metrics such as Accuracy, Precision, F1-score, Recall and False alarm rate.

Accuracy: is defined as the number of correct predictions made by the model. It is the proportion of the total number of correct predictions.

$$Accuracy = \frac{TP + TN}{TP + TN + FP + FN} \quad (6)$$

False Alarm Rate (FAR)/False Positive rate: is a ratio of wrongly classified normal instances.

$$False\ Alarm\ Rate = \frac{FP}{TN + FP} \quad (7)$$

Precision: defines the results classified as positive by the model, how many were actually positive. It is the number of items correctly identified as positive out of total true positives.

$$\text{Precision} = \frac{\text{true positive}}{\text{true positive} + \text{false positives}} \quad (8)$$

Recall: It is the number of items correctly identified as positive out of the total items classified as positive.

$$\text{Recall} = \frac{\text{true positive}}{\text{true positive} + \text{false negatives}} \quad (9)$$

F1-Score: is the weighted average of the precision and the recall, it takes both false negatives and positives into the account and gives a better outlook especially in an uneven class distribution it is given as:

$$\text{F1 Score} = 2\left(\frac{\text{Precision} * \text{recall}}{\text{Precision} + \text{recall}}\right) \quad (10)$$

where True positive (TP) represents data detected as fraudulent, True negative (TN) represents data detected as legitimate, False positive (FP) represents normal data detected as fraudulent, and False Negative (FN) is denoted as fraud data detected as normal.

VII. RESULTS

In this section, an evaluation of the study with some metrics is presented with the two datasets. Dataset I reveals the significance of dataset that is characterized with minimum missing data. This is presented in Tables II and IV. The graphical representation of these datasets is presented in Figure 5.

TABLE III. EVALUATION RESULT ON DATASET 2

Model	*Accuracy(%)*	*F1 score (%)*	*Precision (%)*	*Recall (%)*	*False Alarm rate (%)*
Multi Layer Perceptron	96.4	96.3	99.1	93.6	0.001

TABLE IV. EVALUATION RESULT ON DATASET 2

Model	*Accuracy(%)*	*F1 score (%)*	*Precision (%)*	*Recall (%)*	*False Alarm rate (%)*
Multi Layer Perceptron	77.4	71.4	96.9	56.5	0.002

B *Performance of Dataset 1 and Datset 2 Using MLP*

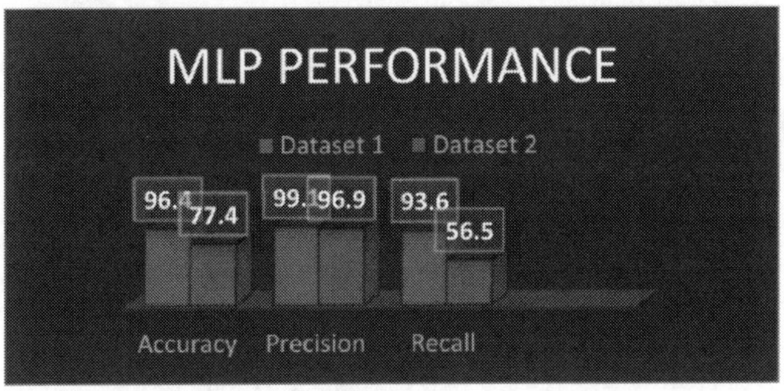

Figure 5.: Performance of Dataset 1 and Dataset 2 using MLP

From the chart above, we can conclude that our model performed appreciably better with dataset using the evaluation metrics.

C *Comparative Evaluation*

The results of this model were thereafter compared with the results of a work that was implemented using Logistic regression machine learning approach with the same dataset 1 is the result.

TABLE V: ECOMPARATIVE EVALUATION OF MLP AND LOGISTIC REGRESSION

Model	Accuracy (%)	Precision (%)	Recall (%)
Multilayer Perceptron	96.4	99.1	93.6
Logistic Regression	Not given	71	64

This model performed impressively against the performance of the Logistic regression research work that used the same dataset. Weighted logistic regression was used as an algorithm level technique and random under-sampling was used as data-level technique to build credit card fraud classifier. The classification used in the research was Logistic Regression and the performance metrics are Recall and Precision. A graphical evaluation report of the two models is illustrated in Figure. 6.

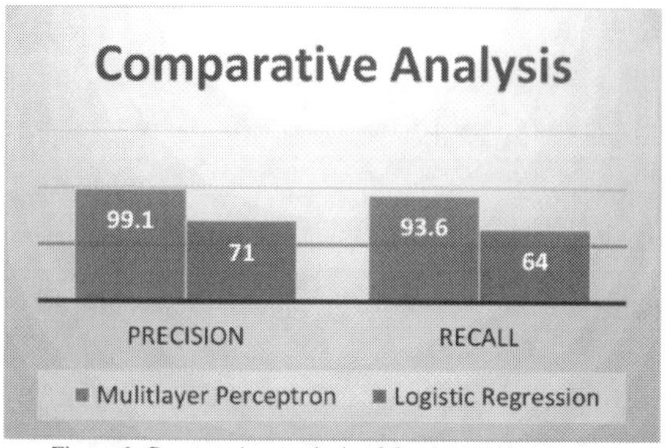

Figure 6: Comparative Analysis of Our Model (MLP) and Logistic Regression

VIII. CONCLUSION

In conclusion, the multilayer perceptron which used information gain method as feature selection technique for obtaining the most relevant features of the dataset was found to be effective in fraud detection. This work will be very useful to the financial sector. This study established a fraud detection framework that is capable of unmasking real-time fraudulent transactions established. This credit card fraud detection framework uses the Multilayer Perceptron to predict fraudulent transaction with a high level of accuracy, precision, recall, good F1-score and very low false alarm rate. Future work could be extended to other algorithms as well as hybridized approach with minimal computational complexity.

REFERENCES

[1] W. S. Albrecht, C. O. Albrecht, C. C. Albrecht and M. F Zimbelman, "Fraud examination," 5th Edition, Cengage Learning, 2014.

[2] F. N. Ogwueleka, "Data mining application in credit card fraud detection system," *Journal of Engineering Science and Technology*, 2014, 6(3):311-322.

[3] H. Shao, H. Zhao and G. Chang, "Applying data mining to detect fraud behaviour in customs declaration," *Proc. of 1st International Conference on Machine Learning and Cybernetics*, 2015, 1241-1244

[4] N. M. Brennan and M. McGrath, "Financial statement fraud: incidents, methods and motives," *Australian Accounting Review*, 2007, 17(2):49-61.

[5] P. L. Clifton, Vincent, S. Kate and G. Ross, "A comprehensive survey of data mining-based fraud detection research," School of Business Systems, Faculty of Information Technology, Monash University, Clayton campus, Wellington Road, Clayton, Victoria 3800, Australia, 2012.

[6] C. S. Throckmorton, V. Mohan, J. M. William and C. Leslie, "Financial fraud detection using vocal, linguistic and financial cues," 2018.

[7] F. Chowdhury and M. S. Ferdous, "Modelling cyber attacks," International Journal of Network Security & Its Applications 9(4):13-31, July 2017.

[8] K. Dinaesh, "Cyber defense mathematical modeling and simulation," *International Journal of Applied Physics and Mathematics, Vol. 2, No. 5, September 2012*

[9] P. Laerte, D. Marcelo, M. Bernardo, F. G. David, and D. T. Deus, "A Formal classification of internet banking attacks and vulnerabilities in combatting financial fraud: A coevolutionary anomaly detection approach," International Journal of Computer Science & Information Technology (IJCSIT), 2015, Vol 3.

[10] S. Maes, K. Tuyls, B. Vanschoenwinkel, and B. Manderick, "Credit card fraud detection using Bayesian and neural networks," In *Proceedings of the 1st International naiso congress on neuro fuzzy technologies* 2002, (pp. 261-270).

How Much Cyber Security is Enough?

Securing mid-sized financial organisations in Australia

Anne Coull
Objective Insight
Australia
email: anne.objectiveinsight@gmail.com

Abstract— **Cyber security is a risk: the risk that the company's information assets will be compromised in a way that affects their data's integrity, availability, and/or confidentiality. Like any other enterprise risk, cyber risk needs to be managed in a way that balances the cost of risk realisation against the cost of mitigating that risk. Defence in depth is a seemingly simple and logical approach to protecting systems and data, but is defence alone enough, and how much is needed? Local and global standards and guidelines direct companies in where to focus their mitigative efforts, but for the uninitiated, these can be confusing. Cyber security is an expensive exercise, with much at stake. By taking a practical approach that combines people, policies, processes as well as technology, organisations can manage the cyber security risk to protect their critical and sensitive information assets, and comply with government regulations, within a reasonable budget.**

Keywords- cyber security; risk management; penetration testing; threat; vulnerability; control; NIST; ASD; APRA; ISO27001; ISO27002; defence in depth.

I. INTRODUCTION

Cyber security and cyber resilience are business challenges and business risks. An effective cyber security strategy incorporates people, policies, processes, and technology into an over-all risk management plan, and integrates these aspects to implement defence in depth [1][31]-[33]. This way, organisations can protect their critical and sensitive information assets, and be proactive in identifying, preventing, detecting, responding, and recovering from cyber threats and attacks [1][7][28][31]-[33].

Small to medium businesses in Australia are on the front-line of the cyber war, and are easy pickings for cyber criminals, as their lack of cyber expertise and investment in cyber security can leave them open to exploitation.

Implementing an effective Cyber Security Risk Management Plan will enable these smaller organisations to balance their IT security expenditure with government regulation and business outcomes [21]. The Australian Government has recently established a set of standards to which businesses in the financial sector must adhere [2]-[6]. For these smaller businesses to survive, they will need to protect their sensitive and critical information assets and satisfy the government regulations within their limited budgets. But how do they know where to start? And, how much cyber security is enough?

While cyber risk can never be reduced to zero, this paper applies practical risk management to enable an organisation to identify where it should be focusing its efforts. In addition, it analyses the requirements and recommendations of the most visible standards and guidelines and draws from these an effective set of controls that, once applied, will protect the organisation from known threats and attacks, reduce the likelihood and impact of successful exploits, and enable the organisation to meet the Australian government's new pre-requisites to do business.

Section 2 assesses the cyber security standards and guidelines available to businesses in Australia's financial sector. Section 3 discusses a practical approach to managing cyber security risk. Section 4 identifies the controls an organisation should apply, within this risk management framework, to mitigate their cyber security risk and reduce the residual risk to an acceptable level.

II. CYBER SECURITY STANDARDS AND GUIDELINES

The following cyber security standards and guidelines were assessed:

1. The Australian Prudential Regulation Authority (APRA):
   a. CPG 234 Management of Security Risk in Information and Information Technology [2];
   b. CPS 234 Information Cyber Security [6];
2. The Australian Signals Directorate (ASD):
   a. Top 4 [7];
   b. Essential 8 [7][8]; and
   c. Top 37 controls [9];
3. AS ISO/IEC 27001:2015 Information technology – Security Techniques – Information security management systems – Requirements [15];
4. AS ISO/IEC 27002:2015 Information technology – Security techniques – Code of practice for information security controls [16];
5. NIST:

a. Cyber Security Framework [19];
b. 800-53 & 800-53A: Security Controls and Objectives [27];
c. 800-53R4 Security and Privacy Controls for Federal Information Systems and Organisations [26];
d. 800-167 Guide to application whitelisting [30];
e. IR 7621: Small business fundamentals [23].

A. AS ISO/IEC 27001:2015 and AS ISO/IEC 27002:2015

The ISO 2700X standards define the objectives and techniques for implementing information security management in an organisation [15][16]. This is the standard applied by the larger banks and financial organisations operating in Australia. It is also the standard used for measuring the security posture of their third-party suppliers. ISO 2700X require that an information security policy will be documented, communicated, and available; Persons will be assigned responsibility for implementing an information security management system that meets the stated objectives and identifies, assesses, and treats the risks associated with the loss of confidentiality, integrity, and/or availability of information by implementing suitable controls to meet the information security objectives [15][16]. ISO 27001 standard specifically identifies the need for competent people to oversee its information security performance, and for all people working in the organisation to be aware of the information security policy and how their individual roles contribute to its effectiveness [15][16].

B. APRA CPS 234

The APRA prudential standard set is aimed at the financial sector in Australia. CPS 234 covers the fundamentals of cyber security, such as the need to have an information security policy and security controls in-place to protect information assets as well as the need for third-party suppliers who hold an organisation's information on their behalf meet these same obligations. CPS 234 requires an organisation to identify and classify its information assets by criticality and sensitivity. Criticality and sensitivity indicate the degree to which the organisation would be impacted by an incident that affects availability, integrity, and/or confidentiality of that asset [2][6]. An asset's classification acts as a guide for selecting controls suitable to protect that asset. The effectiveness of these controls needs to be tested regularly, relative to the rate of systems change within the organisation, and externally in the broader threat landscape [2][6].

APRA requires that an organisation be able to detect and respond to potential cyber incidents and that incidents and vulnerability test results need to be reported to the appropriate Information Security executive(s) and the board. The design and effectiveness of the information security controls need to be internally audited [2][6]. APRA must be notified within 5 days of any material information security incidents and/or when the organisation identifies a material vulnerability in its information security controls that cannot be remediated in a timely manner [6].

Leadership and board commitment are key requirements spelled out in both the APRA CPS 234 and the ISO2700X standards. Ownership and visible support from the top is critical to the success of information security management in an organisation as this assures the necessary resources are made available to establish, implement, maintain and continually improve the security management system [6][16].

C. Australian Signals Directorate Top 4 and Essential 8

The Australian Signals Directorate (ASD) offers a comprehensive list of 37 mitigating cyber security controls that they have classified as essential, excellent, very good, good, and limited [7][8]. ASD claims that their Top 4 cyber mitigations will reduce the risk of a successful cyber exploit by 85% by decreasing the likelihood of a successful intrusion, and then limiting the impact of that intrusion, should it succeed [7]. The essential 8 includes the top 4 plus 4 more essential mitigations [7][8]. The ASD essential 8 mitigations are:

1. Application whitelisting of approved programs to prevent the execution of malicious programs including .exe, DLL, scripts, and installers.
2. Patch operating systems. Patch/mitigate computers (including network devices) with 'extreme risk' vulnerabilities within 48 hours (e.g., Remote code execution in Microsoft windows operating system). Always run the latest version of the operating system, and don't use unsupported versions.
3. Patch applications such as Flash, web browsers, Microsoft Office, Java and PDF viewers. Use the latest version of applications and patch or mitigate extreme risk vulnerabilities within 48 hours.
4. Restrict administrative privileges to operating systems and applications based on user duties. The need for privileged access should be regularly revalidated and confirmed by the person's manager. Privileged accounts must not be used for reading email and web browsing.
5. Harden user applications by configuring web browsers to block Flash, ads, and Java on the internet. Disable any features in MS Office, web browsers, and PDF viewers that are not needed, such as OLE.
6. Important and changed data, software, and configuration settings need to be backed-up daily and stored off site and disconnected from the source network for at least 3 months. Restoration

should be tested at least annually and when the IT infrastructure changes.

7. Use multi-factor authentication for VPNs, RDP, SSH, and other remote access, and for all users performing privileged actions or when accessing sensitive information.
8. Microsoft Office macro settings should be configured to block macros from the internet, and only allow permitted macros from trusted locations or those with a trusted certificate, with limited write access [7][8].

D. *NIST 800-53 and NISTIR 7621 for Small Business*

NIST 800-53 provides a comprehensive framework of guidelines for managing risks – from vulnerability identification and risk assessment through to identifying and implementing mitigative controls. NIST 800-53 divides the cyber security management into 5 phases: identify, protect, detect, respond and recover [19].

NISTIR 7621 for small business offers 25 mitigating cyber security controls. There is natural overlap between the NIST and the ASD essential 8 controls. Both NIST and ASD recommend patching operations systems and applications, whitelisting applications and controlling internet access, ensuring redundancy of systems and data by taking regular backups, limiting access to data, and controlling systems administration privileges. NISTIR 7621 for small business also recommends: the use of both hardware and software firewalls between the organisation's network and the internet; anti-virus and anti-spyware on every device that connects to the organisation's network, encrypting data at rest and in transit. In addition, the NIST guideline extends beyond managing the technology to include mandatory data breach reporting requirements, for example. It also includes controls identified in the ISO 27002 standard, such as restricting physical access to the workspace and data centre [15][16][19][23][26][27][30].

III. Practical Risk Management

Proactive management of cyber security risks within an organisation is best achieved by combining aspects of the standards and guidelines discussed to establish an effective cyber security risk management process that identifies the cyber risks, evaluates the level of the risks for that organisation and implements an appropriate set of mitigating controls to reduce the residual risk to an acceptable level [21][29]. This can be achieved by combining appropriate aspects of the standards and guidelines discussed, within the context of the organisation under consideration.

Risk management is a continuous process. The risk management plan is the basis for effectively identifying, managing, and monitoring its cyber security-related risks [21][29]. An organisation's objective in performing risk management is to enable it to achieve its mission by:

1. More effectively securing the IT systems that store, process, or transmit the company's information;
2. Providing the information needed to make well-informed risk decisions that justify security-related IT expenditure;
3. Facilitating and enabling accreditation, by providing supporting documentation as a result of this risk management plan [21][29].

A. *Cyber Security Risk Management Process Activities*

1) *System characterisation and Scope determination*

Managing cyber risk needs to be done within the context of the organisation, its purpose, scope, and the environment in which it operates. The first step is to understand the business context by defining the mission and operational characteristics of the system: what the system does and how it operates in the organisation's environment, and what is the scope and boundary of the risk management plan [21][29].

2) *Asset identification and analysis*

Within the agreed boundary and scope, identify critical and sensitive information assets and significant and critical systems and activities that need to be protected, and assess their value [6][21][29] in terms of:

i. the functions they perform, as they relate to confidentiality, integrity, and availability;
ii. the value to the business in terms of reputational damage and market-share loss if they were compromised;
iii. their replacement value (if applicable);

3) *Threat identification and analysis*

Perform threat modelling to identify and evaluate relevant threats to confidentiality, integrity, and/or availability of these assets, or the information pertaining to these assets, by considering common, known threats, emerging threats, and threats that relate to the local environment. Threats may be natural events, or man-made: man-made threats can be intentional or accidental; and intentional threats can be external or internal. Intentional threats can be better understood by considering the potential motives driving these behaviours, ability to execute the attack, and opportunities available for the attackers to exploit vulnerabilities to execute these attacks. Commonly known potential threats include social engineering, phishing, hacking, and worms [18][21][24][25][29][31]-[33].

4) *Vulnerability identification and analysis*

Assess the vulnerabilities, or weaknesses in the protection measures for the assets identified that may be exploited by these threats, such as people clicking on links in phishing emails or malicious websites, downloading malware infected files and software, out of date patching on operating systems and applications, and/or lack of whitelisting [21][29][30]. This is an ongoing exercise as new vulnerabilities are identified. Intelligence services can assist with providing updates on recent/current vulnerabilities and exploits.

5) Risk identification

Risks are identified where threats may exploit the vulnerabilities in these assets [21][29].

6) Risk analysis

The level of risk is determined by the likelihood these vulnerabilities will be exploited by these threats, and the impact if this were to happen [21][29]:

Level of Risk Exposure = Likelihood x Impact.

Impact includes the estimated direct and indirect costs to the business, if this were to happen. The NIST Risk Analysis process provides a comprehensive model for risk analysis [27][29] as illustrated in Figure 1. The process starts with the threat source, their intent, and the likelihood they will initiate a threat event to attempt to exploit a vulnerability in the target organisation. The degree to which the attacker is successful in exploiting these vulnerabilities will depend on the effectiveness of the mitigative security controls. The residual risk is the combination of likelihood that the exploit will succeed and the degree of the adverse impact if it does.

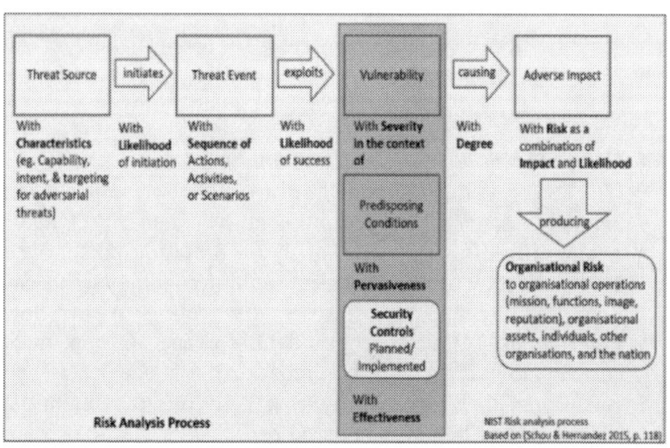

Figure 1. NIST Risk Analysis Process

7) Risk treatment

Prioritise the risks based on business impact. Identify and evaluate countermeasures, or controls that can be applied to reduce the residual risk. Calculate the cost of these controls. The types of controls need to be appropriate for the criticality and sensitivity of the assets, the vulnerabilities and threats to these assets, where they are in the lifecycle, and the potential consequences of a security incident [6][15]-[17].

Controls are selected to:

i. protect critical and sensitive information assets;
ii. mitigate risks and avoid unnecessary operational, financial, and customer losses.
iii. ensure compliance with regulatory and legislation requirements;
iv. gain competitive edge.

8) Monitoring Risk

Following the implementation of the recommended controls, the organisation should monitor, measure and validate the effectiveness of controls and the extent to which they are meeting their objectives [15]-[17].

IV. RECOMMENDED CONTROLS

These controls have been identified from the sources discussed [1]-[16][19][20][22][23][26]-[28][30]-[32] and tested in the Australian cyber landscape for their effectiveness in maintaining cyber security and resilience for a mid-sized Australian organisation with 300-500 employees. These controls apply in both physical (and virtual) data centres and cloud computing architectures, and can be implemented within a reasonable budget and timeframe.

TABLE I. RECOMMENDED CYBER SECURITY CONTROLS

Ownership, accountability, and resourcing	
Objective	***Control***
Information Security Policy	The Information Security Policy is owned and endorsed by the board. It defines how the organisation will mitigate specific elements of its cyber risk, including the behavior it expects from its people. The Information Security Policy is accessible and communicated to all staff on a regular basis, and staff are held to account.
Appropriately staffed & resourced	The cyber security strategy and day-to-day responsibility for implementing and maintaining security protection, detection, response and recovery sits with the CIO, CTO, and/or CISO. This person must have appropriate cyber knowledge.
Trusted staff	Background checks should be conducted on all internal employees. Administration-level privileges should only be provided to trusted staff, for the systems and periods they are required.
Develop a security culture by teaching employees how to protect their data	Induction training to include security policies on use of computers and devices, networks, and internet connections; and expectations of the employee in protecting sensitive and critical information.
	Train employees in appropriate use of corporate devices and resources, such as phones & printers.
	Have all new employees sign a statement that they comprehend these policies, that they will comply with these policies, and that they understand the consequences of non-compliance.
Protection and Prevention	
Objective	***Control***
Protect networks, systems and	Install and regularly update anti-virus and anti-spyware software on every computer and device on the network, and all that will connect to the network.

information from damage by viruses, spyware, and malicious code.	This includes within the office, remote access, and any third-party supplier devices that connect to the organisation's network. Set the anti-virus to automatically update and scan at a regular time.
Provide security for the internet connection: hardware firewall	Install, use, and keep operational a hardware firewall between the internal corporate network and the internet
	Install, use, and keep operational a hardware firewall between internal employee's home network and the internet if employees work from home
	Change the administrator's name and regularly change the administrator's password on the hardware firewall
Provide security for the internet connection: software firewall	Install, configure, use, and keep operational a software firewall between the internal corporate network and the internet. Enable and configure the firewall on Microsoft and IOS systems.
	Install, configure, use, and keep operational a software firewall between internal employee's home network and the internet. Enable and configure the firewall on Microsoft systems.
Patch operating systems and applications	Test and install application and operating system patches. Critical patches should be installed within 48 hours. Use automated scans to identify unpatched vulnerabilities, and determine temporary workarounds until patches are made available.
Control physical access to all computers and network components	Only allow authorised people to have physical access to and use of corporate devices.
	Position computer screens and displays so people walking past cannot read them.
	Know and monitor who has access to the systems, networks, and office space, including cleaners & maintenance, and network repair personnel.
	Store servers and communication hardware in a secure server room, and limit access to those who need it.
	Implement a policy to challenge all unknown personnel.
Secure the wireless access point and network	Set the wireless access point so it doesn't broadcast its SSID (Service Set Identifier).
	Change the default administrative login id and password on the device.
	Use strong encryption for transmitted data so it cannot be easily intercepted and read by electronic eavesdroppers. (WPS-2) (Don't use WEP)
Data storage: Static encryption	Classify, label, and encrypt all sensitive data in storage.
Data storage: Data loss prevention	Establish and train employees on 'rules' in relation to handling and protecting customer data, both at work, and offsite. (e.g., Don't put customer data on home computers)
	Disable USB drive connections
	Monitor data transfer through all channels (email, file copy, print etc.) IDS can assist with this.
	Secure hardware destruction prior to decommissioning
	Utilise the ability to remotely wipe all mobile devices
Encryption in transit	Encrypt data in transit within the network and when shared externally. Options include TLS 1.3 (at the transport layer), WinZip AES 256 for email attachments, and SFTP for external file transfer.
Encryption key management	Securely store the encryption keys and restrict and monitor who accesses these. Tools are available for this purpose but they are only as secure as their own access controls.
Individual user accounts	Each must have a separate, individual user account for each application, computer, and device.
	Passwords need to be a random series of letters, numbers, and special characters, and be at least 8 characters long. Use passphrases.
	Passwords should be changed every 3 months.
	All users should have accounts that DO NOT have administrative privileges.
	Prevent users from installing unauthorised software.
	Administrative rights should only be used by systems administrators for the time and the purpose for which they are needed. Never surf the web from an admin account. It may allow malicious software to be downloaded and installed.
Limit data access to needs to know	Employees should have only access to the specific data and systems they need to do their job. This access should be verified every 3 months
Separation of duties	Protect the business from insider threat by not allowing a single individual to both initiate and approve a financial or other transaction.
Multi-factor authentication	Utilise multi-factor authentication (MFA) on all systems and accounts holding and accessing sensitive and critical data.
Disable macros	Disable macros except in specific, identified circumstances.
Whitelisting	Only download software from trusted sites. Only allow known, listed apps to be installed and run on corporate computers.
Hardware disposal	When disposing of business computers, remove and destroy the hard drives. When disposing of storage media: drives, USB's, paper copies, containing sensitive information, destroy using a cross-cut shredder.
Application development and testing	Have separate build, test, staging, and production environments. Apply security measures to build and test environments. For example: firewall protection; encryption & data masking to protect sensitive information.
	Build security into every phase of the development lifecycle: design, build, test, and implementation
	Perform exploit testing to identify vulnerabilities in applications, prioritise resolution into maintenance schedule.
Secure services and data	Harden Applications. Applications should be developed and implemented to separate the user interface, processing, and data storage layers. Limit communications and data transfer between application layers with subnets, port hardening, and security groups.
Continuous hosting critical systems	Redundant Servers: failover monitoring of critical servers.
	In virtual cloud, pre-image servers for DR redundancy
Harden DNS	Configure DNS server to alternative third-party DNS, such as OpenDNS, Norton DNS, or DNS Resolvers.
Uninterrupted data store	Establish redundant data store (e. Raid5 failover for data, or secondary data store in cloud)
Uninterrupted power	Establish Uninterrupted Power Supply (UPS), with redundant power source
Uninterrupted LAN-to-WAN comms	Redundant LAN-to-WAN connection: ADSL, wireless mobile with alternate ISP
	LAN-to-WAN Domain Router selects alternative connection: ADSL, wireless mobile with alternate ISP & automatically switches over
Uninterrupted LAN	Redundant LAN (cloud or redundant wireless Lan router)
Uninterrupted phone & VoIP	Redundant phone number, VoIP alternative or diversion.

comms	
Identify and track vulnerabilities	Utilise vulnerability scanning tools to identify vulnerabilities relating to patching and OWASP Top 10.
Penetration testing to identify vulnerabilities	Perform penetration testing pre and post release. Perform both internal and external black box and white box penetration testing.
Manage and close vulnerabilities	Prioritise vulnerabilities for resolution and retest based on criticality and sensitivity of assets at risk.
Detection	
Objective	***Control***
Log and analyse activities and events	Define and implement systems and security activity and event logging for all levels, systems, and networks.
	Monitor attempts to access closed and unused ports.
Inbound email authentication	DMARC, DKIM, SPF protocols for inbound DNS authentication, to prevent email spoofing
Email scanning	Incoming emails should be scanned for SPAM and malicious links and content.
Intrusion Detection	Utilise IDS to identify anomalous behaviours and review event logs regularly.
Identify intrusions early	Implement Security Information and Event Management (SIEM) to collate and analyse all log data. Utilise machine learning / artificial intelligence to identify anomalous behaviours across multiple systems as early warning indicators of compromise
Response and Recovery	
Objective	***Control***
Backup important business information	Don't store sensitive information on desktop C: drives Implement a comprehensive backup policy, to backup business information (data), including word processing documents, spreadsheets, configuration information & paper files The 'grandfather' principle has 3 cycles of backup – 1. a snapshot or drive for each day of the week: gets overwritten the same day the following week; 2. a snapshot or drive for each week of the month: gets overwritten the following month; 3. snapshot or drive for each month of the year: gets overwritten the same month the following year Retain the last snapshot or drive for the year, for 8 years. Backup onto separate, removable media or long-term cloud storage. Store backups offsite segregated from primary data. Redundancy for all servers running critical applications Redundancy for critical database(s) O/S & apps should be able to be reinstalled from CD, USB, or snapshot.
	Test the backed-up data to ensure it can be reliably read and restored successfully, at least every 3 months.
Denial of Service Protection	Processes & agreements in place to gain assistance from ISP and/or cloud provider DDoS protection capabilities to identify and block traffic from attacker's IP address(s) (in DoS or DDoS attack)
	Implement & monitor Web Application Firewall (WAF) on all web facing servers.
Cyber security incident management	Plan and implement Cyber Incident Response Process
	Plan for and implement threat awareness and critical incident communications.
Comply with the Australian Privacy Act	Incorporate appropriate data breach notifications into the Incident Management Process.
Business continuity planning (BCP) and testing	Pre-arrange alternative office facilities or secure remote access. For infrastructure housed in a physical data centre, redundant systems in an alternative location will be required. In a cloud computing architecture, terminal servers may be used to facilitate remote access (via secure VPN). Remote systems monitoring to allow system administrators to work remotely or from home
Outsourcing and Supplier Management	
Objective	***Control***
Assure third party security	Assess cyber security capability of third parties interfacing into the organisation systems, and/or storing or processing sensitive or critical data to assure they have at least the same cyber security.

A. *Compliance*

As a result of effectively implementing this Risk Management Plan, with the recommended controls, the organisation will satisfy the requirements for:

- ASD Security certification and accreditation;
- ISO 27001, and ISO 27002 compliance;
- Australian Privacy Standard;
- APRA CPS 234.

V. CONCLUSION

Defence in depth can be an expensive process. It is critical for businesses of all sizes to focus on the real risks that may impact their sensitive and critical data, and to mitigate these in priority order. An effective Risk Management Plan provides a robust framework within which to manage cyber security and cyber resilience. There are many sources of truth when it comes to identifying the right controls for a particular organisation. Taking a structured risk-based approach, based on the information available from NIST, ISO, and ASD will enable an organisation to balance IT security expenditure with business outcomes, and assure the company's survivability in the face of increasing cyber security concerns.

REFERENCES

[1] J. Andress and S. Winterfeld, "Cyber Warfare: Techniques, tactics and tools for security practitioners", second edition, Elsevier, Inc, United States of America, 2014.

[2] APRA, "Prudential Practice Guide CPG 234 – Management of Security Risk in Information and Information Technology", 2013, Available from: https://www.apra.gov.au /sites/default/files/Prudential-Practice-Guide-CPG-234-Management-of-Security-Risk-May-2013_1.pdf, accessed August 2019

[3] APRA, "Prudential Practice Guide CPG 235 – Managing Data Risk", 2013, Available from: https://www.apra.gov.au /sites/default/files/Prudential-Practice-Guide-CPG-235-Managing-Data-Risk_0.pdf, accessed August 2019

[4] APRA, Prudential Standard CPS 232 Business Continuity Management", 2017, Available from: https://www.apra.gov.au/sites/default/files/Prudential-Standard-CPS-232-Business-Continuity-Management-%28July-2017%29.pdf, accessed August 2019

[5] APRA, "Prudential Standard CPS 231 Outsourcing", 2017, Available from: https://www.apra.gov.au/sites/default/files/Prudential-Standard-CPS-231-Outsourcing-%28July-2017%29.pdf, accessed August 2019

[6] APRA, "Prudential Standard CPS 234 - Information Security (Draft)", 2018, Available from: https://www.apra.gov.au/sites/default/files/Draft-CPS-234.pdf, accessed August 2019

[7] ASD, "Strategies to Mitigate Cyber Security Incidents", Australian Cybersecurity Centre (ACSC), Australian Government, 2017, Available from: https://www.cyber.gov.au/publications/strategies-to-mitigate-cyber-security-incidents, accessed August 2019

[8] ASD, "The Essential 8 Explained", ACSC, Australian Government 2017, Available from: https://www.acsc.gov.au/publications/protect/essential-eight-explained.htm, accessed August 2019

[9] ASD, "Australian Government Information Security Manual", ACSC, Australian Government, 2019, Available from: https://www.cyber.gov.au/node/237, accessed August 2019

[10] ASD 2019, "Preparing for and Responding to Denial-of-Service Attacks", ACSC, Australian Government, Available from: https://www.cyber.gov.au/node/166, accessed August 2019

[11] ASD, "Cloud computing security", ACSC, Australian Government, 2019, Available from: https://www.cyber.gov.au/node/55, accessed August 2019

[12] ASD, "Risk management of enterprise mobility including bring your own device", ACSC, Australian Government, 2019, Available from: https://www.cyber.gov.au/node/171

[13] R. Bejtlich, "The tao of network monitoring: beyond intrusion detection", Addison-Wesley 2005.

[14] R. Bejtlich, "The practice of Network Security Monitoring: Understanding Incident Detection and Response", San Francisco: No Starch Press, 2013.

[15] ISO AS ISO/IEC 27001:2015 "Information technology – Security Techniques – Information security management systems – Requirements"

[16] AS ISO/IEC 27002:2015 "Information technology – Security techniques – Code of practice for information security controls"

[17] A. Calder and S. Watkins, "IT Governance: a manager's guide to data security and ISO 27001/ISO 27002", Kogan Page, 2008.

[18] A. Shostack, Threat modelling: designing for security, John Wiley & Sons, Inc. 10475 Crosspoint, BoulevardIndianapolis, IN 46256., 2014

[19] Department of Homeland Security (DHS), "NIST Cyber Security Framework", 2014, Available from: https://www.nist.gov/cyberframework/online-learning/components-framework.

[20] Federal Communications Commission (FCC), "Cyber Security Planning Guide", October 2012, Available from: https://transition.fcc.gov/cyber/cyberplanner.pdf, accessed August 2019

[21] D. Gibson, "Managing risk in information systems", Jones Bartlett Learning, Burlington MA 01803, 2015.

[22] K. Joiner et al., "Four testing types core to informed ICT governance for cyber-resilient systems", IARIA 2018, International journal on advances in security, issn1942-2636 vol.11,no.3&4,year2018, pp.313-327, Available from: http://www.iariajournals.org/security/, accessed August 2019

[23] R. Kissel, NISTIR 7621: "Small Business Information Security: The Fundamentals", 2009, Available from: http://csrc.nist.gov/publications/nistir/ir7621/nistir-7621.pdf, accessed August 2019

[24] Malwaretech, 2017, "How to Accidentally Stop a Global Cyber Attacks", MalwareTech,13 May 2017, Available from: https://www.malwaretech.com/2017/05/how-to-accidentally-stop-a-global-cyber-attacks.html

[25] Mandiant 2013, "APT1: exposing one of china's cyber espionage units", Mandiant, Available from: https://www.fireeye.com/content/dam/fireeye-www/services/pdfs/mandiant-apt1-report.pdf, accessed August 2019

[26] NIST 2013, Security and Privacy Controls for Federal Information Systems and Organizations, "National Institute of Standards and Technology Special Publication 800-53", Revision 4 462 pages (April 2013) CODEN: NSPUE2 Available from: http://dx.doi.org/10.6028/NIST.SP.800-53r4, accessed August 2019

[27] NIST, "NIST special publication 800-31, National Institute of Standards and Technology Special Publication 800-53", 2019, Available from: https://nvd.nist.gov/800-53, accessed August 2019

[28] OWASP, Top 10-2017 Top 10, "Open Web Application Security Project", 2017, Available from: https://www.owasp.oeg/index.php/top_10-2017_Top_10, accessed August 2019

[29] C. Schou and S. Hernandez, "Information Assurance handbook: Effective computer security and risk management strategies", McGraw Hill Education. United States of America, 2015.

[30] A. Sedgewick, M. Souppaya, and K. Scarfone, "NIST Special Publication 800-167: Guide to Application Whitelisting", U.S Dept Commerce 2015, Available from: http://dx.doi.org/10.6028/NIST.SP.800-167, accessed August 2019

[31] Verizon Enterprise Solutions 2018, 2018 "Data Breach Investigations Report", Available from: https://enterprise.verizon.com/resources/reports/dbir/, accessed August 2019

[32] Verizon Enterprise Solutions 2019, 2019 "Data Breach Investigations Report", Available from: https://enterprise.verizon.com/resources/reports/dbir/, accessed August 2019

[33] S. Winterfeld and J. Andress, "The basics of cyber warfare: understanding the fundamentals of cyber warfare in theory and practice", Elsevier, Inc, United States of America, 2013.

Cyber Security Controls

The role of policy, collaboration and engagement in cyber security

Leonie Shepherd
Technology
Objective Insight
Australia
anne.objectiveinsight@gmail.com

Abstract— **In Australia, Cyber-attacks are increasing with devastating impact to some business. The Australian Signals Directorate's Australian Cyber Security Centre (ACSC) [4] is running a survey to understand what small to medium sized businesses want or need to tackle cybercrime. They report that "the level of knowledge about good cyber security practices remains fairly low with the majority of businesses believing they are safe from cybercrime because they use antivirus software". These companies would employ people who can assist in minimizing cyber-attacks when they are engaged via effective policies and frameworks with a focus on engagement between the owners and users of the policies to ensure they are fit for purpose, easy to understand and follow. The ACSC also drives cyber security awareness. However enhanced collaboration across organizations and industry to combine skills and knowledge would further assist in effective cyber resilience with metrics help to focus people on the desired outcomes.**

Keywords-APRA; CPS234; policy; engagement.

I. INTRODUCTION

Every person that accesses the systems and data in organizations represent some kind of cyber security risk. Organizations rely on their people to identify potential cyber risks and take the appropriate steps aligned to their requirements. Therefore business and technology processes need to be regularly reviewed to identify where things can go wrong with a focus on the user of the policy and framework via workshops and awareness programs for example.

The use of entity level controls will assist in minimizing cyber risks. The nature of controls can be either preventative or detective and act as management's primary line of defense. This includes effective frameworks, policies and procedures that are fit for purpose and the reality of the situations they are meant to cover with options for contributions to assist in improving their effectiveness as a part of changing organizational culture to be more cyber resilient.

A control is an action taken by management to mitigate an inherent risk and/or satisfy an obligation. A control either reduces the likelihood of the risk occurring or reduces the potential impact if the risk occurs. It needs to be proportionate to the risks faced and designed to support strategic objectives. The ACSC survey highlights potential gaps and weaknesses in current processes and capabilities that result in cyber-attacks. This is one of a number of initiatives by the Australia Government. The Australian Prudential Regulatory Authority (APRA), who has a remit by the Australian government to regulate consumer banks, business banks, insurance companies, hedge funds, investment banks and superannuation providers, introduced Standard CPS234 for all APRA regulated entities effective 1 July 2019. The key obligation under CPS234 is that regulated entities must maintain information security in a manner commensurate with the size and extent of threats to its information assets, and which enables the continued sound operation of the entity. It applies to all information assets regardless of whether they are material business activities or not and assets managed by third parties [1]. APRA regulated businesses also rely on their people to know and do the right thing to protect companies from cyber-attacks. The Office of the Australian Information Commissioner (OAIC) [2] report that only 5% of data breaches notified under the NDB scheme from 1 April 2018 to 31 March 2019 were due to system faults however 35% were due to human error.

The rest of the paper is structured as follows; Section II introduces the need to focus on the people that organizations rely on to be more cyber resilient and the requirements of APRA regulated entities as cyber-attacks have increased on financial organizations Section III presents a proposal to more effectively collaborate and engage across and within organizations to help them to be more cyber resilient. Section IV concludes the paper.

II. COLLABORATE AND ENGAGE

Effective engagement between policy owners and the people required to understand and follow the policy will assist in minimizing potential cyber risks. This includes creating a culture where people can and will work together to share specialized knowledge and experience just as the cyber criminals work together. Furthermore, it is increasingly important for organizations to collaborate with each other and with their people to gain new insights and connections to better protect their systems and data as the cost of cyber-crime increases. This includes supporting effective governance of outsourced services and reviewing contracted arrangements aligned to policy and frameworks.

A. *APRA regulated organizations*

APRA regulated organizations, under CPS234, are required to ensure their policies, standards, guidelines and procedures pertaining to information security are in order and aligned to their exposure to threats. An effective policy framework is important to manage potential risks, as it includes responsibilities of stakeholders to whom the framework applies including Board, senior management, governing bodies and individuals. This would include categorizing and managing data classifications and supporting employees to understand and manage their data appropriately, particularly customer related or sensitive information. Therefore, policies need to be accessible, effective, streamlined, simplified so that they are easy to understand and follow, enforceable, written in plain English and tied to employee metrics (key performance indicators) to support behavior changes.

In an APRA regulated entity, Boards are ultimately responsible for information security. However, they rely on their employees and sometimes on a third party provider to understand and adhere to their organizational policies and procedures. They rely on frameworks being reviewed and tested by the framework owner on an annual or more frequent basis where required and effective governance. The use of outsourced service providers does not eliminate management's responsibility for maintaining effective controls over material inherent risks or compliance with laws and regulations [1].

B. Notifiable data breachess

Process level controls need to be in place to ensure or verify that appropriate actions have been taken when executing a process or to recover from errors or irregularities. For example, APRA says that the cyber security measures in CPS234 will help APRA-regulated entities to repel cyber adversaries, as well as handle incident response swiftly and effectively if a breach occurs [1]. This follows an increased number of cyber-attacks. Since Australia's Notifiable Data Breaches (NDB) scheme launched in February 2018, the Office of the Australian Information Commissioner (OAIC) advise that 964 data breaches were reported between 1 Apr 2018 and 31 March 2019, which is a 712% increase in reported data breaches. The main sources of the data breaches were attributed to malicious or criminal attacks (60%), phishing and spear phishing (153), credentials obtained by unknown means (28%) and human error (35%). OAIC report that 83% of data breaches affected fewer than 1,000 people. However, 86% of notifications involved disclosure of contact information. The finance sector accounted for 41% of data breaches compared to a 35% average for all sectors. OAIC advise "The predominance of human factors in data breaches emphasizes the importance of education and training for all employees who handle personal information." [2]

The goal of CPS234 is continued information security management and improvement, investment aligned to the sophistication of the cyber-attacks and risk management. APRA expects these entities to ensure the security of all customer data". APRA must be notified as soon as possible but no later than 72 hours after becoming aware of an information security incident that did or had the potential to materially affect a stakeholder [1]. OAIC report that "most data breaches—including those resulting from a cyber incident—involved a human element, such as an employee sending information to the wrong person or clicking on a link that resulted in the compromise of user credentials". [2].

III. PROPOSAL

Considering how long cyber security has been highlighted, yet more organizations are victims of cyber-attacks, perhaps there is an opportunity to more effectively collaborate and engage across organizations and within organizations with a focus on the people they rely on to assist them to be cyber resilient, for example via awareness. This may include guidance on how organizations, which hold customer or sensitive data, could run a diagnostic gap analysis against their current cyber security governance framework. For example, running an assessment to identify potential gaps and weaknesses in current processes and capabilities related to:

1. Reviewing roles and responsibilities such as actionable roles and escalation processes
2. Information security capability such as how internal and third party risk assessments are conducted. How vendors are tiered according to risk
3. Policy framework such as the location of the organisational frameworks covering vulnerabilities and threats – how is this stored and maintained, who has access to it in what format. This includes the owner details correctly and clearly recorded for queries and feedback
4. Implementation of controls such as how vulnerabilities and threats are detected then classified and measured.
5. Review and update information security policies, procedures and controls for example including one or a combination of the following:

a. Walk through processes from start to finish with the people performing the activities to collect evidence of how activities that minimise cyber security risks are performed. This provides assurance that all controls and potential control gaps are identified. Once controls are identified and documented, link them to the relevant risk. This includes ensuring adequate cyber security mechanisms where a supplier manages data or systems
b. Ask questions aimed at getting relevant information from the people performing the activities in order to identify the points in the process where things can go wrong and the actions that have been designed to prevent, detect and recover from these errors.
c. Review existing policies, procedures, standards and guidelines for adequacy of information security controls such as via conducting workshops to

discuss changes to the business environment, risk, controls and any potential issues

6. Review contracts with service providers. Test their security controls and evaluate their governance processes if they manage organizational assets.

7. Run awareness campaigns aimed at ensuring policies and frameworks make sense, clearly set out what is required, support delivery of what is necessary and clarify where and how to make a positive contribution to improve it. Combine this with metrics supporting behavior changes. Ongoing monitoring would provide feedback on the effectiveness of the campaigns..

IV. CONCLUSION

Using APRA CPS234 guidelines or similar, organizational testing of information security capability and policy framework in terms of people, processes and technology at the most fundamental level is important to combine the various initiatives. Clearly defined, documented policies, standards and procedures with the end-user in mind support management requirements (information threats, technical and procedural vulnerabilities). Aim for a balance of benefit versus risk of each control when reviewing results as a part of ensuring confidentiality, integrity (accuracy and freedom from unauthorized change or usage) and availability (access and usability when required).

REFERENCES

[1] Australia Prudential Regulation Authority (APRA), "Prudential Standard CPS 234 - Information Security (Draft)", 2018, Available from: https://www.apra.gov.au /sites/default/files/Draft-CPS-234.pdf

[2] Office of the Australian Information Commissioner (OAIC) "Notifiable Data Breaches scheme 12-month insights report", Available from: https:///www.oaic.gov.au/privacy/notifiable-data-breaches/notifiable-data-breaches-statistics/notifiable-data-breaches-scheme-12month-insights-report//

[3] Smart Collaboration: Breaking Down Silos - Heidi K. Gardner

[4] The Australian Signals Directorate's Australian Cyber Security Centre (ACSC), available via https://www.cyber.gov.au/

Detecting Spectre Vulnerabilities by Sound Static Analysis

Daniel Kästner, Laurent Mauborgne, Christian Ferdinand
AbsInt GmbH
Email: info@absint.com
Science Park 1, 66123 Saarbrcken
Germany

Henrik Theiling
Sysgo AG
Email: office@sysgo.com
Am Pfaffenstein 14, 55270 Klein-Winternheim
Germany

***Abstract*—Spectre attacks are critical transient execution attacks affecting a wide range of microprocessors and potentially all software executed on them, including embedded and safety-critical software systems. In order to help eliminating Spectre vulnerabilities at a reasonable human and performance cost, we propose to build on an efficient industrial code analyzer, such as Astrée, which enables an automatic analysis of big complex C codes with high precision. Its main purpose is to discover run time errors, but to do so, it computes precise over-approximations of all the states reachable by a program. We enriched these states with tainting information based on a novel tainting strategy to detect Spectre v1, v1.1 and SplitSpectre vulnerabilities. The selectivity and performance of the analysis is evaluated on the embedded real-time operating system PikeOS, and on industrial safety-critical embedded software projects from the avionics and automotive domain.**

***Keywords*–Spectre; taint analysis; abstract interpretation; static analysis; embedded software; operating systems; safety; cybersecurity.**

I. INTRODUCTION

In the past year, a series of cybersecurity attacks have been publicly reported, which exploit transient instruction execution, i.e., instructions which should not have an observable effect since they are speculatively executed or have to be flushed because of an exception [1] [2]. They have become known as Spectre or Meltdown attacks and they are highly problematic because they are rooted in hardware features present in most current hardware architectures. They can be considered confidentiality breaches: essentially, a malicious program can exploit Meltdown and Spectre to get hold of secrets stored in the memory of other running programs. Since the initial publication of [1] [2] there was a continuous stream of novel versions of transient execution attacks, so the full extend of the problem is still not fully known.

In the past, security properties have mostly been relevant for non-embedded and/or non-safety-critical programs. Recently due to increasing connectivity requirements (cloud-based services, car-to-car communication, over-the-air updates, etc.), more and more security issues are rising in safety-critical software as well. Security exploits like the Jeep Cherokee hacks [3] which affect the safety of the system are becoming more and more frequent. Because of the increasingly pervasive monitoring of personal data including location data or health information, confidentiality breaches in embedded systems like mobile phones, automobiles, or airplanes have to be considered increasingly critical. Furthermore, data leakage might also have impact on safety, e.g., if administrator or maintenance passwords are leaked.

While Meltdown (so far) has only been reported on Intel and AMD processors, Spectre attacks affect a wide range of target architectures. As of today, four different classes of Spectre attacks have been reported, some of which comprise several distinct attack vectors. For some of the attacks, mitigation measures have been suggested that can be practically applied. The Spectre v1, Spectre v1.1 and SplitSpectre attacks are based on speculative execution, in particular, on branch prediction on array bound index checks. Vulnerabilities to these kinds of attacks can be discovered by static analysis. A naive mitigation strategy consists of flushing the cache or inserting memory barriers before every conditional instruction, which, however, would cause unacceptable runtime overhead. In our work we show that with low analysis effort it is possible to precisely identify Spectre v1/v1.1 and SplitSpectre vulnerabilities: there has to be an index bound check which depends on user-supplied data such that the accessed array element is used to access an element of another array. We will show that these vulnerabilities can be detected with very low false alarm rates, so that they can be safely mitigated with low runtime overhead.

The methodology we apply is abstract interpretation, a formal method for sound semantics-based static program analysis [4]. It supports formal soundness proofs (it can be proven that no error is missed) and scales to real-life industry applications. Abstract interpretation-based static analyzers provide full control and data coverage and allow conclusions to be drawn that are valid for all program runs with all inputs. Such conclusions may be that no timing or space constraints are violated, or that runtime errors or data races are absent: the absence of these errors can be guaranteed [5]. Nowadays, abstract interpretation-based static analyzers that can detect stack overflows [6] and violations of timing constraints [7] and that can prove the absence of runtime errors and data races [8] [9], are widely used for developing and verifying safety-critical software.

A. *Related Work*

Related work on applying static analysis to detect Spectre attacks has been reported in [10]. The difference to our approach is that [10] works on binary code, using mainly the BAP code analyzer [11], which cannot soundly analyze all possible behaviors, but relies on bounds to unroll loops, meaning that the approach cannot, in general, find all possible vulnerabilities. Our approach works at the source code level since here the analyzer can be sound and still be very precise about function pointer calls and other pointer accesses which reduces the false alarm rate, compared to approaches at the binary level. Another difference is that in our work we could also cover the SplitSpectre vulnerability which was made public only a few months ago. Also the code under analysis is different: we are focusing on real-life industrial code, which is at the same time safety-critical and subject to cybersecurity requirements.

Taint analysis of big c programs was presented in [12], but it was based on a type system, and still a prototype that did not lead to an industrial quality tool.

B. Contributions

We discuss the impact of Spectre vulnerability on industrial running code, and explain how it can be mitigated. The target application used in our work is the real-time operating system PikeOS, which is used in aerospace, medical, automotive, railway, and industrial applications up to highest criticality levels. An operating system deployed in highly critical aerospace and automotive applications is subject to severe safety and cybersecurity requirements. We demonstrate that – without specific counter measures – even such a system is vulnerable to Spectre attacks and we show that by using our static analysis framework these vulnerabilities can be efficiently eliminated. Apart from the OS layer, we also evaluate our approach on real-life safety-critical applications from the avionics and automotive sectors.

As discovering the places to insert the mitigations is non-trivial (in fact, it can be proven to be undecidable), we propose to extend the sound static analyzer Astrée with a dedicated taint analysis, to help find a small number of places where mitigations should be considered. Our contribution includes the use of sets of taint hues, which allows to track complex taint states, and provides more precise hints for Spectre vulnerabilities. The precision and scalability of the tainting follows from the precision and scalability of Astrée on industrial code. Astrée runs on C programs, but the taint strategy presented in this article is applicable to other programming languages as well.

C. Overview

This article is structured as follows: in Section II we will give an overview of the Spectre vulnerabilities, focusing on the Spectre-PHT variants targeted by the approach presented in this article. Section III describes the kernel structure of the PikeOS operating system and discusses the basic concepts for mitigating Spectre vulnerabilities. After a brief introduction of static program analysis and abstract interpretation in Section IV, we describe the design and the work flow of the Astrée analyzer in Section V. Section VI starts with discussing static analysis of cybersecurity properties in general, then summarizes the key concepts of taint analysis, and concludes with a precise description of our taint analysis-based Spectre detection algorithm. The experimental results are presented in Section VII, Section VIII concludes.

II. SPECTRE

In this section, we give an overview of Spectre attacks with a focus on Spectre vulnerabilities and illustrate them with typical code examples. In doing so we follow the systematization from [13]. Spectre belongs to the class of transient execution attacks which use covert channels for transmitting data from transient execution stages to a persistent architectural state. Instructions whose execution has been started by the CPU but whose results are never committed to the architectural state are called transient instructions. They can occur due to out-of-order execution, speculation, but also due to exceptions and interrupts. Transient execution attacks transfer microarchitectural state changes caused by the execution of transient instructions to an observable architectural state. Spectre-type attacks exploit branch misprediction events; in contrast Meltdown-type attacks exploit transient out-of-order instructions following a CPU exception. To overcome the increasingly confusing naming of newly discovered transient execution vulnerabilities the article [13] proposes a naming scheme based on the microarchitectural element exploited by the attack:

- **Spectre-PHT**: V1 (CVE-2017-5753, Bounds Check Bypass) [14], V1.1 (CVE-2018-3693, Bounds Check Bypass on Stores) [15], and the newly discovered *SplitSpectre* [16] exploit the *Pattern History Table* (PHT)
- **Spectre-BTB**: V2 (CVE-2017-5715, Branch Target Injection) [14] exploits the *Branch Target Buffer* (BTB)
- **Spectre-STL**: V4 (CVE-2018-3639, Speculative Store Bypass) [17] exploits CPU memory disambiguation, specifically store-to-load forwarding (STLF)
- **Spectre-RSB**: ret2spec [18] and Spectre-RSB [19] exploit the Return Stack Buffer (RSB).

Note that Spectre V1.2 can actually be considered a Meltdown attack since it depends on a `#PF` exception [13].

In our work we are targeting Spectre-PHT since other vulnerabilies can be handled differently: Variant 2 can be fixed in one central point or by switching on compiler mitigations, so we need no analyzer. For V3 (Meltdown) and V3a, we expect a microcode update, and otherwise, software cannot protect against this anyway, so again, an analyzer does not help. For V4, if the microcode permits it, we can use the 'speculative store bypass disable'. Otherwise, V4 would need a binary analyzer, which is currently out of scope of this work. Similarly, for Spectre-RSB a binary-level analyzer would be required. The advantage of a source-level detection of Spectre V1/V1.1/SplitSpectre vulnerabilities is that it is possible to precisely and efficiently detect and mitigate them without the imprecisions and manual interactions to be considered for binary-level analysis.

The basic idea of Spectre v1/1.1 is to exploit that speculative execution of memory accesses modifies the cache in trusted code, which can then be detected from untrusted code using timing attacks, i.e., measuring timing of memory accesses to determine what the trusted code accessed. The vulnerability is a breach of security: the memory accesses that cause the cache to be modified in trusted code are not actually properly executed since they are protected by a range check. They are only speculatively executed, i.e., the effect of this speculative execution should have been discarded by the processor. But despite being executed only speculatively, the processor does not undo the effect on the cache. This, in effect, allows the timing attack to see the result of memory accesses that are properly protected by a check.

The scenario in which this vulnerability can be exploited is the following: there is trusted code that has two array accesses, the first of which is indexed based on data from untrusted code. This happens frequently in communication between trusted and untrusted code, e.g., with file handle ids, or other ids to address resources in trusted code. An example is given in Figure 1:

```
ErrCode vulnerable1(unsigned idx)
{
    if (idx >= arr1.size) {
        return E_INVALID_PARAMETER;
    }
    unsigned u1 = arr1.data[idx];
    ...
    unsigned u2 = arr2.data[u1];
    ...
}
```

Figure 1. Code with Spectre vulnerability.

In the code listing of Figure 1, `idx` is untrusted data that is used to index `arr1`. The array access is properly protected by an `if()` on the array size and generates an error message, so the code has no obviously broken security problems with the array access. However, the processor may still, despite the conditional, speculatively execute `arr1.data[idx]`. This speculative execution is discarded later, when the code exits the function with an error code, but the effect on the cache is not undone. Since the index is out of range, the array access can read much more memory that just the contents of `arr1`. Usually, the whole address space may be speculatively read by code like the above.

To read in user space what was the result of the access, the second array access comes into play: the value read from `arr1` is used to index `arr2`, so depending on the value of the first read, the second array access again modifies the cache. Untrusted code can then time which cache lines were touched to find out the value of `u1`, and since the index to `arr1` is under the control of untrusted code, untrusted code can effectively read any memory cell accessible in the trusted code.

All this is based on the speculative execution of the two array accesses, the result of which are discarded, but the cache effect is not undone, making this exploitable.

To fix this vulnerability in software, array indices in trusted code, no matter how well protected by a range check, must be fortified by mapping the array index into the array range. This limits the scope of the attack to the array itself, which is probably OK since with a value that is in range, trusted code would have accessed the array anyway. E.g., assume we have a function or macro `FENCEIDX` to map a value into $0..size-1$, we can rewrite the code from Figure 1 as shown in Figure 2 to protect against Spectre V1:

```
ErrCode vulnerable1(unsigned idx)
{
    if (idx >= arr1.size) {
        return E_INVALID_PARAMETER;
    }
    unsigned fidx =
        FENCEIDX(idx, arr1.size);
    unsigned u1 = arr1.data[fidx];
    ...
    unsigned u2 = arr2.data[u1];
    ...
}
```

Figure 2. Code from Figure 1 with protection against Spectre.

If the array access in this code is speculatively executed, the value of `u1` will be read only from `arr1`.

`FENCEIDX` can be implemented very efficiently on many architectures, so the impact on performance is negligible. The real problem is finding which array accesses to fortify, because a single missed vulnerable array access allows untrusted code to break into the trusted address space.

III. Protecting PikeOS against Spectre

PikeOS is SYSGO's embedded operating system and hypervisor. It is available for various 32-bit and 64-bit architectures: Intel and AMD x86, ARM, PowerPC, and SPARC. Some of these are affected by the Spectre vulnerability.

The PikeOS kernel was chosen for this work as a use case for examining how Spectre vulnerabilities can be detected with a static analyzer. The kernel is well suited because it is exactly functioning at different levels of trust, i.e., it receives via system calls information from untrusted user code and works with this information in the trusted kernel code. This is exactly the scenario where Spectre and similar vulnerabilities can be exploited. By being an operating system kernel for highly critical embedded systems, this is an interesting industrial use case.

A. *Manual Spectre Mitigation*

To examine how static analysis can help mitigate Spectre vulnerabilities in software, the PikeOS was first manually searched for patterns that are potentially vulnerable to Spectre V1. It turns out that the PikeOS kernel has only 700 array indirections, so manually checking each one for Spectre V1 is still feasible. When a potential vulnerability is identified, the counter-measure is to introduce a macro call that maps a user-provided array index to a value smaller than the array size, i.e., to rewrite `a[i]` as `a[FENCEIDX(i,n)]` where `n` is the array size. In the PikeOS kernel, we found 22 potential Spectre V1 vulnerabilities that we fixed this way. Different architectures implement `FENCEIDX(i,n)` in different ways to be as efficient as possible, and unaffected architectures just map it back to `i`.

The heuristics that was used for manual identification of a vulnerability may have caused false positive identifications, i.e., not all of these are guaranteed to be exploitable. This was done so that no vulnerability was missed by using an overly complicated identification strategy, i.e., we tried to make it easy for humans to judge the absence of a vulnerability in order to avoid mistakes. Whenever it looked like there could be one, the `FENCEIDX` was introduced. Note that a single failure to identify a vulnerability would leave the whole PikeOS kernel vulnerable.

The most recently documented SplitSpectre attack is most probably not applicable in PikeOS or any OS kernels, because the two parts of the exploit are distributed among trusted and untrusted code, separated by a system call layer in our case, where no value is leaking even on speculative paths. It is more likely to be exploitable in just-in-time compilation scenarios.

B. *Kernel Code Structure*

One complication for a static analyzer in the case of an operating system kernel is that the kernel is not a sequential application. So the typical static analyzer for application code will not be able to be applied directly the PikeOS kernel code.

On the other hand, the PikeOS kernel is a typical target for Spectre vulnerabilities, so adapting the static analyzer to the structure of an operating system kernel is another necessary step for a Spectre analyzer.

The structure of a kernel is typically split into two parts: the boot phase, where the kernel initializes data and hardware. This part is sequential, and the static analyzer needs this phase for its own boot-strapping of the values and contexts that the kernel executes in. In this phase, there is no user input, so no Spectre vulnerabilities can be found here. After the boot phase, the kernel basically turns into a library of callbacks that are triggered either by user-requests in the form of system calls, or by system events like interrupts. The system calls are the interesting ones for the Spectre analysis, as it is here where user provided data enters the PikeOS kernel.

IV. Static Program Analysis

Some years ago, static analysis meant manual review of programs. Nowadays, automatic static analysis tools are gaining popularity in software development as they offer a tremendous increase in productivity by automatically checking the code under a wide range of criteria. Here, the term *static analysis* is used to describe a variety of program analysis techniques with the common property that the results are only based on the software structure.

Purely syntactical methods can be applied to check syntactical coding rules as contained in coding guidelines, such as MISRA C [20], SEI CERT C [21], or Common Weakness Enumeration (CWE) [22]. They aim at a programming style that improves clarity and reduces the risk of introducing bugs. Compliance checking by static analysis tools has become common practice. Some of the rules require a deeper understanding of the code as they focus on semantical properties which requires knowledge about variable values, pointer targets etc.

To address such rules, and – even more importantly – to identify semantical code defects, semantics-based static analyses can be applied. Semantics-based methods can be further grouped into *unsound* vs. *sound* approaches, the essential difference being that in *sound* methods there are *no false negatives*, i.e., no defect will be missed (from the class of defects under consideration). Abstract interpretation is a formal method for sound semantics-based static program analysis [4]. It supports formal correctness proofs: it can be proved that an analysis will terminate and that it is sound, i.e., that it computes an over-approximation of the concrete semantics. Imprecisions can occur, but it can be shown that they will always occur on the safe side.

The difference between syntactical, unsound semantical and sound semantical analysis can be illustrated at the example of division by 0. In the expression $x/0$ the division by zero can be detected syntactically, but not in the expression a/b. When an *unsound* analyzer does not report a division by zero in a/b it might still happen in scenarios not taken into account by the analyzer. When a *sound* analyzer does not report a division by zero in a/b, this is a proof that b can never be 0.

V. Astrée

One example of a sound static runtime error analyzer is the Astrée analyzer [9] [23]. Its main purpose is to report program defects caused by unspecified and undefined behaviors according to the C norm (ISO/IEC 9899:1999 (E)). The reported code defects include integer/floating-point division by zero, out-of-bounds array indexing, erroneous pointer manipulation and dereferencing (buffer overflows, null pointer dereferencing, dangling pointers, etc.), data races, lock/unlock problems, deadlocks, etc.

The design of the analyzer aims at reaching the zero false alarm objective. For keeping the initial number of false alarms low, a high analysis precision is mandatory. To achieve high precision Astrée provides a variety of predefined abstract domains, e.g.: The interval domain approximates variable values by intervals, the octagon domain [24] covers relations of the form $x \pm y \leq c$ for variables x and y and constants c. The memory domain empowers Astrée to exactly analyze pointer arithmetic and union manipulations. It also supports a type-safe analysis of absolute memory addresses. With the filter domain digital filters can be precisely approximated, the interpolation domain tracks table lookups and interpolation functions. An automaton domain is available for precisely and efficiently analyzing finite-state machines. Floating-point computations are precisely modeled while keeping track of possible rounding errors.

Any remaining alarm has to be manually checked by the developers – and this manual effort should be as low as possible. Astrée explicitly supports investigating alarms in order to understand the reasons for them to occur. Alarm contexts can be interactively explored, the computed value ranges of variables can be displayed for each different context, the call graph is visualized, and a program slicer is available to identify the program parts contributing to a selected defect. By fine-tuning the precision of the analyzer to the software under analysis the number of false alarms can be further reduced.

To deal with concurrency defects, Astrée implements a sound low-level concurrent semantics [25] which provides a scalable sound abstraction covering all possible thread interleavings. The interleaving semantics enables Astrée, in addition to the classes of runtime errors found in sequential programs, to report data races, and lock/unlock problems, i.e., inconsistent synchronization. The set of shared variables does not need to be specified by the user: Astrée assumes that every global variable can be shared, and discovers which ones are effectively shared, and on which ones there is a data race. After a data race, the analysis continues by considering the values stemming from all interleavings. Since Astrée is aware of all locks held for every program point in each concurrent thread, Astrée can also report all potential deadlocks.

Practical experience on avionics and automotive industry applications are given in [9] [26] [27]. They show that industry-sized programs of millions of lines of code can be analyzed in acceptable time with high precision for runtime errors and data races.

VI. Taint Analysis-based Spectre-Detection

Taint analysis was first introduced as a dynamic analysis technique (e.g., in PERL), to try to find out which part of a code could be affected by some inputs. The original technique consisted in flipping normally unused bits, that would be copied around by operations and assignments. The same idea can be extended to static analysis by enhancing the concrete semantics of programs with tainting, the formal equivalent of the unused flipped bit in the dynamic approach. In the context of abstract interpretation, it is easy to abstract this extra information in an efficient and sound way, using dedicated abstract domains. Conceptually, taint analysis consists in discovering data dependencies using the notion of taint propagation. Taint propagation can be formalized using a non-standard semantics of programs, where an imaginary taint is associated to some input values. Considering a standard semantics using a successor relation between program states, and considering that a program state is a map from memory locations (variables, program counter, etc.) to values in $\mathcal{V}$, the *tainted* semantics relates tainted states, which are maps from the same memory locations to $\mathcal{V} \times \{\text{taint}, \text{notaint}\}$, and such that if we project on $\mathcal{V}$ we get the same relation as with the standard semantics.

To define what happens to the *taint* part of the tainted value, one must define a *taint policy*. The taint policy specifies:

- **Taint sources** which are a subset of input values or variables such that in any state, the values associated with that input values or variables are always tainted.
- **Taint propagation** describes how the tainting gets propagated. Typical propagation is through assignment, but more complex propagation can take more control flow into account, and may not propagate the taint through all arithmetic or pointer operations.
- **Taint cleaning** is an alternative to taint propagation, describing all the operations that do not propagate the taint. In this case, all assignments not containing the taint cleaning will propagate the taint.
- **Taint sinks** is an optional set of memory locations. This has no semantical effect, except to specify conditions when an alarm should be emitted when verifying a program (an alarm must be emitted if a taint sink may become tainted for a given execution of the program).

A. Taint Analysis in Astrée

Astrée has been equipped with a generic abstract domain for taint analysis. It allows Astrée to perform normal code analysis, with its usual process-interleaving, interprocedural and memory layout precision, while carrying and computing taint information at the byte level. Any number of taint hues can be tracked by Astrée, and their combinations will be soundly abstracted.

Tainted input is specified through directives attached to program locations. Such directives can precisely describe which variables, and which part of those variables is to be tainted, with the given taint hues, each time this program location is reached. Any assignment is interpreted as propagating the join of all taint hues from its right-hand side to the targets of its left-hand side. In addition, specific directives may be introduced to explicitly modify the taint hues of some variable parts. This is particularly useful to model cleansing function effects or to emulate changes of security levels in the code.

The result of the analysis with tainting can be explored in the Astrée GUI via tooltips for all expressions appearing in the code, or explicitly dumped using dedicated directives. Finally, the taint sink directives may be used to declare that some parts of some variables must be considered as taint sinks for a given set of taint hues. When a tainted value is assigned to a taint sink, then Astrée will emit a dedicated alarm, and remove the sinked hues, so that only the first occurrence has to be examined to fix potential issues with the security data flow.

The main intended use of taint analysis in Astrée is to expose potential vulnerabilities with respect to security policies or resilience mechanisms. Thanks to the intrinsic soundness of the approach, no tainting can be forgotten, and that without any bound on the number of iterations of loops, size of data or length of the call stack. It seems particularly well suited to help detecting Spectre-PHT vulnerabilities, as these only occur in places where user input may interfere.

B. Detecting Spectre Vulnerabilities by Taint Analysis

The first step in Spectre-PHT vulnerabilities is to be able to control a variable through user (or public) input. Finding such variables can be approximated using tainting, so we first introduce tainting directives for identified public input. In the case of PikeOS, this is easily done, as the project analyzed by Astrée consists in one big loop with random calls to the OS: for each such call, we taint the parameters. In the code excerpt

```
void main(void)
{
  while (1) {
    switch (rand) {
      case 1:
        unsigned page;
        __ASTREE_initialize((page));
        __ASTREE_taint((page; controlled));
        os_call(page);
        break;
      ...
      case 148:
       int p;
       unsigned size;
       __ASTREE_initialize((p,size));
         __ASTREE_taint((p, size; controlled));
       os_call148(&p, size);
    }
  }
}
```

Figure 3. Example code with taint sources marked.

of Figure 3, `page`, `p`, and `size` are helper variables which are considered initialized with some unknown value. The Astrée directive `__ASTREE_initialize` models this effect and prevents alarms about uninitialized variable accesses. The directive `__ASTREE_taint` takes a comma-separated list of variables to be tainted and the taint hue to be used as parameters. The effect is that the system calls are analyzed with unknown, possibly attacker-controlled values.

The second condition is that such data controlled by the attacker are compared to a bound, so that speculative execution can be exploited. The idea here is to use the facility for Astrée to deal with more than one taint hue, to distinguish between possibly controlled, and possibly controlled and tested to be smaller than a bound. Since it would be quite demanding to manually add tainting directives for that to the source code under analysis, we added inside Astrée an automatic detection of comparison with bounds, which automatically changes the taint from *controlled* to *dangerous*.

Now the question is, how far in the code should variables stay dangerous? Speculative execution does not last forever, and in all known attacks so far, the memory access using dangerous variables must occur during speculative execution, which is one of the reasons why [10] introduced their speculative execution window. But we work on the source code level, and we aim at target architecture independence. One reasonable limit, though, is the length of the branches: when there is a test, there are two possible outcome, the branches, and when the control flow becomes the same whatever the outcome (the branches are merged) then the variable should not be considered dangerous anymore. The implementation challenge with that view, is that tainting, by design, cannot be removed on joins. So, we came up with some non-standard use of the multi-hues tainting facilities offered by Astrée: we decided to taint public input with two hues (let's call them 1 and 2), and that flagging a memory location as dangerous consists in *removing* a hue (let's say it is hue 2). In that way, as long as the memory is tainted with only hue 1, it is considered dangerous, but as soon as we merge with a context where it is tainted with hue 1 and 2, it becomes merely controlled by the attacker again.

The third step is that the dangerous variable must be used to compute some memory address. Once again, we automatically discover in Astrée when a dangerous value is used to compute a memory location, and in that case, flag that address with a new taint hue. At each place where an address tainted with that hue is dereferenced, we emit a Spectre vulnerability alarm, and remove the tainting for that address, so that end-users can concentrate on the first occurrence, where they can, e.g., introduce fences that will anyway mitigate the vulnerability for all subsequent dereferences of the same address.

To illustrate the tainting algorithm we use the following example code shown in Figure 4:

```
volatile int controlled;
__ASTREE_volatile_input((controlled; [1,2]));
int victim_function( size_t x) {
  if (x< array1_size ) {
    temp &= array2 [array1[ x ]] * 512];
  }
  return x;
}                       ALARM: Spectre vulnerability
void main(){
  unsigned int val, retval;
  init(&val);          //reads val from the environment
    ASTREE_taint((val; controlled));
  retval = victim_function(val);
}
```

Figure 4. Code excerpt with taint coloring.

In that code, `val` is tainted with hues 1 and 2, to denote that it may be controlled by the attacker. The taint is propagated to argument `x` of the victim function, and when `x` is compared to the size of the array, the tainting is transformed into hue 1 (hue 2 is removed from the tainting of `x`). This means that `x` is considered dangerous after the test. Then when `x` is used to compute an offset of `array1` before dereferencing, Astrée emits a Spectre vulnerability alarm.

It should be noted that we warn as soon as we find a single dereference of a dangerous address, whereas Spectre 1 requires two dereferences, but in practice that did not cause many false positives, and it seems that this criterion is necessary anyway to be safe with respect to SplitSpectre.

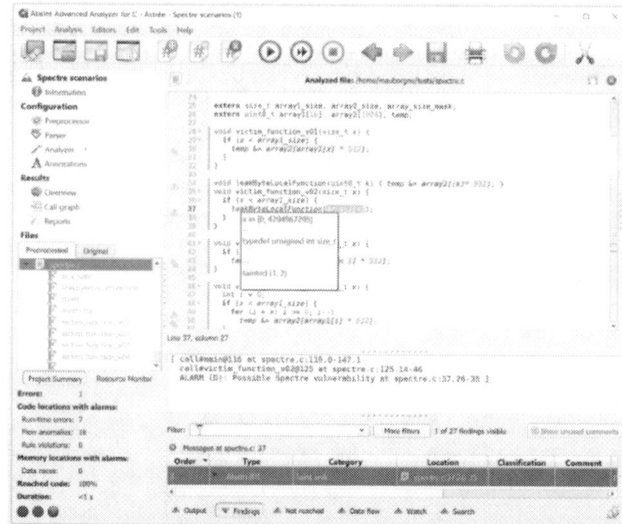

Figure 5. Astrée GUI showing Spectre vulnerability alarm

A screen shot of a Spectre vulnerability alarm in Astrée is shown in Fig.5. The taint hues derived for variables in the code are shown in the tool tips.

This approach does not provide absolute safety from Spectre attacks. The first limitation is that tainting can only taint *reachable code*, and Spectre may be exploited on unreachable code (speculative execution may cause the execution of normally unreachable code). Note that Astrée displays unreachable code as parts of its normal output. If needed, the code can be made reachable to be covered by the analysis. Second, it targets a specific set of Spectre vulnerabilities, not all possible flavors of Spectre vulnerabilities. It embeds the Spectre detection into the runtime error analysis which is needed in safety-critical systems anyway, and reports vulnerabilities with high precision and on the basis of a sound analysis. This helps to significantly reduce the attack surface with little overhead.

VII. EXPERIMENTS

Our main experiment runs on the PikeOS sources, which are about 400 000 lines of preprocessed C code. Astrée can run with different levels of precision. Using a low precision level doesn't seem to hurt the precision of Spectre detection too much. In such mode, Astrée analyzes the whole code in 2h30, using 17 GB of memory. During the analysis, Astrée does much more than warn about Spectre vulnerabilities, it also checks for compliance to coding rules, or warns about potential runtime errors. But the extra precision needed for that analysis is not lost, as it allows the detection of Spectre vulnerabilities to be very targeted: Astrée only reports 68 locations with possible Spectre vulnerabilities.

A. Reviewing the Spectre Alarms

A very interesting aspect of that experiment is that PikeOS was already carefully analyzed by experts to root out all possible vulnerabilities. As expected due to Astrée's soundness, all vulnerabilities found by the experts were also reported by Astrée. The precision of the analysis allowed the locations reported by Astrée to be reviewed in less than an hour. The review led to interesting conclusions:

- A number of false positives corresponded to places where the index used for the array access was shifted (using a right shift operation), so that even when the test for rang of the index failed, the final array access was always in range. In most case, the actual size of the array used in the code was not available to Astrée, so that Astrée could not have concluded that here were no vulnerability. It was a simple matter for the experts to assert that the right shift was enough to prevent a Spectre vulnerability, but we found that is was a good thing that such accesses be checked.
- A couple of alarms corresponded to calls from trusted code, so the data should be protected early enough, but it seemed to the expert that it would be a good idea to add fences for that cases anyway (which they hadn't before running Astrée).
- One interesting alarm exposed a possible Spectre 1.1 vulnerability. It was quite hard to discover, as the test on the input variable occurred two calls before its use in an array access. That makes it likely that the branch speculation would be finished before reaching the arrays access, but not impossible. It is one of those cases where a human can easily get lost with indirections and complex control flow, but where an automatic analyzer prevails.

B. Analysis Overhead

In order to asses the efficiency of our approach, we also ran an analysis of PikeOS without Spectre detection enabled, and finished only 5 minutes faster (2h25 instead of 2h30), using the same amount of memory.

In addition to the analyses of PikeOS we ran experiments on industrial avionics and automotive code. In both cases we manually selected some global variables as taint sources since no information about actual user-controlled values was available to us.

The avionics project consists of 2 million lines of preprocessed C code. It ran through in 2h43 (21 GB), compared to 2h36 without Spectre detection. The run with Spectre detection enabled found 113 possible vulnerabilities.

The automotive project consists of about 2.7 million lines of preprocessed C code. Without Spectre detection, it ran through in 1h42, and in 1h47 with Spectre detection enabled, and found 1271 vulnerabilities.

The immediate conclusion is that adding taint analysis in general, and Spectre detection in particular is quite costless for Astrée. Also, it seems that we found a good granularity for our detection criteria, since the number of findings is quite small with respect to the size of the code.

C. Further Experiments

For lack of time, we did not run the analysis of PikeOS with its mitigations yet, but that will be simple enough, as we will just include an Astrée untainting directive inside the fence macros used by Sysgo. This way Astrée will be able to confirm that the mitigation implemented in the code covers the Spectre attacks under consideration.

We also ran Astrée on simple code snippets on Spectre vulnerability published on Paul Kocher's web page [28], and Astrée shows the vulnerabilities in less than a second.

VIII. Conclusion

Spectre belongs to the recently discovered class of transient execution attacks which exploit common performance-enhancing microprocessor features. It can cause confidentiality breaches by leaking secret data through covert channels from transient execution stages to observable architectural states. It affects a wide range of microprocessors, including processors used for safety-critical embedded applications, trusted with particularly sensitive information.

In this article we have discussed the impact of Spectre on the safety-critical real-time embedded operating system PikeOS and outlined a mitigation strategy based on static taint analysis. We have presented a novel tainting strategy to detect Spectre V1, V1.1 and SplitSpectre vulnerabilities and discussed its implementation in the sound static analyzer Astrée. We have conducted experiments on the source code of the PikeOS operating system where the analyzer detects all vulnerabilities existing in the code while producing only few false alarms. Additional experiments on industrial avionic and automotive software confirm that the analysis is applicable to industry-size safety-critical application software at very little overhead.

Acknowledgment

This work was funded within the project ARAMiS II by the German Federal Ministry for Education and Research with the funding ID 01—S16025. The responsibility for the content remains with the authors.

References

[1] P. Kocher et al., "Spectre attacks: Exploiting speculative execution," ArXiv e-prints, Jan. 2018.

[2] M. Lipp et al., "Meltdown," ArXiv e-prints, Jan. 2018.

[3] Wired.com, "The jeep hackers are back to prove car hacking can get much worse," https://www.wired.com/2016/08/jeep-hackers-return-high-speed-steering-acceleration-hacks/ [retrieved: July 2019], 2016.

[4] P. Cousot and R. Cousot, "Abstract interpretation: a unified lattice model for static analysis of programs by construction or approximation of fixpoints," in Proc. of POPL'77. ACM Press, 1977, pp. 238–252. [Online]. Available: http://www.di.ens.fr/cousot/COUSOTpapers/POPL77.shtml[retrieved:July2019].

[5] D. Kästner, "Applying Abstract Interpretation to Demonstrate Functional Safety," in Formal Methods Applied to Industrial Complex Systems, J.-L. Boulanger, Ed. London, UK: ISTE/Wiley, 2014.

[6] D. Kästner and C. Ferdinand, "Proving the Absence of Stack Overflows," in SAFECOMP '14: Proceedings of the 33th International Conference on Computer Safety, Reliability and Security, ser. LNCS, vol. 8666. Springer, September 2014, pp. 202–213.

[7] J. Souyris et al., "Computing the worst case execution time of an avionics program by abstract interpretation," in Proceedings of the 5th Intl Workshop on Worst-Case Execution Time (WCET) Analysis, 2005, pp. 21–24.

[8] D. Delmas and J. Souyris, "ASTRÉE: from Research to Industry," in Proc. 14th International Static Analysis Symposium (SAS2007), ser. LNCS, no. 4634, 2007, pp. 437–451.

[9] D. Kästner et al., "Finding All Potential Runtime Errors and Data Races in Automotive Software," in SAE World Congress 2017. SAE International, 2017.

[10] G. Wang, S. Chattopadhyay, I. Gotovchits, T. Mitra, and A. Roychoudhury, "oo7: Low-overhead defense against spectre attacks via binary analysis," CoRR, vol. abs/1807.05843, 2018. [Online]. Available: http://arxiv.org/abs/1807.05843[retrieved:July2019].

[11] D. Brumley, I. Jager, T. Avgerinos, and E. J. Schwartz, "BAP: A binary analysis platform," in Computer Aided Verification - 23rd International Conference, CAV 2011, Snowbird, UT, USA, July 14-20, 2011. Proceedings, 2011, pp. 463–469. [Online]. Available: https://doi.org/10.1007/978-3-642-22110-1_37[retrieved:July2019].

[12] D. Ceara, L. Mounier, and M. Potet, "Taint dependency sequences: A characterization of insecure execution paths based on input-sensitive cause sequences," in Third International Conference on Software Testing, Verification and Validation, ICST 2010, Paris, France, April 7-9, 2010, Workshops Proceedings, 2010, pp. 371–380. [Online]. Available: https://doi.org/10.1109/ICSTW.2010.28[retrieved:July2019].

[13] C. Canella et al., "A systematic evaluation of transient execution attacks and defenses," CoRR, vol. abs/1811.05441, 2018. [Online]. Available: http://arxiv.org/abs/1811.05441[retrieved:July2019].

[14] P. Kocher et al., "Spectre attacks: Exploiting speculative execution," S&P, 2019.

[15] V. Kiriansky and C. Waldspurger, "Speculative buffer overflows: Attacks and defenses," arXiv:1807.03757, 2018.

[16] A. Mambretti et al., "Let's not speculate: Discovering and analyzing speculative execution attacks," IBM Research Report RZ 3933 (#ZUR1810-003), Oct 2018.

[17] J. Horn, Speculative Execution, Variant 4: Speculative Store Bypass, https://bugs.chromium.org/p/project-zero/issues/detail?id=1528 [retrieved: July 2019], 2018.

[18] G. Maisuradze and C. Rossow, "Ret2spec: Speculative execution using return stack buffers," in Proceedings of the 2018 ACM SIGSAC Conference on Computer and Communications Security, ser. CCS '18. New York, NY, USA: ACM, 2018, pp. 2109–2122. [Online]. Available: http://doi.acm.org/10.1145/3243734.3243761[retrieved:July2019].

[19] Microsoft Edge Team, "Mitigating speculative execution side-channel attacks in microsoft edge and internet explorer," https://blogs.windows.com/msedgev/2018/01/03/speculative-execution-mitigations-microsoft-edge-internet-explorer [retrieved: July 2019], Jan 2018.

[20] MISRA (Motor Industry Software Reliability Association) Working Group, MISRA-C:2012 Guidelines for the use of the C language in critical systems, MISRA Limited, Mar. 2013.

[21] Software Engineering Institute SEI – CERT Division, SEI CERT C Coding Standard – Rules for Developing Safe, Reliable, and Secure Systems. Carnegie Mellon University, 2016.

[22] The MITRE Corporation, "CWE – Common Weakness Enumeration," https://cwe.mitre.org [retrieved: July 2019].

[23] A. Miné et al., "Taking Static Analysis to the Next Level: Proving the Absence of Run-Time Errors and Data Races with Astrée," in 8th European Congress on Embedded Real Time Software and Systems (ERTS 2016), Toulouse, France, Jan. 2016.

[24] A. Miné, "The Octagon Abstract Domain," Higher-Order and Symbolic Computation, vol. 19, no. 1, 2006, pp. 31–100.

[25] A. Miné, "Static analysis of run-time errors in embedded real-time parallel C programs," Logical Methods in Computer Science (LMCS), vol. 8, no. 26, Mar. 2012, p. 63.

[26] A. Miné and D. Delmas, "Towards an Industrial Use of Sound Static Analysis for the Verification of Concurrent Embedded Avionics Software," in Proc. of the 15th International Conference on Embedded Software (EMSOFT'15). IEEE CS Press, Oct. 2015, pp. 65–74.

[27] D. Kästner et al., "Analyze This! Sound Static Analysis for Integration Verification of Large-Scale Automotive Software," in Proceedings of the SAE World Congress 2019 (SAE Technical Paper). SAE International, 2019.

[28] Paul Kocher, "Spectre Mitigations in Microsoft's C/C++ Compiler," http://www.paulkocher.com/doc/MicrosoftCompilerSpectreMitigation.html [retrieved: July 2019], 2018.

Hardware Implementation of Lightweight Chaos-Based Stream Cipher

Guillaume Gautier*, Maguy Le Glatin*, Safwan El Assad†, Wassim Hamidouche*,
Olivier Deforges*, Sylvain Guilley‡, Adrien Facon‡
* Univ Rennes, INSA Rennes, CNRS, IETR - UMR 6164, F-35000 Rennes, France
Email: guillaume.gautier@insa-rennes.fr, maguy.le-glatin@insa-rennes.fr,
wassim.hamidouche@insa-rennes.fr, olivier.deforges@insa-rennes.fr
†Polytech Nantes, CNRS, IETR - UMR 6164, F-44000 Nantes, France
Email: safwan.elassad@univ-nantes.fr
‡ Secure-IC SAS, F-35510 Cesson-Sévigné, France
Email: sylvain.guilley@secure-ic.com, adrien.facon@secure-ic.com

Abstract—**Due to the proliferation of connected devices, the development of secured and low-resource cryptographic systems has become a real challenge. In fact, ciphering algorithms have not been thought to be implemented on embedded platforms with limited computing, memory and energy resources. This paper addresses a hardware implementation of a chaos-based stream cipher is initially optimized for software. First, the structure of the cipher is investigated. Then, its hardware implementation on a Zynq7000 platform is proposed considering both throughput performance and logic resources usage. The proposed design is compared to hardware implementations of existing stream ciphers including chaos-based ones, Advanced Encryption Standard (AES), Rabbit, Salsa20 and Trivium.**

Keywords–Chaos-based stream ciphers; Hardware implementation; Lightweight stream cipher; Computational performance.

I. INTRODUCTION

The need of encryption methods has nearly always existed to protect sensitive information. The number of connected devices is constantly and rapidly increasing. Those devices are communicating between each other through multiple channels exchanging information, such as confidential messages. In this context, the protection of sensitive data exchanged over networks is necessary. This can be done thanks to cryptography. It consists in making the information unintelligible for a person from outside the application by coding it with a secret key. Therefore, it becomes necessary to develop new lightweight cryptographic systems that can be embedded on these connected devices with low energy and computing resources.

In the literature, multiple ciphers are defined and implemented on hardware devices. We especially studied the stream ciphers in which the output is obtained by performing an eXclusive OR (XOR) between the input of the cipher and the output of a random generator. For example, Advanced Encryption Standard (AES), the state of the art encryption standard, is available in multiple versions [1], [2], each optimizing a trade-off between surface and speed. Moreover, some ciphers, like Trivium [3], are designed to be hardware friendly and minimize logic resources. Some ciphers, based on chaos theory, have also hardware implementations [4], [5]. Those ciphers usually require a high logic resources to digitize chaotic systems.

Based on works in [6], a LightWeight Chaos-Based Stream Cipher (LWCB SC) is proposed in this paper. This design is implemented on Field-Programmable Gate Array (FPGA) hardware platform. The system includes some counter-measures against Side Channel Attacks (SCA) [7], such as Correlation Power Analysis (CPA) and Differential Power Analysis (DPA). The proposed hardware implementation achieves a throughput of 565 Mbps at an operating frequency of 18.5 MHz .

The rest of this paper is organised as follows. The existing stream ciphers are first presented in Section II. Section III investigates the design and details of the hardware implementation of the chaos-based stream cipher. The performance of the proposed system is assessed in Section IV in terms of both throughput and used logic resources. Section IV accesses the performance of the proposed implementation in terms of throughput and used logic resources. Finally, Section V concludes this paper.

II. RELATED WORK

A. Existing stream ciphers

There are several hardware implementation of the state of the art stream ciphers. This section gives a brief review of the existing implementations.

1) AES: AES [8] developed in 2001 is the most widely used system. It is considered as a stream cipher only in its CounTeR (CTR) mode. It takes 128 bits as input and can use a key of 128, 192 or 256 bits. Its round function consists of three layers including key addition layer, byte substitution layer called S-Box and diffusion layer.

2) Rabbit: The Rabbit stream cipher [9] is one of the most effective algorithms of the eSTREAM project. This project was launched in 2004 to create new stream ciphers for dedicated designs. The cipher is not based on S-Boxes but on 8-32 bits state variables and counters.

3) Salsa20: Salsa20 [10] is based on a hash function. This latter is implemented with simple operations as additions, XOR and rotation. This cipher is very fast but presents some security weaknesses. Indeed, several attacks have been concluded against it.

4) Trivium: Trivium [3] is also a cipher from the eS-TREAM Project. It is particularly well suited for applications requiring a flexible hardware implementation. The 288-bit internal state is stored in three shift registers which are the heart of the cipher and can be viewed as a circular register.

B. Existing chaotic systems

Several chaotic systems have been developed and used for designing chaotic hardware key generation for secure cryptography systems. Lorenz's [4] and Lü's [5] systems are the famous ones. A chaotic system can be considered as discrete or continuous. The previously cited systems are continuous and defined by a differential equations.

In [4], a cipher to encrypt images is developed and implemented on an FPGA platform. It uses a key generator based on the Lorenz's chaotic system. Another example of such system is presented in [5] where a Lü's-system-based-chaotic key generator is used.

III. Proposed Hardware Chaos-Based Stream Cipher

The proposed solution is based on the generator previously presented in [6]. This generator consists of two cells that use different chaotic maps called Skew Tent map and PieceWise Linear Chaotic (PWLC) map. These maps are encapsulated into an Infinite Impulse Response (IIR) filter to form the two cells. Finally, the outputs of the two cells are XORed to generate the key stream [6].

The solution described in this paper aims to improve the security of the chaos-based system introduced in [6] by increasing its resilience against SCA. Figure 1 illustrates the block diagram of the enhanced chaos-based generator where the new blocks are highlighted in red. The Skew Tent map is replaced by 4D map defined by a discrete Chebyshev polynomial T_4 of degree 4. A second Linear Feedback Shift Register (LFSR) block is added to overcome some inconsistencies of the 4D map. The outputs of the two cells are weakly coupled before being fed back to the recursive cells illustrated in green in Figure 1.

The cipher text C is created with a simple XOR operation between the plain text P and a key stream X_G generated by the proposed system

$$C = P \oplus X_G.$$

A. Hardware-friendly architecture of the generator

The block diagram of the proposed generator is depicted in Figure 1. We have defined a hardware high level module that instantiates the two cells of the generator, the weak coupling and the key stream's output. The generator module takes as input a secret key and an Initial Vector (IV).

The output key stream X_G corresponds to the sum of the outputs of the two chaotic maps X_{4D} and X_P after a number of iteration tr, defined in the secret key

$$X_G(n) = \begin{cases} X_{4D}(n) + X_P(n) & \text{if } n > tr, \\ 0 & \text{otherwise,} \end{cases}$$

with n is the iteration number, $X_{4D}(n)$ and $X_P(n)$ are the outputs of the 4D and PWLC cells at iteration n, respectively.

To introduce more resilience against algebraic attacks and SCA, we define a weak coupling block $[B]$

$$\begin{bmatrix} XC_{4D}(n) \\ XC_P(n) \end{bmatrix} = \begin{bmatrix} 2^N - B_{11} & B_{12} \\ B_{21} & 2^N - B_{22} \end{bmatrix} \begin{bmatrix} X_{4D}(n-1) \\ X_P(n-1) \end{bmatrix},$$

with N is bit depth of the system, B_{ij} are coefficients defined in the secret key, $XC_{4D}(n)$ and $XC_P(n)$ are the outputs of weak coupling block at iteration n.

The block diagrams of the two cells are delimited in orange in Figure 1. Both cells are composed of a recursive cell illustrated in green, a map and LFSRs. The next two paragraphs present the hardware implementations of the chaotic maps: 4D and PWLC.

1) 4D map: The 4D map is defined by a discrete version of the Chebyshev polynomial of degree 4

$$4D_{MAP}(X) = (X - 2^{2N-1})^4 - 2^{2N-2} \times (X - 2^{2N-1})^2, \quad (1)$$

where X corresponds to Xin_{4D} in Figure 1.

To implement the new 4D map, (1) is expressed to minimize the logic resources of the hardware implementation

$$\begin{aligned} 4D_{MAP}(X) &= (X - 2^{2N-1})^4 - 2^{2N-2} \times (X - 2^{2N-1})^2 \\ &= Y^2 - 2^{2N-2} \times Y \\ &= [Y \times Y - Y << (N-2)] >> (3N-6), \end{aligned}$$
$$\text{with } Y = (X - 2^{N-1})^2 = X \times X + 2^{N-2} - X << 2^{N-1}. \quad (2)$$

Implementation of (2) requires only two multipliers of 32 and 64 bits inputs, respectively.

2) PWLC map: The PWLC map is defined by (3)

$$PLWCmap(X, P_P) = \begin{cases} C_1 \times X & \text{if } 0 < X < P_P, \\ C_2 \times (X - P_P) & \text{if } P_P < X < 2^{N-1}, \\ C_2 \times (2^N - P_P - X) & \text{if } 2^{N-1} < X < 2^N - P_P, \\ C_1 \times (2^N - X) & \text{if } 2^N - P_P < X < 2^N, \\ 2^N - 1 & \text{otherwise,} \end{cases} \quad (3)$$

where X is the input of the PWLC map Xin_P and P_P is the parameter of the PWLC map defined in the secret key, C_1 and C_2 are two constants derived from P_P.

In the proposed solution, the ratios C_1 and C_2 are precomputed by the key generator to avoid the implementation a resource-intensive divider. Then, to use the minimum number of multipliers, without reducing the throughput of the generator, the inputs of the multiplier are selected by multiplexers.

B. A counter-measure against SCA

To protect the generator against CPA and DPA attacks [7], masking operations are added to the recursive cells. The aim of masking operations is to randomize intermediate results for the same couple (secret key, IV). The masking is performed by adding a random value to the outputs of the weak coupling XC_{4D} and XC_P

$$XM_{4D}(n) = XC_{4D}(n) + mask_{4D}(n),$$

where XM_{4D} is the output of the 4D-cell mask operation at iteration n, $mask_{4D}(n)$ is a random value, generated by XOR Shift Random Number Generator of integer values in the interval $[0, 2^N - 1]$. The same calculation is performed for the output of the PWLC-cell mask $XM_P(n)$ with $XC_P(n)$ and $mask_P(n)$.

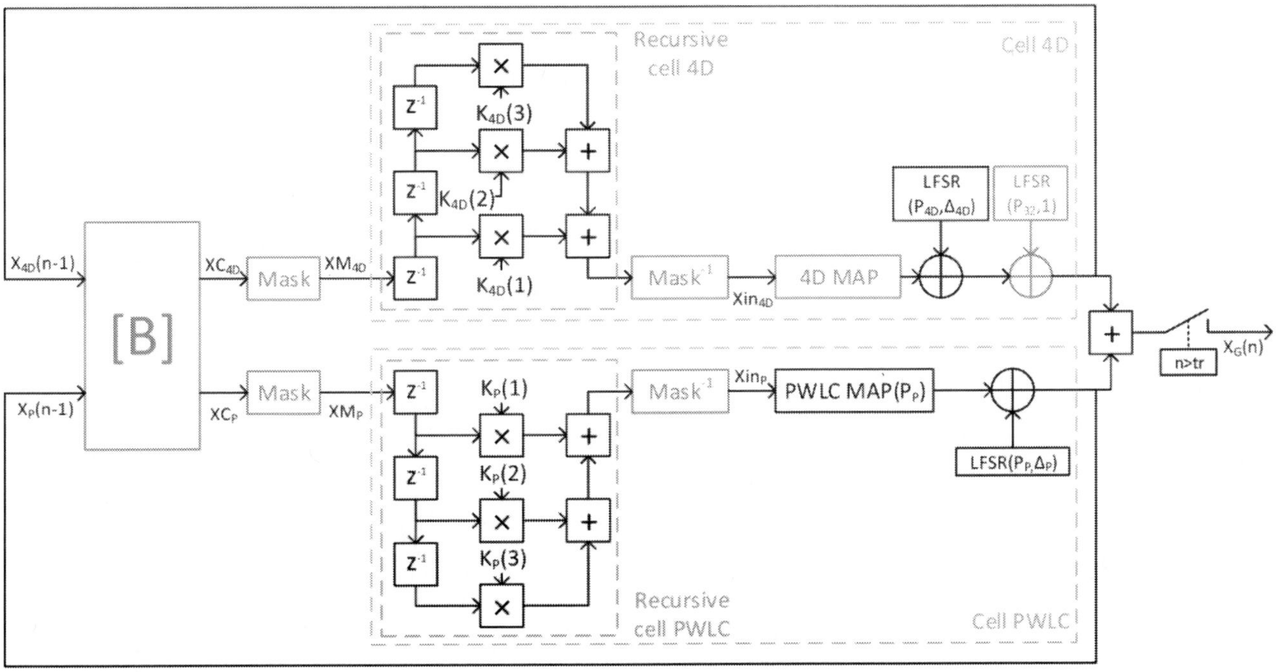

Figure 1. Improved PCNG diagram. In red are shown the differences with [6].
In green are highlighted the recursive cell. Orange dotted line delimits the two cells.

To obtain the same key stream X_G for the same couple (key, IV), the mask operations are reverted before the chaotic maps. The inverse mask operation is performed after the recursive cells by subtracting the transform of the mask value from the output value of the recursive cell.

$$Xin_{4D}(n) = \sum_{i=1}^{D} XM_{4D}(n-i) \times K_{4D}(i) - \sum_{i=1}^{D} mask_{4D}(n-i) \times K_{4D}(i),$$

where $K_{4D}(i)$ is the ith coefficient of the recursive cells given in the secret key and D is the number of delays in the recursive cells. Identically, $Xin_{4D}(n)$ is a function of $XM_{4D}(n-i)$, $K_{4D}(i)$ and $mask_{4D}(n-i)$.

IV. Results and Discussion

In this section, an internal module of the cipher is implemented and tested. Some comparisons with the state-of-the-art are also provided. To evaluate the performance in terms the resources usage and speed, Xilinx Vivado set of tools is used. In these experiments, the bit depth N is set to 32 bits and the number of delay D inside the recursive cells is set to 3.

A. *Implementation of the LWCB SC*

Table I gives the hardware resources used for the PCNG. It uses in total 2,363 Look-Up Tables (LUTs) and 96 DSP blocks. Most of the resources are used by the recursive cells with 1,087 LUTs and 42 DSP blocks for the PWLC cell and 1,001 LUTs and 44 DSP blocks for the 4D one.

TABLE I. Hardware resources usage of the proposed implementation

Component	LUTs	DSP Blocks
Output Adder	102	0
PWLC Cell	1,087	42
4D Cell	1,001	44
4D Mask	24	0
PWLC Mask	39	0
Coupling Matrix $[B]$	110	10
Total	2,363	96

The proposed implementation produces one sample of the PCNG at each clock cycle and can operate at 18.5 MHz with a throughput of 565 Mbps.

B. *Comparison with other existing stream ciphers*

Table III and II present a comparison with existing implementations of the ciphers presented in Section II.

TABLE II. Speed performance comparison of several systems

Cipher	Max Freq (MHz)	Throughput (Mbps)
LWCB SC	**18.5**	**565**
Lorenz's chaotic system [4]	15	124
Lü's chaotic system [5]	23	183
AES [1]	644	84,449
	886	11,776
AES [2]	290	232
Rabbit [11]	NC	9,380
Trivium [12]	240	254
Trivium [13]	201	201
Salsa20 [14] (Spartan 3)	19	911
Salsa20 [14] (Spartan 6)	48	2,519

TABLE III. HARDWARE RESOURCES USAGE COMPARISON OF SEVERAL SYSTEMS

Cipher	Device	Area (nb of LUTs)	DSP Blocks
LWCB SC	**Zynq7000**	**2,363 (4.44%)**	**96 (43.64%)**
Lorenz's chaotic system [4]	Virtex II	2,718	40
Lü's chaotic system [5]	Virtex II	1,926	40
AES [1]	Virtex VI	9,276	NC
	Spartan 6	9,375	NC
AES [2]	Spartan 2	444	NC
Rabbit [11]	Virtex V	2,272	24
Trivium [12]	Spartan 3	100	NC
Trivium [13]	Spartan 3	376	NC
Salsa20 [14]	Spartan 3	3,374	NC
	Spartan 6	2955	NC

It can be noted that the fastest cipher is AES [1]. The AES implementations presented in [1], [2] operate at 644 MHz and 886 MHz and the throughput is equal to 84,448 Mbps and 11,776 Mbps, respectively. Rabbit [11] implementation reaches AES performance with a throughput of 9,380 Mbps. Even though, Trivium [12], [13] reaches a high frequency the throughput is not better than other slow frequency ciphers. For example, Salsa20 [14] implementations present a throughput of 911 Mbps and 2,519 Mbps with an operating frequency of 19 MHz and 48 MHz, respectively. These frequencies are the same as those achieved by the implementations of ciphers based on chaotic key generators [4], [5]. However, these ciphers are still, in term of throughput less efficient than all the others implementations, as they have at 124 Mbps and 183 Mbps throughput.

A correlation between the speed performance and the hardware resources usage can be noted. In fact, the implementation of AES [1] which is the fastest is also the one using the most resources. This is also the case with the implementations of Rabbit [11] and Salsa20 [14], which use approximately 3,000 LUTs for a quite important throughput. Moreover, the implementations using the less resources are the Trivium's [12], [13] with only 100 and 376 used LUTs. The compact implementation of AES [2] has nearly the same results with 444 LUTs for the same speed performance.

For the implementations of the ciphers based on a chaotic generator [4], [5], this relation is not satisfied. Indeed, they use 2,718 and 1,926 LUTs, it achieves the same than Rabbit and Salsa20 implementations which have better speed performance.

V. Conclusion and Future Work

In this paper, we have proposed a hardware implementation of a new version of the LWCB SC on a FPGA platform. The new design can operate at a maximum frequency of 18.5MHz with a throughput of 565 Mbps. In addition it uses a reduced area of the platform of 2,363 LUTs.

The comparison with the state-of-the-start shows that the speed performance reached by the LWCB SC is below those of AES and the existing ciphers from the eSTREAM project. However, it is the same frequency and a better throughput than the ciphers based on a chaotic generator. The results in terms of resources usage reveal that the LWCB SC uses the same area as the state-of-the-art.

In future work, we will investigate some enhancements in order to improve the performance of the LWCB SC in terms of resources usage and speed performance. The synchronous pipeline of the system and a new design of the cell could be considered to improve its performance. Furthermore, tests against attacks such as CPA and DPA will be carried-out to validate the security of this implementation.

Acknowledgment

This work was funded by the Research Pole of the "Pôle d'Excellence Cyber" with the support of the French Ministry of the Armed Forces and the Brittany Region.

References

[1] U. Farooq and M. F. Aslam, "Comparative analysis of different AES implementation techniques for efficient resource usage and better performance of an FPGA," Journal of King Saud University - Computer and Information Sciences, vol. 29, no. 3, Jul. 2017, pp. 295–302.

[2] P. Chodowiec and K. Gaj, "Very Compact FPGA Implementation of the AES Algorithm," in Cryptographic Hardware and Embedded Systems - CHES 2003. Berlin, Heidelberg: Springer Berlin Heidelberg, 2003, vol. 2779, pp. 319–333.

[3] C. De Canniere and B. Preneel, Trivium. Berlin, Heidelberg: Springer Berlin Heidelberg, 2008, pp. 244–266.

[4] C. Tanougast, "Hardware Implementation of Chaos Based Cipher: Design of Embedded Systems for Security Applications," in Chaos-Based Cryptography. Berlin, Heidelberg: Springer Berlin Heidelberg, 2011, vol. 354, pp. 297–330. [Online]. Available: http://link.springer.com/10.1007/978-3-642-20542-2_9

[5] S. Sadoudi, C. Tanougast, M. S. Azzaz, A. Dandache, and A. Bouridane, "Real-time FPGA implementation of Lorenz's chaotic generator for cipher embedded systems," in 2009 International Symposium on Signals, Circuits and Systems. Iasi, Romania: IEEE, Jul. 2009, pp. 1–4.

[6] G. Gautier et al., "Enhanced Software Implementation of a Chaos-Based Stream Cipher," SECURWARE 2018.

[7] J. Fan et al., "State-of-the-art of secure ECC implementations: a survey on known side-channel attacks and countermeasures," in 2010 IEEE International Symposium on Hardware-Oriented Security and Trust (HOST). Anaheim, CA, USA: IEEE, Jun. 2010, pp. 76–87.

[8] C. Paar and J. Pelzl, Understanding cryptography: a textbook for students and practitioners. Heidelberg ; New York: Springer, 2010.

[9] M. Boesgaard, M. Vesterager, and E. Zenner, "The Rabbit Stream Cipher," in New Stream Cipher Designs. Berlin, Heidelberg: Springer Berlin Heidelberg, 2008, vol. 4986, pp. 69–83.

[10] D. J. Bernstein, "The Salsa20 Family of Stream Ciphers," in New Stream Cipher Designs. Berlin, Heidelberg: Springer Berlin Heidelberg, 2008, vol. 4986, pp. 84–97. [Online]. Available: http://link.springer.com/10.1007/978-3-540-68351-3_8

[11] D. Stefan, "Hardware Framework for the Rabbit Stream Cipher," in Information Security and Cryptology. Berlin, Heidelberg: Springer Berlin Heidelberg, 2010, vol. 6151, pp. 230–247.

[12] D. Hwang, M. Chaney, S. Karanam, N. Ton, and K. Gaj, "Comparison of FPGA-Targeted Hardware Implementations of eSTREAM Stream Cipher Candidates," p. 12.

[13] K. Gaj, G. Southern, R. Bachimanchi, and E. Department, "Comparison of hardware performance of selected Phase II eSTREAM candidates," p. 11.

[14] J. Sugier, "Implementing Salsa20 vs. AES and Serpent Ciphers in Popular-Grade FPGA Devices," in New Results in Dependability and Computer Systems. Heidelberg: Springer International Publishing, 2013, vol. 224, pp. 431–438.

Eavesdropping Hackers: Detecting Software Vulnerability Communication on Social Media Using Text Mining

Andrei Lima Queiroz
Applied Intelligence Research Centre
Technological University Dublin
andrei.queiroz@tudublin.ie

Susan Mckeever
Applied Intelligence Research Centre
Technological University Dublin
susan.mckeever@tudublin.ie

Brian Keegan
Applied Intelligence Research Centre
Technological University Dublin
brian.x.keegan@tudublin.ie

***Abstract*—Cyber security is striving to find new forms of protection against hacker attacks. An emerging approach nowadays is the investigation of security-related messages exchanged on Deep/Dark Web and even Surface Web channels. This approach can be supported by the use of supervised machine learning models and text mining techniques. In our work, we compare a variety of machine learning algorithms, text representations and dimension reduction approaches for the detection accuracies of software-vulnerability-related communications. Given the imbalanced nature of the three public datasets used, we investigate appropriate sampling approaches to boost detection accuracies of our models. In addition, we examine how feature reduction techniques, such as Document Frequency Reduction, Chi-square and Singular Value Decomposition (SVD) can be used to reduce the number of features of the model without impacting the detection performance. We conclude that: (1) a Support Vector Machine (SVM) algorithm used with traditional Bag of Words achieved highest accuracies (2) The increase of the minority class with Random Oversampling technique improves the detection performance of the model by 5% on average, and (3) The number of features of the model can be reduced by up to 10% without affecting the detection performance. Also, we have provided the labelled dataset used in this work for further research. These findings can be used to support Cyber Security Threat Intelligence (CTI) with respect to the use of text mining techniques for detecting security-related communication.**

Keywords–cyber security threat intelligence; software vulnerability; machine learning; text mining; social media, hacker communication.

I. Introduction

There is no guarantee that we are using software products free of vulnerabilities. Some vulnerabilities are built in to software products and can remain unknown or dormant for long periods. In recent years, significantly large data breaches have been associated with vulnerabilities on companies software assets. For instance, a data breach on the Equifax credit company, which is believed to have originated from an exploitation of a vulnerability on Equifax defence applications after being shared (or sold) on Dark Web underground forums [1]. This issue affected the private information of more than 140 million people. Another example of such a problem was found in the Facebook web application, which affected the data of 50 million users. This time, the flaw was found in a feature called *"View As"*, which allowed a hacker to exfiltrate users access token. The bug responsible for this vulnerability was introduced within the application around July 2017 and was discovered by the companys software engineers almost one year later [2].

Although considerable work has been carried out during the software engineering lifecycle in order to address vulnerability issues, we still remain exposed to vulnerable products without knowing. As a result, many of these vulnerabilities can go undetected, unpatched or exploited for long periods of time. We, the software users, have no knowledge if hackers have found these issues before they were made public.

In the age of information, criminals are taking advantage of the communication channels on social media to either sell hacker tools or promote cyber-attacks against enterprise assets [3][4]. Hackers can buy and sell products that might be used to take advantage of these vulnerabilities or use these channels to exchange and learn how to take advantage of such vulnerabilities. However, it is not just black hat hackers who are part of this system. There are white hat hackers using social media, particularly Twitter, to inform the users and software vendors about the problems found [5].

In order to use this information to act proactively against such threats, researchers are focusing on supervised machine learning classification models for detecting malicious conversations on social media and specialised on-line hacker communities. This type of research is experiencing considerable growth within the cyber security domain as machine learning approaches for text are changing and improving rapidly with the availability of rich distributed representation models for words and sentences such as word2vec, sentence2vec. However, some studies fail to follow appropriate structured methods to build, evaluate and improve these models. Another issue identified is that there is a lack of labelled data (gold standard) for this type of research, which makes it difficult to compare the classification performance of models applied to the same problem.

With this in mind, this research proposes to: (1) Identify the features, classifiers and practices that gives best detection accurancies for software-vulnerability-related communication in on-line social media channels; (2) Using appropriate techniques to address the inherent imbalance of datasets, which has a higher proportion of negative instances (non-malicious communication) than positive instances (malicious communication); (3) Using appropriate strategies to address the high feature dimensionality inherent from the textual nature of the social media user content, which includes document frequency reduction, feature selection and features extraction; and (4)

Apply robust labelling strategies so that the datasets used here can be used for further research in this field.

The core contribution of this paper is to conduct an empirical comparison of text mining techniques for improving Cyber Security Intelligence (CTI) so as to act proactively against exploitation of software. Other research work on this subject has used a smaller number of datasets to compare their findings. In our approach, we use three different datasets from different sources (Surface Web, Deep Web and Dark Web). Also, the term software in the context of this work, is used in a broad context, which refers to all type of computer programs ranging across the software layers and found in any computer-like devices, such as web servers, embedded system, mobile phone, cars, ATM, network protocols.

The structure of this paper is as follows: Section 2 discusses related work in the area of text mining and cyber security. Section 3 explains our approach for this work, the techniques to be applied and the datasets used. Our experimental work and results are presented in Section 4, with conclusions and future work in Section 5.

II. Related work

Some works have been using similar techniques to investigate hacker forums and other social media. Nunes et al. [6] proposed one of the first works that address the use of classification models to detect malicious hacker communication in on-line communities. Their model has reached good performance in terms of recall, 92% for forums and 80% for products in marketplaces by using semi-supervised co-training technique and SVM. In more recent work, Deliu et al. [4] used the same SVM algorithm to determine which messages are *relevant* and *irrelevant* for cyber security and, on top of that, they used the Latent Dirichlet Allocation (LDA) unsupervised method to cluster the posted messages in topics, such as leaked credentials, malicious server, virus and malware.

In a similar way Cherqi et al. [7] have used supervised learning approach to detect *hacker related* and *non-hacker related* content in marketplaces on Dark Web forums. The authors have used some domain-specific features such as price, origin, destination and rating of products to increase the performance of the model. These type of features are specific to Dark Web marketplaces and it is not easily found on other social media platforms metadata or post content. For this reason, we have decided to use only word features as they can be applied to all datasets used in this work.

A problem we have identified in the area of text mining/classification for cyber security is the lack of consistent labelled datasets. Existing work relies on labelling annotation done by key-word matching where the ambiguity of the messages and subjectivity is not addressed [4][8]. In our work, we have decided to address this issues by labelling all instances three times with different people. In the end, the final label has been assigned by the majority of votes.

Another issue with these works is that they generally lack on presenting more information about the distribution of instances in each class, whether it is imbalanced or not. This issue has a direct effect on the classification performance of the model [9]. As a result, it makes harder to reproduce the experiment and to perform a comparison among other models.

Finally, we want to highlight that these works have a broad goal in terms of detecting malicious hacking, including carding, data breach, DDoS, whilst our proposed work has a more specific focus on software-vulnerability related communication.

III. Approach

In this section, we explain the methodology and techniques used to perform the creation of the classification models. Also, we describe the data and the methodology to provide the labels (categories) for each instance of the dataset.

A. Datasets

The three datasets used in this work are referred to as D1, D2 and D3 for the remainder of the paper. The original data for D1 and D3 is publicly available in [10][11], while D2 was first used in [12]. These datasets represent social media message boards from surface, Deep Web and Dark Web, including forum, micro blogs, and market place. All content is related to communication regarding technical and personal references to computing, security, internet services, and technology. Among these messages, we identify that few are related to malicious activities in software products or have mentioned security problems (flaws, vulnerabilities).

A summary description of each original dataset is described below:

D1 - CrackingArena Forum - This is one of the largest hacker forums existing in 2018 with 44,927 posts and 11,977 active users. It contains communication related to security issues in computing, which makes the data suitable to cyber security research on the interaction patterns among cyber criminals. The variety of covered topics in the forum ranges from social engineering, cracking/exploit tools to tutorials, which makes this forum a viable source for pinpointing the characteristics of newly emerged hacker assets. The posts in this forum date from 8/4/2013 to 24/2/2018 and is available on [10].

D2 - Security Experts - The data contains posts from 12 security-expert users on Twitter. Six of them are part of the well-known-security experts with average number of followers of 18,800, and the other six are part of the lesser-known security experts, with an average number of followers of 1,100. Their tweets are mostly related to security aspects of technology, including software vulnerabilities and hacking. The collected tweets have a one year range from early March 2016 to early March 2017. The total number of Tweets gathered is 11,833.

D3 - Dream Market - With 91,463 posted products from 2,092 sellers in 2016, this is a well-known market place for selling illegal products, such as illicit drugs, fake IDs, stolen credit card numbers and copyrighted software. It also advertises hacker products used in malicious hacker activities. This market place can be accessed only via the ToR network. The posts range from 12/4/2013 to 10/4/2017 and is available on [11].

To prepare the original datasets for analysis, we performed a series of processing steps: (1) keywords-filtering; (2) label annotation; and (3) final label assignment. The steps are described as follows:

*1) **Key-words filtering**:* Providing the label for all instances of the raw datasets would be expensive and time-consuming. In addition, based on initial observation, the number of relevant messages (software-vulnerability-related communication) is far less represented within the datasets compared to the non-relevant. To address these issues, we have decided to filter the dataset using security-specific keywords. The list of keywords used are related to the most common security problems that hackers use to exploit software and applications. They can be found in the Open Web Application Security Project (OWASP) top 10 Application Security risks [13] and the SANS top 25 software errors [14].

The volume of posts is high in each dataset, with a small proportion of instances related to software vulnerabilities. The aim of filtering the instances with this list of keywords is to: (1) reduce of the number of messages, thus, reducing the time and human resource needed for the label annotation task, and (2) increase the proportion of the instances of the less represented class (relevant messages).

*2) **Label annotation task**:* Our three datasets had to be re-labelled in order to be usable for the task of software vulnerability detection. Accurate labels are critical to the success of supervised learning. Existing work has relied on labelling annotation done by the authors, where some discussion is provided to form a consensus in doubtful messages [6], or by assigning a specific label to instances in a keywords-matching approach [4], where messages that match specific words, e.g., Hacker, are marked as being from positive class.

In this work, we are following a systematic approach, where each instance (post) in the datasets has been labelled by three different human labellers (computing researchers). Those three different opinions are considered in further step for defining the final label.

Due the ambiguity of some messages, it is not always straightforward to assign a binary label as **Yes** for (malicious software-vulnerability-related communication) or **No** (non-malicious software-vulnerability-related communication). For this reason, we have created a third label called **Undecided**. In order to complete the task they should decide whether the message is related to software-vulnerability-related communication. The following rules should be applied:

- Yes, for messages that appears as malicious messages of vulnerabilities in software assets.
- No, for messages not related to hacker activity or are out of the scope of our research (Data breach, copyrighted software cracked, stolen accounts and credit card accounts).
- Undecided, for messages that the labeller does not have enough information or confidence to mark as Yes or No.

In Table I we have examples of messages and their respective labels. The message M1, marked as Yes, is related to a type of vulnerability (Stack Buffer Overflow) affecting a software product. Message M2, also marked as Yes, is related to a release of a Proof Of concept (PoC) of a vulnerability called *dirtycow*. The messages M3 and M4 are related to personal opinion and have no direct relation to real vulnerabilities in software. It is fair to note that despite of M3 and M4 have *hack* and *hacker* keywords, they are not considered malicious communication, thus marked as No. In M5, there is not enough information to decide whether either the ssh_scan tool is vulnerable or can be used against a vulnerable software, as well as M6, where we cannot confirm that the error mentioned leads to a vulnerability into the sneaker software product, thus they are marked as Undecided. We acknowledge that the model will only be as good at detecting hacker messages as the knowledge of the labellers, for this reason, people who understand the ambiguity and subtlety of the messages is a critical step.

Following this labelling approach, we have reduced the subjectivity (using multiples labellers) and uncertainty (having Undecided as third label).

*3) **Final label assignment**:* The assignment of the final label was given by the partial agreement voting scheme which consists of:

- At least 2 of 3 labels being equal for assigning the final label, e.g.: (NO, NO, Undecided), the final label is NO.
- Total disagreement labels, e.g., (NO, YES, Undecided), excludes the instance from the final dataset.
- When the final label is Undecided, we changed to YES. From a security perspective, we rationalise that it is better to capture these uncertain messages as malicious problem. Using this model in real-situation, the undecided messages would be captured as malicious and then examined by a human expert. Also, it helps to adjust the balance between the classes as the number positive instances (YES) is lower than the negative (NO) in our binary classification model.

In the end, after completing all processing steps on the original data, the description of the new datasets D1 to D3 can be seen in Table II.

B. Methodology

*1) **Training and Test split**:* Our approach is to produce classification models that will assess user posts as potential software vulnerability threats or not. We have used a supervised learning approach, using our three labelled datasets for training and evaluation. Also, the 10-fold cross validation on each dataset. For the random partitioning of the datasets into the 10 groups or folds, we ensured stratification, such that the ratios of positive instances to negative instances are the same in each fold and as per the entire dataset.

*2) **Metrics**:* The main objective of the classification models presented in this research is to detect malicious communication regarding the exploitation of software on social media (hacker forums, market places, micro blogs). In this context, the impact of a false negative (FN), or non-detection of malicious communication, is higher than the impact of a false positive (FP), or malicious communication being detected as normal communication. Under these circumstances, our model is prioritising the classification of the positive classes (malicious communication) rather than negative class (regular communication).

However, a model with high rate of FP (also known as false alarm), is not desirable either, as it implies that a model is wrongly detecting a threat where there is not. If this situation occurs often, either a time-consuming expert investigation will be needed or unnecessary security actions will be taken.

TABLE I. LABELLING TASK EXAMPLES

ID	*Message*	*Label*
M1	Multiple remote memory corruption vulns in all Symantec/Norton antivirus products, including stack buffer overflows	Yes
M2	PoC for dirtycow vuln [URL]	Yes
M3	Reading about lawyers argue about our Jeep hack is endless fun	No
M4	it is amazing a hacker can put up with a sociologist ;)	No
M5	Just released ssh_scan v0.0.10. Release notes can be found here	Undecided
M6	I like sneaker's error 0xC0000156	Undecided

TABLE II. DATASET DESCRIPTION (AFTER PROCESSING)

ID	*Type*	*Source*	*No instances*	*Distrib. (pos/neg)*	*Avg. No. words*
D1	Technical communication	Hacker Forum	1,682	10/90%	50
D2	Expert communication	Twitter	1,921	15/85%	13
D3	Market Place	Dark Web	1,927	16/84%	169

[*] Available in http://tiny.cc/8ws67y

For this reason we use *average class accuracy*, also known as *balanced accuracy*, *average recall*, and *macro-average recall*. This metric is the sum of the recall of the positive and negative classes divided by the number of classes as seen in (2) and recall being (1). This metric is suitable for imbalanced datasets as it prevents the majority class from dominating the results.

$$Recall = \frac{TruePositive}{TruePositive + FalseNegative} \quad (1)$$

$$Avg.ClassAcc = \frac{Recall(pos.Class) + Recall(neg.Class)}{No.Classes} \quad (2)$$

*3) **Traditional Text Representation**:* Bag-of-words (BoW), Words n-grams (W_ngram) and Char n-grams (C_ngram) are commonly used as text representation for text mining and classification tasks. In all cases, the text is split into a set of tokens, with normalised occurrence counts per token in a single vector produced to represent each post.

In BoW approach, the text is tokenised into an unordered set of words, where each separate word represents a single feature. In Words n-grams approach, which is an improvement upon BoW, it uses tokens which are split into a set of features consisting of N continuous sequential words occurrences. Finally, in Char n-grams, the process is the same as Words n-gram, however, it acts on the character level within the words.

The next step represents each post (document) as a vector with the frequency of its containing word (or characters, depending on the features representation). We are using the range of 1 to 4, N=(1,4), with W_ngram and C_ngram representations.

In our work, we are using these traditional approaches and Word Level Distributed models for text representation (Section III-B4) for performing the experiment of our baseline classification models.

*4) **Word Level Distributed Text Representation**:* Unlike traditional text representations, Word Level Distributed Representation models, or Word Embedding (WEMB) models, capture syntactical and semantic information of words.

One of the first WEMB models is the Word2vec [15]. It has been widely used as feature representation in classification models. This model is based on a three-layer neural network and has two types: One that leverages the surrounding information to predict the central word (CBOW) and other that uses the central word to predict the surrounding information (Skip-gram). Another popular WEMB model for text representation is Glove [16], which is a co-occurrence matrix model that provides a word representation by using global matrix factorisation.

In this work, we are using public available pre-trained WEMB models, one being the Word2vec (skip-gram) and the other the Glove (co-occurrence). The goal is to verify whether the WEMB characteristics enhance classification performance of our applied model in comparison to traditional text representations.

Table III has the description of the pre-trained WEMB models used in this experiment as type, source, dimension and size. These models are identified by the names on ID column for the remainder of this work.

In addition, in order to create a vector that adequately represents the entire document (post message on social media), we are using the *averaging* technique, which has shown good performance in [17]. This technique consists in averaging vectors of the pre-trained WEMB model for each word of the document. Table IV indicates the percentage of the words in each dataset that was found within the pre-trained WEMB models.

TABLE III. WEMB PRE-TRAINED MODELS DESCRIPTION

ID	*Type*	*Source*	*Dimension*	*Trained size*	*Vocab. size*
SG	SkipGram[1]	Google News	300	100B	3M
G1	Glove	Wikipedia 2014	300	6B	400K
G2	Glove	Common Crawl	300	42B	1.9M
G3	Glove	Twitter	200	27B	1.2M

[1] Word2vec

TABLE IV. PROPORTION OF WORDS FOR EACH DATASET WITHIN PRE-TRAINED WEMB MODELS

ID	*D1*	*D2*	*D3*
SG	57%	81%	74%
G1	62%	85%	80%
G2	75%	92%	89%
G3	61%	83%	76%

*5) **Classification Algorithm**:* This work is using two classical learning-based algorithms from the supervised learning domain which are known for good performance in text classification [18].

The first, the Support Vector Machine (SVM), is based on a maximal margin classifier algorithm. Also, SVMs are very effective for using in high dimensional space, which is the case of text classification [19]. The second, the Naive Bayes (NB) classifier, is based on the Bayes theorem, which is considered one of the simplest and efficient algorithms and is commonly used for text classification task [20].

*6) **Baseline Results**:* For the baseline results, two classification algorithms were used, SVM and NB. For text representation, we used three traditional techniques, BoW, Words-N-gram and Char-N-gram; and four pre-trained WEMB models. In addition, the values of n-grams (char and word) ranges from 1 to 4 and the datasets D1 to D3 are used to compare the models.

The results shown in Figure 1 are for the models combining different traditional features representation and algorithms. They are presented in modified boxplot format, where the middle line of the box represents the mean (instead of median) of the *avg. class accuracy* for all datasets (each one is represented with a different mark). The best result is given by the model SVM+C_NGRAM, 0.78, which is not a largely improvement compared to SVM+BOW, 0.76, and NB+BOW, 0.72. In order to compare them, we have performed the Friedman Statistical test to determine whether there is any difference on the results achieved. With p-value=.097 (for α = .05), the null hypothesis is not rejected, meaning that there is no statistical certainty that any model is outperforming any another. Considering this, the baseline for the remainder of this work is the SVM+BOW. This model is computationally less expensive compared to the others (due the reduced number of features), and also allowed us to perform the next set of experiments without the need of extra/special hardware to accelerate the process.

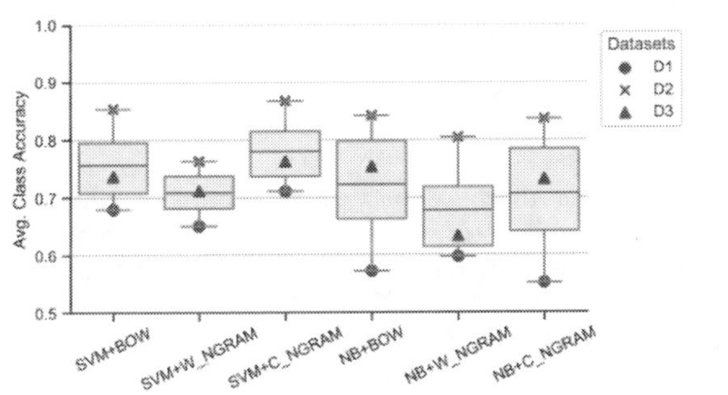

Figure 1. Baseline results.

Additionaly, in Figure 2, we compared the baseline with other models using WEMB for feature representation as shown in Table III. It is seen that the model using WEMB did not outperform SVM+BOW, which uses Bag of Words representation. The best model among those using WEMB is SVM+G2, recording the mean avg. Class Accuracy of 0.64, whilst SVM+SG, SVM+G1 and SVM+G3 recorded 0.59, 0.62 and 0.61 respectively.

C. Imbalanced Datasets

The datasets used in this research have imbalanced classes, with the majority class being from the negative class (see

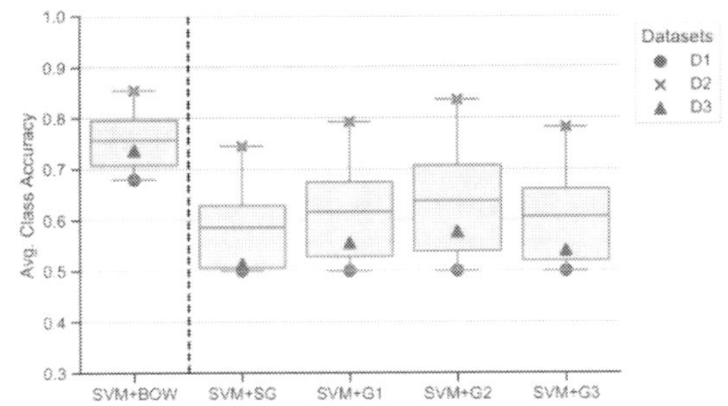

Figure 2. SVM using Bag of words (BOW) and Word Embedding (SG, G1, G2, G3) as features representation

Distribution in Table II), or in other words, they are general conversation and offer no significant value to the purpose of this research.

As a result of this imbalance, the classification performance is affected. Without sufficient knowledge to learn from the minority classes (positive), classifiers may over-assign instances to the majority classes (negative). As seen in Figure 3, Neg. Recall is higher than Pos. Recall in all datasets, with negative instances being at least 5 times higher in number than positive instances in all datasets. One of our aims is to apply techniques that can address the imbalanced nature of dataset in order to increase Pos. Recall without damaging overall average recall.

We use random over-sampling to increase the number of positive instances in datasets in D1, D2, D3. This technique has been proven to enhance positive recall of models trained on imbalanced datasets [21]. In our experimental set, we randomly resampled each fold three times, recording the average of the results for each run in order to minimise any random selection influence. Also, we have not performed this technique into the test fold data.

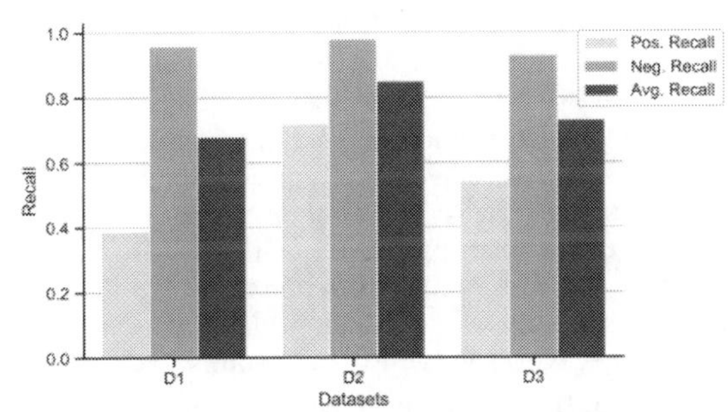

Figure 3. Pos., Neg., and Avg. Recall for SVM+BOW

D. Dimensionality Reduction

The feature space of our model in all datasets are high dimensional and sparse. The average number of features for each model by feature representation can be seen in the Table V.

For many learning algorithms, training and classification time increases directly with the number of features and consequently a high numbers of features may even negatively impact on classifier accuracy. A simple technique to reduce

TABLE V. AVG. NO. FEATURES PER TEXT REPRESENTATION

Text Representation	*D1*	*D2*	*D3*
BoW	9,422	4,880	18,119
Word n-grams n=(1,4)	168,082	49,610	542,259
Char n-grams n=(1,4)	96,063	36,372	104,981

the number of features is the use of document frequency (DF) reduction. DF reduction uses the number of features that occur within the documents (posts messages on social media) and removes the features that occur most often and least often.

Figure 4 shows the average for DF reduction in the number of features across all datasets, as we adjust the threshold for the least often features from 0.1% up to 1%.

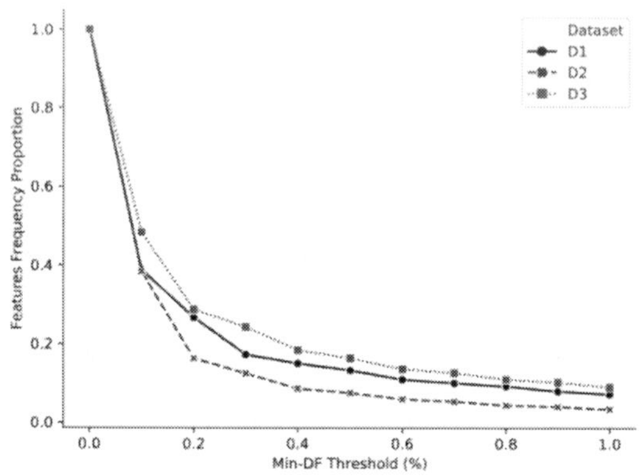

Figure 4. Feature reduction

At the 0.1% threshold, where the 0.1% frequent words are excluded, we see a reduction of at least 50% (0.5) of features in all datasets. In our experimental section, we have evaluated the impact of this reduction in relation to the classification performance of the model.

There are two other approaches that can be used to further reduce the number of features of our classification model, namely, feature selection and features reduction.

Feature selection involves techniques that choose the best subset of the existing features. Typically, they rank the features using algorithms that correlate the features to the target class label and choose the top ranked features. Also, it helps eliminate noisy of less predictive features to significantly reduce the dimensionality without losing classification performance. In this work, we have used the chi-square technique.

In contrast to feature selection, feature extraction is a dimension reduction approach that transforms the existing features to a set of alternative, more compact features, while retaining as much information as possible. Common methods include the unsupervised Principal Component Analysis (PCA) and Singular Value Decomposition (SVD) approaches, which perfom a transformation of the data into a reduced feature space that captures most of the variance in the data. In this work, we have used SVD technique.

IV. Experiment and Results

The experiments are using the datasets D1 to D3 and follows the methodology described in Section III-B.

A. Dataset resampling

Chen et al. [21] have demonstrated that oversampling techniques can increase the positive recall. However, an excess of oversampling can lead to an overfit of the model. In order to find the optimal oversampling size, we have explored different resampling proportions for the positive class. Figure 5 shows the result.

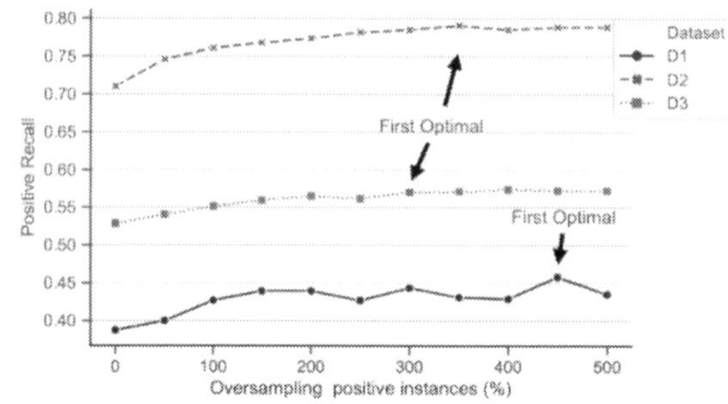

Figure 5. Optimal point

In order to find the best oversampling size, we defined the *first optimal rule* . This rule consists of setting the optimal point as being the one that most improves the positive recall and has less resampled instances. Following this rule, D1 and D2 and D3 have their first optimal point set as 450%, 350% and 300% respectively.

With this technique, we have achieved an increase of the positive recall of 6% for D1 and D2, and 3% for D3, representing an average increase of 5%. Finally, the new proportion of the classes is shown in Table VI.

TABLE VI. RE-SAMPLED DATASET

	D1 (+/-) %	*D2* (+/-) %	*D3* (+/-) %
Before	(10/90)	(15/85) %	(16/84) %
After	(44/56)	(32/62) %	(37/63) %

B. Dimensionality Reduction

In order to make the model more efficient in terms of computational performance, all unnecessary features need to be removed. To achieve this, the detection accuracy after Document Frequency (DF) reduction needs to be verified in order to maintain the previous detection accuracy. In Figure 6, we have compared the positive recall for each of our datasets before and after the DF reduction. We removed all least frequent words, appearing in $<$ (less than) 0.1% of the documents and the most frequent words appearing in $>$ (more than) 20% of the documents. As seen in Figure 6, after reduction, the positive recall has been maintained in D1 and D2, and for D2 it has increased by 1%.

In the following, we have applied two other techniques on top of the reduced dataset post Document Frequency. First, the chi-square feature selection and second, the SVD feature extraction. For chi-square, we have used 50% of the number of actual features and for SVD, we reduced the dimensionality to 10% of the actual features space. These results are consistent with [17], which has found the same values for the same techniques. In Figure 7, the results indicate that we can use this

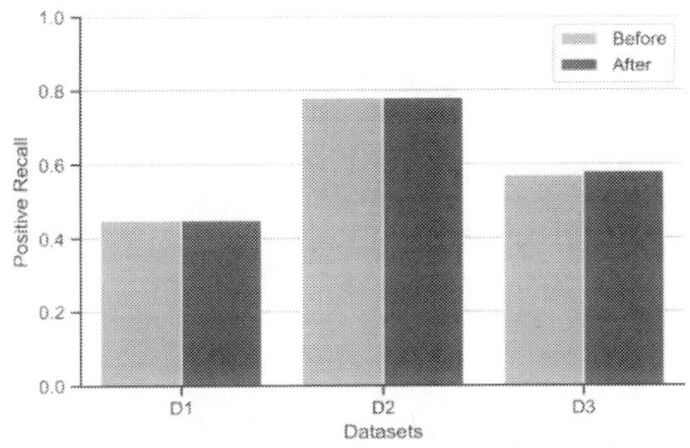

Figure 6. Document Frequency Reduction

technique to further reduce the dimensionality of the model. The trade-off for this is a minor reduction in the classification performance (less than 1%) using DF + SVD.

The summary of the results for all steps taken in this work can be seen in Table VII. It is seen that, for all datasets, the use of re-sampling technique improves over the baseline model in both metrics, positive recall and avg. class accuracy. In addition, the use of one of the three dimensionality reduction (DF, DF+Chi2 or DF+SVD) after re-sampling do not heavily change the performance already recorded.

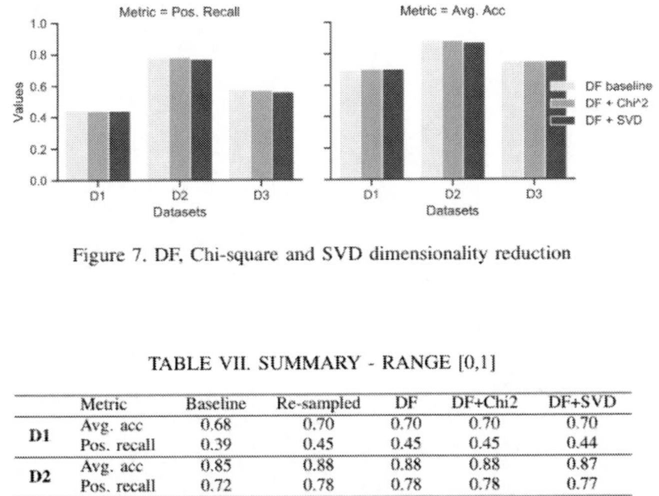

Figure 7. DF, Chi-square and SVD dimensionality reduction

TABLE VII. SUMMARY - RANGE [0,1]

	Metric	Baseline	Re-sampled	DF	DF+Chi2	DF+SVD
D1	Avg. acc	0.68	0.70	0.70	0.70	0.70
	Pos. recall	0.39	0.45	0.45	0.45	0.44
D2	Avg. acc	0.85	0.88	0.88	0.88	0.87
	Pos. recall	0.72	0.78	0.78	0.78	0.77
D3	Avg. acc	0.73	0.75	0.75	0.75	0.75
	Pos. recall	0.54	0.57	0.58	0.57	0.56

V. CONCLUSION AND FUTURE WORK

The main goal of this work is the investigation of how machine leaning and text mining techniques can be applied to detection of software-security-related communication in on-line channels. With this respect, it has been concluded:

(1) SVM and traditional BOW text representation performed better than a more robust SVM + WEMB model, such as Word2vec and Glove. We believe this happened due to the use of pre-trained models, trained in a generic and non-security related source (such as Wikipedia, Google news) Table III), thus, it does not capture the entire meaning of security-related words and jargon. With respect to the result of the four classification models using pre-trained WEMB features representation, the SVM + G2 achieved the best results among them. This is due to the higher percentage of words the G2 model has in common with the datasets (D1 to D3) compared to the other WEMB models (SD, G1 and G3), as seen in Table IV.

(2) The random sampling technique has proven to be useful for training models with imbalanced quantity of instances within the classes. In this experiment, we have an increase of the positive recall by 5% in average by oversampling the minority class. Models trained in D2 and D3 achieve best positive recall (with less oversampling) by increasing 350% and 300% the number of the minority class, respectively, whilst D1 reach its best in 450%.

(3) The detection performance of the models can be achieved with a small quantity of features. By DF reduction, where the least (appearing in less than 0.1% documents) and the most often (appearing more than 20% in documents) features were removed, we have at least a drop of 50% of the total features, while maintaining the same classification performance. To further reduce the dimensionality of the model, chi-square and SVD techniques can be used at the levels of 50% and 10% of the number of features respectively.

We believe that these findings can bring further directions to CTI initiatives with respect to the creation of accurate and efficient classification models. In addition, in this paper, we took a systematic approach to apply a variety of core text mining techniques (feature representation, reduction and resampling) in order to determine a reference for other researchers. Also, we have published our three labelled dataset to be used by others to compare their approaches and results.

The next steps would be comparing the performance of these models against deep learning classification models, such as convolutional neural networks (CNNs) and recurrent neural networks (RNNs), and use other form of text representation not used in this work, such as Sent2vec. We also want to perform a multiclass classification using the three classes of our dataset (Yes, No and Undecided) to see how well the model can perform the detection of uncertain messages (those marked as Undecided).

ACKNOWLEDGMENT

Andrei Lima Queiroz would like to thank the scholarship granted by the Brazilian Federal Programme Science without Borders supported by CNPq (Conselho Nacional de Desenvolvimento Científico e Tecnológico), No 201898/2015-2.

REFERENCES

[1] CNBC. The great Equifax mystery: 17 months later, the stolen data has never been found, and experts are starting to suspect a spy scheme. URL: https://www.cnbc.com/2019/02/13/equifax-mystery-where-is-the-data.html [Accessed: Jul, 2019].

[2] Facebook Newsroom. Security Update. URL: https://newsroom.fb.com/news/2018/09/security-update/ [Accessed: Jul, 2019].

[3] A. Algarni and Y. Malaiya, "Software vulnerability markets: Discoverers and buyers," International Journal of Computer, Information Science and Engineering, vol. 8, no. 3, 2014, pp. 71–81.

[4] I. Deliu, C. Leichter, and K. Franke, "Collecting cyber threat intelligence from hacker forums via a two-stage, hybrid process using support vector machines and latent dirichlet allocation," in 2018 IEEE International Conference on Big Data (Big Data). IEEE, 12 2018, pp. 5008–5013.

[5] C. Sabottke, O. Suciu, and T. Dumitras, "Vulnerability disclosure in the age of social media: Exploiting twitter for predicting real-world exploits," in 24th USENIX Security Symposium (USENIX Security 15). Washington, D.C.: USENIX Association, Aug. 2015, pp. 1041–1056.

[6] E. Nunes, A. Diab, A. Gunn, E. Marin, V. Mishra, V. Paliath, J. Robertson, J. Shakarian, A. Thart, and P. Shakarian, "Darknet and deepnet mining for proactive cybersecurity threat intelligence," CoRR, vol. abs/1607.08583, 2016, [accessed: Jul, 2019]. [Online]. Available: http://arxiv.org/abs/1607.08583

[7] O. Cherqi, G. Mezzour, M. Ghogho, and M. El Koutbi, "Analysis of hacking related trade in the darkweb," in 2018 IEEE International Conference on Intelligence and Security Informatics (ISI), Nov 2018, pp. 79–84.

[8] R. P. Lippmann, W. M. Campbell, D. J. Weller-Fahy, A. C. Mensch, G. M. Zeno, and J. P. Campbell, "Finding malicious cyber discussions in social media," Lincoln Laboratory Journal, vol. 22, no. 1, 2016, pp. 46–59.

[9] A. Okutan, G. Werner, S. J. Yang, and K. McConky, "Forecasting cyberattacks with incomplete, imbalanced, and insignificant data," Cybersecurity Journal, vol. 1, no. 1, Dec 2018, p. 15.

[10] AZSecure-data.org. Cracking Arena [Hacker forum]. URL: https://www.azsecure-data.org/other-forums.html [Accessed: Jul, 2019].

[11] ——. Dream Market [Market Place]. URL: https://www.azsecure-data.org/other-data.html [Accessed: Jul, 2019].

[12] A. Queiroz, B. Keegan, and F. Mtenzi, "Predicting software vulnerability using security discussion in social media," in 16th European Conference on Information Warfare and Security, ECCWS, Dublin, Ireland, Jun. 2017, pp. 628–634.

[13] OWASP. Top 10 Application Security Risks - 2017. URL: https://www.owasp.org/index.php/Top_10-2017_Top_10 [Accessed: Jul, 2019].

[14] SANS. Top 25 Most Dangerous Software Errors. URL: https://www.sans.org/top25-software-errors [Accessed: Jul, 2019].

[15] T. Mikolov, K. Chen, G. Corrado, and J. Dean, "Efficient estimation of word representations in vector space," in 1st International Conference on Learning Representations, ICLR 2013, Scottsdale, Arizona, USA, May 2-4, 2013, Workshop Track Proceedings, 2013. [Online]. Available: http://arxiv.org/abs/1301.3781

[16] J. Pennington, R. Socher, and C. D. Manning, "Glove: Global vectors for word representation," in In EMNLP. Association for Computational Linguistics, 2014, pp. 1532–1543.

[17] H. Chen, S. Mckeever, and S. J. Delany, "The use of deep learning distributed representations in the identication of abusive text," in 13th International AAAI Conference on Web and Social Media ICWSM-2019, vol. 13, no. 1, Munich, Germany, Jun. 2019, pp. 125–133.

[18] T. Joachims, "Text categorization with support vector machines: Learning with many relevant features," in Machine Learning: ECML-98, C. Nédellec and C. Rouveirol, Eds. Berlin, Heidelberg: Springer Berlin Heidelberg, 1998, pp. 137–142.

[19] C. Cortes and V. Vapnik, "Support-vector networks," Machine Learning Journal, vol. 20, no. 3, Sep 1995, pp. 273–297.

[20] D. D. Lewis, "Naive (bayes) at forty: The independence assumption in information retrieval," in Machine Learning: ECML-98, C. Nédellec and C. Rouveirol, Eds. Berlin, Heidelberg: Springer Berlin Heidelberg, 1998, pp. 4–15.

[21] H. Chen, S. Mckeever, and S. J. Delany, "Harnessing the power of text mining for the detection of abusive content in social media," in Advances in Computational Intelligence Systems. Cham: Springer International Publishing, 2017, pp. 187–205.

A Secure Storage Scheme for Healthcare Data Over the Cloud Based on Multiple Authorizations

Zeyad A. Al-Odat*, Sudarshan K. Srinivasan*, Eman M. Al-Qtiemat*, Sana Shuja†
*Electrical and Computer Engineering, North Dakota State University
Fargo, ND, USA
†Electrical Engineering, COMSATS Institute of Information Technology,
Islambad, Pakistan
Emails: *zeyad.alodat@ndsu.edu, *sudarshan.srinivasan@ndsu.edu, *eman.alqtiemat@ndsu.edu,
†SanaShuja@comsats.edu.pk

***Abstract*—This paper introduces a secure storage scheme for healthcare data with multiple authorizations. The proposed design divides the healthcare data into small parts and distributes them over multiple cloud locations. The Shamir's Secret Sharing and Secure Hash Algorithm are employed to provide the security and authenticity requirements to the proposed design. The design comprises two phases, the distribution phase, and the retrieving phase. The distribution phase comprises three operations of dividing, encrypting, and distribution. The retrieving phase performs collecting and verifying operations. To increase the security level, the encryption key is divided into secret shares using Shamir's Secret Sharing. Moreover, the Secure Hash Algorithm is used to verify the healthcare data after retrieving from the cloud. The experimental results show that the proposed design can reconstruct a distributed healthcare data with a significant speed while conserving the security and authenticity properties.**

***Keywords*—*Healthcare*; *Security*; *Shamir's Secret Sharing*; *Authorization*.**

I. Introduction

The global healthcare system is changing every day, particularly the conversion into a digital healthcare environment that contains all patient's data and their corresponding records [1]. This change is stimulated by the new technologies, increased number of populations, and the change in people's lifestyles. The emerging technology offers a convenient environment for supporting healthcare management, digital clinics, monitoring, and preserving of health records [2].

Cloud computing is an emerging technology that is updated frequently and adopted with new technologies rapidly [3]. The big healthcare data is considered as a big data application over cloud computing. Therefore, all challenges, analyses, and concerns that are related to cloud computing are applied to the big healthcare data [4].

The security and privacy of big data are important because numerous amount of data is stored at the same pool of storage locations [5]. The security and privacy concerns of the healthcare data over the cloud are increasing, in addition to the concerns of healthcare institutions that found the security and privacy requirements of the healthcare data over the cloud are not adequate [2][6].

Big data security is guaranteed by different technologies, including the following: 1) Encryption, 2) Centralized key management, 3) User access control, 4) Intrusion detection and prevention, and 5) Physical security. Moreover, everyone is responsible for security, e.g., policies, agreement list, and security software. The security requirements of physical components are guaranteed by the Cloud Service Provider (CSP), which grants proper accesses to the data owners [7].

One of the main methods to share big data is distribution technology. The big data is divided into parts and distributed over several storage locations [8]. However, many criteria need to be addressed in this scheme including data security and retrieval. The data need to be secured against unauthorized access and protected from data tampering and alteration. Data security is achieved using encryption techniques, e.g., Advanced Encryption Standard (AES) while data integrity is achieved using the Secure Hash Algorithm (SHA). However, an attacker can hack the encryption key and access the big data. In the case of healthcare data, the attacker will gain access to the patients' sensitive information, e.g., social security numbers [9].

In this paper, we introduce a secure and authentic healthcare storage scheme over the cloud. In our design, the Shamir's Secret Sharing (SSS) and SHA are employed to provide the security requirements of the proposed scheme. The SSS is used to divide the encryption key into parts and distributes these parts over authorized entities. The $SHA-512$ is used to check the data integrity after retrieval [10].

The rest of paper is organized as follows: Section II provides a background information about the secure hash algorithm and Shamir's Secret Sharing; a literature review is presented in Section III; Sections IV exhibits the proposed methodology; results and discussions are conferred in Section V; Section VI concludes the paper.

II. Background

Before going through the details of our proposal, brief descriptions about The *SSS* and *SHA* will be presented in the subsequent text.

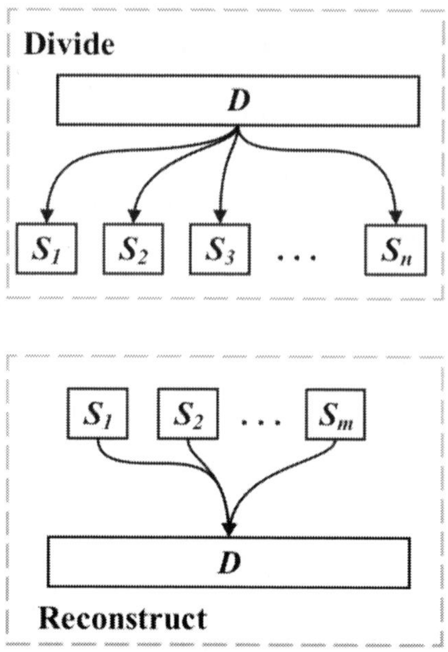

Figure 1. Shamir's Secret Sharing structure

A. Shamir's Secret Sharing

The SSS is a secret sharing technique that is proposed by Adi Shamir [11]. The *SSS* divides data (D) into a number of pieces (S_n) where D is easily reconstructable from the minimum number of pieces (S_m). The SSS is a (m, n) based scheme, where m is the minimum number of pieces that are needed to reconstruct the data (D) and n is the total number of pieces that the data (D) is divided to. Additionally, D is completely undetermined if the number of known pieces is fewer than $m - 1$, which means that m pieces must be available to reconstruct the original data D. Figure 1 shows the general structure of the SSS algorithm, where it involves two operations, the divide and reconstruct. The upper part of the figure shows that the data D is divided into n pieces. Then, to reconstruct the data D from these parts a minimum of m pieces is needed. More details will be presented in Section IV.

B. Secure Hash Algorithm

The SHA is a cryptography function that is used for integrity scrutiny. The SHA takes a message (M) of arbitrary size, then through compression function calculations produces the message hash (H). The SHA is used to provide the authenticity and integrity of the data, i.e., ensure that the data have not tampered during transmission or storing.

The secure hash algorithms follow two construction models. The first construction model is Merkle Damgard (*MD*), which is used to construct the hash functions *MD4*, *MD5*, *SHA-1*, and *SHA-2* [12]. The second one is the Sponge structure model that is used to construct the $SHA - 3$ hash function [13]. In our proposal, we use the MD structure model to provide data integrity and authenticity. Figure 2 shows the general structure of the MD structure model. The message M of size $< 2^{128}$ is preprocessed first by padding the input message to make its size a multiple of the block size (B). Then the padded message M^* is divided into equal size blocks (B_n).

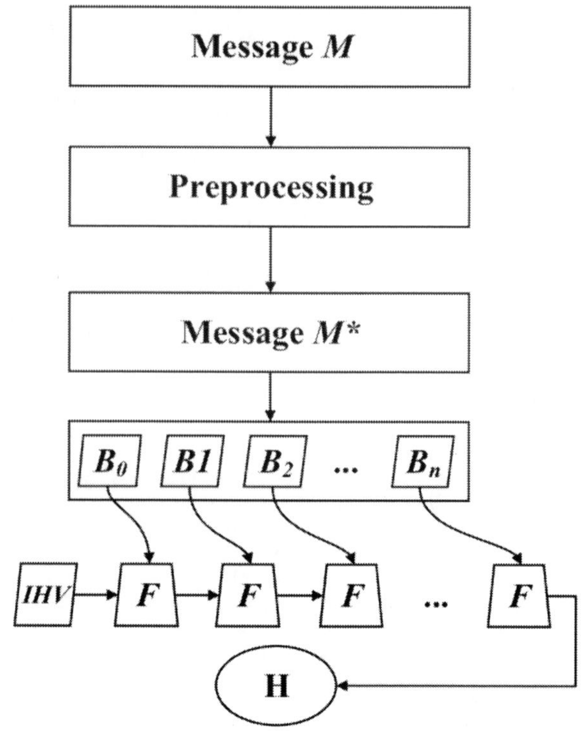

Figure 2. General structure of the Secure Hash Algorithm (SHA)

In the *MD* hash standards, the maximum message size that each algorithm accepts is dependent on the block size, where the 512-bit block size accepts messages of size less than 2^{64}-bit, while the others accept a message size of 2^{128}-bit. All hash standards perform the following steps:

1) **Message padding**. In this phase, the message is padded with a sufficient number of zeros to make the message size multiple of the block size.
2) **Message divide**. In this phase, the message is divided into equal size blocks (B), where the block size is dependent to the desired hash function.
3) **Compression function calculation**. All blocks are processed sequentially using compression function (F). The Initial Hash Value (IHV) is used to process the first block (B_0), then the output of processing each block is used as (IHV) to the next block calculation.
4) **Output hash generation**. The output of the last block calculation is taken as the output hash (H).

For more details about secure hash algorithms and their compression functions, the reader is referred to [14].

C. Threat Model

Two major threats are related to this work.

1) Privacy Threat. The healthcare data owners (patients, medical institutions, authorized entities) have concerns about the privacy of their data. These concerns include the encryption key exposure by an adversary and the *CSP* threat. Once the attacker gains access to the encryption key, all sensitive healthcare information will be exposed. Furthermore, the *CSP* can access the uploaded data and distributes them without the knowledge of the data owners. Therefore, the level of trust between the data owners and *CSPs* is reduced [15].
2) Integrity Threat. The healthcare data might be exposed to intentional or unintentional data tampering. The data owners are not aware of their uploaded data over the cloud and they consider that the *CSP* will take full responsibility for the uploaded data. However, the stored healthcare records may be tampered by an external adversary or due to software or hardware failures of the cloud service [16].

In our work, we preserve the healthcare data privacy over the cloud and provide a scheme that increases the level of trust between the data owners and the *CSP*.

III. Related Work

A secure leakage resilient s-health system has been proposed to protect the privacy keys from seizing that might happen because of some leakage attacks [17]. This approach presented a new cryptographic public key called leakage-resilient anonymous Hierarchical Identity-Based Encryption (HIBE). The security of this construction has been proven against chosen-plaintext attacks. Also, performance analysis has been done to demonstrate the practicability of this technique.

To solve security challenges, many approaches have been suggested based on Attribute-Based Encryption. Charanya *et al.* employed multiple parties in cloud computing to assure that eHealth data are secure [18]. Attributes and key policy have been used to encrypt health data, the only one who has this information can decrypt the health data. Decryption can be done only after verifying the attributes and key policy by using both a key distribution center and the secure data distributor. However, both of the aforementioned approaches consider the key privacy not all health data privacy.

An efficient data-sharing scheme called MedChain has been presented to control efficiency issues in the existing approaches such as sharing data streams, which are generated by monitoring devices [19]. This technique collects blockchain, digest chain, and structured peer to peer network techniques for sharing both types of healthcare data. For flexible data sharing, a session-based healthcare data-sharing scheme is designed. an evaluation process has been applied on MedChain illustrated that it can fulfill higher adequacy and satisfy the security-based requirements in data sharing.

A novel framework has been proposed for control accessing the Personal Health Records (PHRs) in the cloud computing environment [20]. To enable fine-grained and scalable access control for PHRs, Attribute-Based Encryption (ABE) techniques have been utilized to encrypt the PHRs for patients. Authors divided their system into various security domains, each domain is responsible for a subset of the users. Each patient has full control over his data, and the complexity of key management is reduced significantly. The proposed scheme is flexible, it supports efficient and on-demand repeal of user access rights.

Chen *et al.* have presented a secure dynamic access structure that can guarantee accurate access to the cloud server's medical records with multi-user settings [21]. Cryptography based on Lagrange multipliers has been used for encrypting the records to assure the maximum control of patients over their medical data. Mainly, this work focused on improving the encryption of PHRs and enhancing user dynamic access rules. This approach is very flexible in case of multi-user access and addition or modification of PHR.

The delay time of accessing the patient record can cause a death toll and decrease the health service level delivered by the medicinal professionals. A new study has been introduced that combines the Triple Data Encryption Standard (3DE) and Least Significant Bit (LSB) to enhance security measure that is applied to the patient's data [22]. For the experiment, a simulation program has been developed by using Java programming language. The experiment shows that patient's data and is saved, shared, and controlled in a secure way using the proposed combined method.

A new approach has been introduced to protect the identity and the privacy of the medical data using an effective encryption technique [23]. Also, an authorization framework has been discussed to control the access control mechanism of medical data. Encryption was done by using ARCANA that provides hierarchically access to many data resources. The XACML access model has been employed to subedit the access control framework. The AT&T scheme has been implemented to control the access mechanism of the patient's health data.

In the subsequent section, a secure healthcare storage and sharing scheme based on multiple authorizations will be presented.

IV. Proposed Methodology

The proposed design comprises two phases, distribution and retrieving. In the distribution phase, the healthcare data are signed, encrypted and distributed over multiple cloud locations. Also, the encryption key (E) is divided into parts and distributed over n authorized entities (*AEs*). In the retrieving phase, the healthcare data are collected from the storage locations using the (*SE*), and least number of authorized entities are requested to provide their secret part (E_n). The proposed design is implemented with aligning to Figure 3 and

Figure 5. To better understand the figures and the details of the proposed work, please refer to Table I that shows the used notations in this section.

TABLE I. NOTATIONS

Symbols	Meaning
D	The healthcare Data
SHA	Secure Hash Algorithm (*SHA-512*)
H	Hash value after applying the *SHA-512*
H^*	Hash value after retrieving D
SSS	Shamir's Secret Sharing
D_i	i part of Data D
E	Encryption Key
E_n	n parts of Encryption key E
$L(x)$	Lagrange polynomial to find $L(0)$
CSP	Cloud Service Provider
AE	Authorized Entity
SE	Service Entity that responsible for Data collection

A. Distribution Phase

In the distribution phase, the *SHA-512* compression function is applied to the healthcare data file. Then, the calculated hash value (H) is appended to the healthcare data (D), as shown in Figure 3. Afterward, the healthcare data file is divided into smaller blocks (D_1, D_2, $\ldots$, D_i), where the hash value (H) is appended to the last block (D_i). Each of the healthcare data parts is encrypted using the encryption key (E) and distributed over multiple cloud locations for storage and sharing.

The Encryption key (E) plays a major rule in the security of the healthcare data D. Therefore, the encryption key (E) is divided into shares (E_1, E_2, ..., E_n) using the SSS algorithm. Then, these shares are distributed over n authorized entities (AEs), where m number of shares must be present to calculate the original encryption key. According to the SSS algorithm, the number of shares (m) that are needed to reconstruct E is represented by a polynomial of power ($m-1$), as shown in Figure 4. The figure shows the pseudo-code of the general procedure to divide the encryption key (E) into shares (E_n). Firstly, the minimum number of shares (m) that are needed to reconstruct E is determined. Then, an (m-1) random numbers (a_{m-1}) are generated to construct the polynomial equation ($f(x)$) that is used to generate the required shares (n). Noting that, the value of a_0 is equal to the value of E. Afterward, the total number of shares (n) is determined, and n pairs of shares $(t, f(t))$ are generated using the polynomial function ($f(x)$). The generated secret shares are distributed over several authorized entities (*AEs*) including patients, physicians, medical institutions, and any other authorized entities, which are determined ahead of the secret shares generation process.

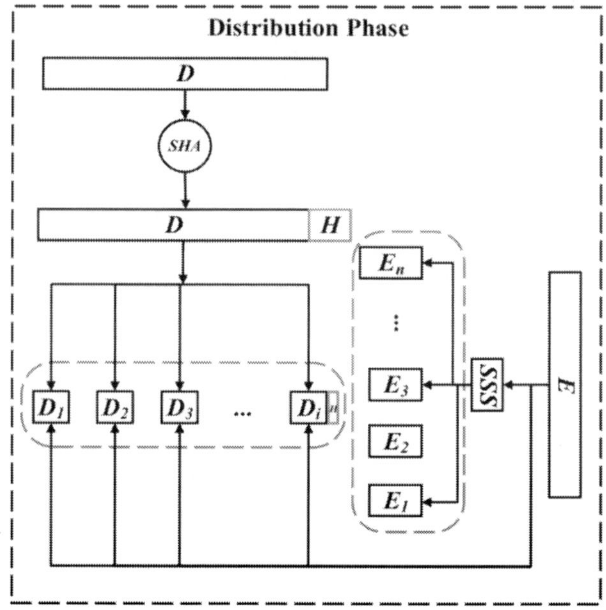

Figure 3. Schematic diagram of the Distribution phase

Algorithm 1: SSS

Input: Encryption Key (E)
Output: E_1, E_2, ..., E_n

Determine(m) ; `//Least number of shares`
for $i \leftarrow 1$ ***to*** $m-1$ **do**
  $a_i = Rand()$
$f(x) = a_0 + a_1x + a_2x^2 + ... + a_{m-1}x^{m-1}$
Determine(n) ; `//Total number of shares`
for $t \leftarrow 1$ ***to*** n **do**
  $E_t = (t, f(t))$

Figure 4. Pseudo Code of the SSS algorithm

B. Retrieving Phase

In the cloud, the healthcare data parts are distributed over multiple storage locations. To keep track of all parts a unique identifier is given to each part after partitioning. In our proposal, one of the authorized entities, called Service Entity (*SE*), is responsible for data parts collection and parsing. The *AEs* have the correct order of the data parts and their locations over the cloud, and every time a retrieval job is requested the *SE* duty is assigned to one of the *AEs*. However, the *SE* is unable to decrypt the healthcare data because of the multiple authorization scheme that we deployed using the *SSS* algorithm. To ensure that the *SE* is not considered as a weak part in the design, the *SE* duty is assigned to one of the data owners every time a data retrieval request is performed.

To retrieve the healthcare data, one of the authorized entities sends an access request to the service entity. The service entity sends a secret-key share request to all authorized entities (AEs). According to the predefined configurations in the distribution phase, m number of secret shares must be provided to reconstruct the encryption/decryption key. Once collected, the encryption/decryption key (E) is computed using Lagrange

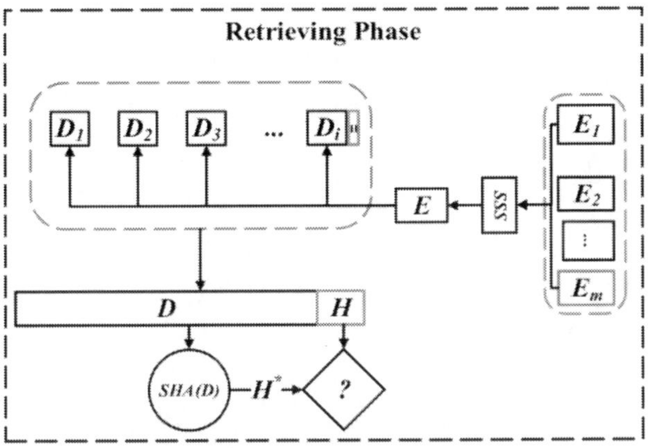

Figure 5. Schematic diagram of the Retrieving phase

polynomials equation, as shown in (1).

$$L(0) = \sum_{j=0}^{m-1} f(x_j) \prod_{\substack{q=0 \\ q \neq j}}^{m-1} \frac{x_q}{x_q - x_j}, \quad (1)$$

where $L(0)$ represents the retrieved key (E), and each point pair $(x, f(x_j))$ refers to one share.

Afterward, the healthcare data parts are collected from the storage locations, assembled according to their identifiers, and decrypted using the retrieved E-key. Moreover, one more step is needed to verify the integrity of the healthcare data. The secure hash algorithm is used to accomplish the last step, where the SHA-512 is used to compute the hash value (H^*) of the retrieved healthcare data D. The computed hash value (H^*) and the appended hash value (H) are compared to determine whether they are equal. If D is correctly gathered and not modified during transmission, the values of H and H^* are equal. Otherwise, D is corrupted and contains tampered contents. In the case of retrieving an individual record, the *SE* determines which data part the requested record belong to. Then, the data part block is decrypted to retrieve the required record.

V. Results and Discussion

The experiments were tested using a configurable experimental environment for High-Performance Computing (HPC) using Center for Computationally Assisted Science and Technology (CCAST) at the North Dakota State University. On CCAST, we reserved a cluster lease with 2-Intel Xeon processors 2.5GHz with 56 threads and 64GB of RAM. We tested the proposed design using a sample of synthesized data. The size of this sample is equal to *5GiB*.

A. Experimental analysis

To test the speed of the proposed design, we measured the elapsed time to collect and hash the test sample data. The results show that the proposed design requires 26.5 seconds to compute the hash value for the collected sample data. The time needed to collect the sample data parts and decrypts them is equal to 475.26 seconds. Overall, the total time to hash and collect the sample data parts shows the significant speed of our proposal over other designs in the literature, neglecting the time needed to collect the encryption key (E). Moreover, the decentralized approach that we proposed using the *SSS* algorithm provides a secure and authentic mechanism to store and monitor the healthcare data over the cloud.

B. Security Analysis

The security of the proposed design is expressed from the healthcare data owners perspective. For each security threat, we built a security model to verify the efficiency of the proposed design. This model includes the employed security functions (SSS and SHA-512) and experimental results. The security analyses results were deduced according to four deductions.

Deduction 1: The healthcare data parts are distributed over multiple locations and identified by a unique identifier for each part.

The first level of security is accomplished using the service entity, where the (*SE*) is the only one who is responsible for data summing according to their identifiers.

Deduction 2: The encryption key (E) is divided into shares and distributed over multiple authorized entities.

The second level of security is obtained using the SSS algorithm, where the decentralized encryption key scheme protects the encryption key (E) even if parts of the secret shares are exposed to an adversary.

Deduction 3: The healthcare data are integral and authentic, thanks to the *SHA-512*.

The third level of security is achieved by using the *SHA-512*. After retrieving the healthcare data, the *SHA-512* compression function is applied to make sure the retrieved data are tamper-free and gathered in the correct order.

Deduction 4: The level of trust between the healthcare data owners and the *CSPs* is increased.

The healthcare data owners make sure that the *CSP* has no access to the stored data. This is because the data are encrypted and the encryption key is distributed over multiple users. Moreover, the proposed design allows the healthcare data parts to be distributed over different *CSPs* which is supported by the data identifiers and the *SE*.

The employment of the SHA and SSS algorithms consolidates the healthcare data storage and sharing and increases the level of trust between the *CSP* and client. The proposed design accomplished the security requirements of data integrity and CSP prevention. Moreover, the use of SSS consolidates the proposed design against centralized control.

VI. Conclusions and Future Work

In this paper, a secure storage scheme for healthcare data was presented. The proposed design employed the *SSS* algorithm and *SHA-512* to provide the security requirements to the proposed design. The *SSS* is used to divide the encryption key into secret shares and distributes these shares on multiple authorized entities. Also, the *SHA-512* ensures that the healthcare data parts are tamper-free and collected in the correct order after retrieval. The proposed design is tested using a synthesized data sample using a high-performance computing environment. The results showed a significant speed in retrieving the healthcare data, and the security analysis provides the security proof of the proposed design.

In the future, further experiments will be conducted to include different samples. The security requirements will be extended to include the case of third-party auditor (*TPA*). Moreover, a data replication scheme over the cloud will be applied to the proposed design using division and replication of data in the cloud for optimal performance and security.

Acknowledgments

This publication was funded by a grant from the United States Government and the generous support of the American people through the United States Department of State and the United States Agency for International Development (USAID) under the Pakistan - U.S. Science & Technology Cooperation Program. The contents do not necessarily reflect the views of the United States Government.

Computing services, financial and administrative support from the North Dakota State University Center for Computationally Assisted Science and Technology (CCAST) and the Department of Energy through Grant No. DE-SC0001717 are gratefully acknowledged.

References

[1] C. Burghard, "Big data and analytics key to accountable care success," *IDC health insights*, pp. 1–9, 2012.

[2] J. G. Ronquillo, J. Erik Winterholler, K. Cwikla, R. Szymanski, and C. Levy, "Health it, hacking, and cybersecurity: national trends in data breaches of protected health information," *JAMIA Open*, vol. 1, no. 1, pp. 15–19, 2018.

[3] M. Ahmadi and N. Aslani, "Capabilities and advantages of cloud computing in the implementation of electronic health record," *Acta Informatica Medica*, vol. 26, no. 1, p. 24, 2018.

[4] K. Abouelmehdi, A. Beni-Hessane, and H. Khaloufi, "Big healthcare data: preserving security and privacy," *Journal of Big Data*, vol. 5, no. 1, p. 1, 2018.

[5] C. Tankard, "Big data security," *Network security*, vol. 2012, no. 7, pp. 5–8, 2012.

[6] W. Wilkowska and M. Ziefle, "Privacy and data security in e-health: Requirements from the users perspective," *Health informatics journal*, vol. 18, no. 3, pp. 191–201, 2012.

[7] R. Lu, H. Zhu, X. Liu, J. K. Liu, and J. Shao, "Toward efficient and privacy-preserving computing in big data era," *IEEE Network*, vol. 28, no. 4, pp. 46–50, 2014.

[8] Y. Li, K. Gai, L. Qiu, M. Qiu, and H. Zhao, "Intelligent cryptography approach for secure distributed big data storage in cloud computing," *Information Sciences*, vol. 387, pp. 103–115, 2017.

[9] Z. A. Al-Odat, S. K. Srinivasan, E. Al-Qtiemat, m. a. latha dubasi, and s. shuja, "Iot-based secure embedded scheme for insulin pump data acquisition and monitoring," in *The Third International Conference on Cyber-Technologies and Cyber-Systems*. IARIA, 2018, pp. 90–93.

[10] Z. Al-Odat, M. Ali, and S. U. Khan, "Mitigation and improving sha-1 standard using collision detection approach," in *2018 International Conference on Frontiers of Information Technology (FIT)*. IEEE, 2018, pp. 333–338.

[11] A. Shamir, "How to share a secret," *Commun. ACM*, vol. 22, no. 11, pp. 612–613, Nov. 1979. [Online]. Available: http://doi.acm.org/10.1145/359168.359176

[12] I. B. Damgård, "A design principle for hash functions," in *Advances in Cryptology — CRYPTO' 89 Proceedings*, G. Brassard, Ed. New York, NY: Springer New York, 1990, pp. 416–427.

[13] G. Bertoni, J. Daemen, M. Peeters, and G. Van Assche, "Sponge functions," in *ECRYPT hash workshop*, vol. 2007, no. 9. Citeseer, 2007, pp. 1–93.

[14] F. PUB, "Secure hash standard (shs)," *FIPS PUB 180*, vol. 4, pp. 1–27, 2012.

[15] B. L. Filkins *et al.*, "Privacy and security in the era of digital health: what should translational researchers know and do about it?" *American journal of translational research*, vol. 8, no. 3, p. 1560, 2016.

[16] Y. X. Yan, L. Wu, W. Y. Xu, H. Wang, and Z. M. Liu, "Integrity audit of shared cloud data with identity tracking," *Security and Communication Networks*, vol. 2019, pp. 1–11, 2019, doi.org/10.1155/2019/1354346.

[17] Y. Zhang, P. Lang, D. Zheng, M. Yang, and R. Guo, "A secure and privacy-aware smart health system with secret key leakage resilience," *Security and Communication Networks*, vol. 2018, pp. 1–13, 2018.

[18] R. Charanya, S. Nithya, and N. Manikandan, "Attribute based encryption for secure sharing of e-health data," in *Materials Science and Engineering Conference Series*, vol. 263, no. 4, 2017, p. 042030.

[19] B. Shen, J. Guo, and Y. Yang, "Medchain: Efficient healthcare data sharing via blockchain," *Applied Sciences*, vol. 9, no. 6, p. 1207, 2019.

[20] M. Li, S. Yu, K. Ren, and W. Lou, "Securing personal health records in cloud computing: Patient-centric and fine-grained data access control in multi-owner settings," in *International conference on security and privacy in communication systems*. Springer, 2010, pp. 89–106.

[21] T.-S. Chen *et al.*, "Secure dynamic access control scheme of phr in cloud computing," *Journal of medical systems*, vol. 36, no. 6, pp. 4005–4020, 2012.

[22] A. Babatunde, A. Taiwo, and E. Dada, "Information security in health care centre using cryptography and steganography," *arXiv preprint arXiv:1803.05593*, 2018.

[23] J. Vora *et al.*, "Ensuring privacy and security in e-health records," in *2018 International Conference on Computer, Information and Telecommunication Systems (CITS)*. IEEE, 2018, pp. 1–5.

Annealed Cyber Resiliency

Cyber Discernment for the Launch Providers of Space Systems

Steve Chan
Decision Engineering Analysis Laboratory
San Diego, California
email: schan@dengineering.org

Bob Griffin
Tucson, Arizona
email: bobgriffin@me.com

Abstract—**Out-of-the-box and outside-the-wire thinking is required to identify sophisticated synthetic aberrations, which would bypass prototypical cyber defense systems. The various tools and techniques are somewhat important within the ecosystem, but an assessment methodology that embodies diligence, persistence, and learning over time can be even more vital than the various tools and techniques. This paper posits that the depth and breadth of any cyber investigation foray can well be achieved by employing an approach that is termed Cyber Discernment. In Cyber Discernment, a methodological robust decision engineering framework, Karassian Netchain Analysis (KNA), among others, is utilized to understand Negative Influence Dominating Sets (NIDS) or areas of instability and Positive Influence Dominating Sets (PIDS) or islands of stability. By ascertaining PIDS and understanding how best to mitigate NIDS, a form of *annealed cyber resiliency, enhanced cyber security,* and *latent cyber stability* can be achieved, thereby mitigating against unintended consequences, undesired elements of instability, and "perfect storm" crises lurking within the system.**

Keywords-space systems; strategic infrastructure; critical infrastructure; advanced persistent threats; outside-the-wire.

I. INTRODUCTION

Generally speaking, systems residing within the "space" ecosystem constitute attractive "persistent targets" (for "Advanced Persistent Threats (APTs)" due to their serving as an "Achilles heel" or central point of failure for large-scale systems, their potential lack of stringently enforced cyber security regulation, and their relatively large and pervasive attack surface area. Considering that much of the world's strategic infrastructural and critical infrastructural systems rely upon space-based systems, it would seem axiomatic the attacks would be channeled in this direction. Technically, space systems do not require substantively different cyber security systems from that of other strategic and/or critical infrastructure; however, as these space systems often serve as underlying infrastructure for other strategic and/or critical infrastructural systems (hence, "outside-the-wire," which is military jargon for being beyond the relatively safe confines of a controlled environment), they are not necessarily construed to be intrinsic to the referenced strategic and/or critical infrastructural systems and, therefore, are not necessarily subject to the same cyber security standards.

Typically, space systems are relatively sophisticated pieces of equipment (e.g., hardening, compute capabilities, communications packages, etc.). Despite the involved sophisticated technology, cybersecurity standards for space system assets are not necessarily strictly regulated by any governing body; the relative lack of regulation segues to an arena, wherein space systems may lack common cybersecurity standards and may be subject to a myriad of cyberattacks. This is distinct from other domains, such as Industrial Control Systems (ICS), which are regulated by the Federal Energy Regulatory Commission (FERC) and subject to, on a voluntary basis, the electric utility industry's North American Electric Reliability Corporation (NERC), which is the successor to the North American Electric Reliability Council (also known as NERC). The United Nations International Telecommunication Union (ITU) regulates the assigned frequencies for satellite communications and registers the orbits of satellites, but apart from this aspect, there are relatively few standards at play, and cyber vulnerabilities remain a challenge [1].

While the seemingly lack of standards for such sophisticated systems is already of great concern, the recent trend of low-cost satellites — utilizing commercial-off-the-shelf (COTS) technology — being launched into orbit may be of even greater concern. These "cubesats" have a fairly low barrier to entry with regards to engineering from a technical standpoint and are relatively inexpensive to launch (less than $100K). Considering the COTS nature of the satellite, it is likely that open-source software (OSS) is used prevalently by the components with the concomitant associated vulnerabilities. As has been debated over time [2], there are advantages and disadvantages to OSS. First, the wide distribution of COTS products and its associated OSS means that many people have access to the code base, and an attacker can extensively analyze the paradigm for vulnerabilities. Second, COTS products and its associated OSS need to be actively maintained, patched, and upgraded, particularly as cyber attackers are becoming increasingly adept. Just as Managed Service Providers (MSPs) and Managed [Cyber] Security Service Providers (MSSPs) are leveraging early warning indicators, such as the National Vulnerability Database (NVD) and Sentient Hyper Optimized Data Access Network (SHODAN), cyber attackers are also leveraging these assets for exploitation opportunities and as attack accelerants [3]; security patches are often not applied, and software vulnerabilities or backdoors (which may have been intentionally embedded) persist.

While the National Institute of Standards and Technology (NIST) Cybersecurity Framework is well-documented and widely adopted on a voluntary basis, currently, there is no mandatory reporting, via the Code of Federal Regulations for the Department of Defense-Defense Industrial Base Cybersecurity Activities (32 CFR Part 236). In other words, there is no mandatory reporting of cyber incidents by space systems organizations, which are responsible for space systems that enable other strategic and/or critical infrastructures.

Section I provided an introduction to the paper. Section II presents the criticality of time synchronization for event correlation. Section III delineates the cyber risks and responsibilities within an exemplar satellite launch project. Section IV posits a robust decision engineering framework for addressing cyber in a defense-in-depth fashion. Section V summarizes the paper and alludes to future work.

II. The Criticality of Time Synchronization for Event Correlation

Among the various cyber-attack vectors, the criticality of Assured, Position, Navigation, and Timing is affirmed by the legislative direction of the National Defense Authorization Act for Fiscal Year 2019. In essence, it recognizes that "strategic high-end competitors possess the capability to disrupt systems that depend on [Global Positioning System] GPS which could pose an unacceptable level of risk … in GPS-denied environments." Accordingly, a paradigm of "cyber-robust[ness]" is being emphasized by the U.S. Army's Program Executive Office, Missiles and Space to "counter emerging threats."

At the core of the GPS issue is the fact that GPS-based clocks have become foundational to critical infrastructural systems (some are construed as mission-critical strategic infrastructural systems). Yet, despite this criticality, GPS-based clocks are susceptible to a variety of issues and represent a potential cyber "Achilles heel" for the modern-day mission-critical strategic infrastructural and critical infrastructural systems. Along this vein, the term of art "cyber," particularly within the context of the discussed case of the GPS-based clock, should be more clearly delineated. Among a variety of sources, the U.S. Army Cyber Warfare Field Manual (FM) 3-38 [4], "Cyber Electromagnetic Activities" (supplanted by FM 3-12 "Cyberspace and Electronic Warfare") contends that "Cyber Electromagnetic Activities" encompass not only conventional cyber activities (e.g. Distributed Denial-of-Service or DDoS attack, which is an attack by which multiple compromised computer systems attack a targeted resource, such as a GPS-based clock. The torrent of incoming messages, connection requests force the targeted resource to slow down or shut down, thereby denying service for legitimate use), but also activities involving electronic warfare (e.g., GPS jamming, GPS spoofing, etc.) and spectrum management operations. Professor Todd Humphreys at the University of Texas, Austin demonstrated in 2012 that a software-defined small-scale spoof attack might be quite inexpensive to build and execute [5], and the U.S. Maritime Administration noted in 2017 that a large-scale spoof attack occurred in the Black Sea (a body of water and marginal sea of the Atlantic Ocean between the Balkans, Eastern Europe, the Caucasus, and Western Asia) against 20 ships [6]. Spectrum management operations refers to the management of the spectrum. By way of example, the U.S. spectrum is managed by the Federal Communications Commission (FCC) for non-governmental applications as well as by the National Telecommunications and Information Administration (NTIA) for governmental applications. Spectrum management is a burgeoning problem due to the growing number of spectrums uses, such as over-the-air broadcasting, government and research uses (e.g. defense, public safety), commercial services to the public (e.g. wireless broadband), and industrial, scientific, as well as medical services. This is delineated in Figure 1 below.

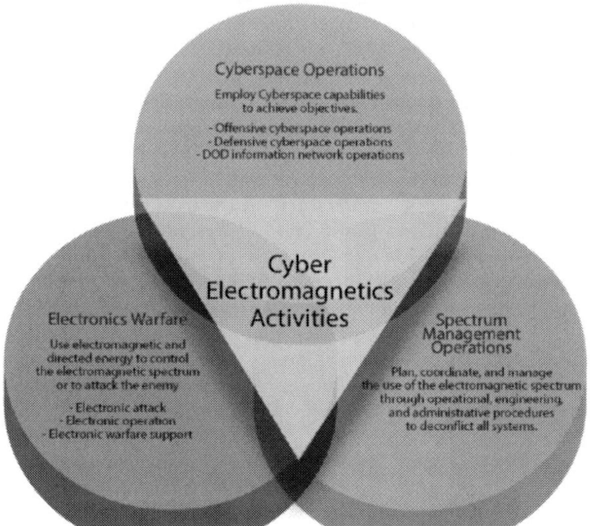

Source: FM 3-38, p 1-2.

Figure 1. Cyber Electromagnetic Vulnerabilities

As can be seen by way of various vulnerability databases (e.g. NVD), such as that produced by the National Cybersecurity and Communications Integration Center (NCCIC) Cyber Emergency Response Team (ICS-CERT), there exists several GPS clock vulnerabilities that can affect the accuracy of the clock. This is unacceptable as correct correlation of data (i.e. event correlation) [7] to time (i.e., accurate timestamping) [8] is needed to establish a meaningful baseline against which anomalies can be detected. To rearticulate this matter, by way of example, logs are predicated upon timestamps, as can be seen in Figure 2. If these timestamps are manipulated, then the sequencing of the log entries would be incorrect; any subsequent utilization of detection methodologies [9][10] for forensic investigation would be greatly inhibited.

Figure 2. Exemplar Log for Forensic Investigation

There have been a variety of attacks against space systems, and interestingly, the attackers' interest has not necessarily focused upon the space system itself, but rather upon the technology, which was enabled by the space system. For example, Kaspersky Labs discovered that Turla, a Russia-based cyber-espionage group, had compromised a satellite internet provider and obfuscated their ensuing cyber-espionage operations against countries ranging from the U.S. to various former Eastern Bloc countries [11]. By using a ground antenna, Turla could detect Internet Protocol (IP) addresses from satellite internet users and proceed to initiate a Transmission Control Protocol/Internet Protocol (TCP/IP) connection from the compromised IP address. This type of attack is not easily discernable, as it does not perceivably impact a satellite internet user's performance (which depends upon whether the attacker and legitimate satellite internet users are using the IP address concurrently), and it is unlikely to be flagged by conventional intrusion detection systems (IDS).

III. CYBER SECURITY RISKS AND RESPONSIBILITIES WITHIN AN EXEMPLAR SATELLITE PROJECT

Unfortunately, the expanding ecosystem of cyber electromagnetic spectrum cyber vulnerabilities presents a dilemma for those involved in satellite projects. Satellite projects were technologically challenging enough from just a capabilities perspective (e.g., Ka-band systems are susceptible to weather due to signal absorption by moisture in the air and by wetness on antenna surfaces [12], [13]), but the spectrum of cyber-attack pathways given the growing complexity of systems [14] and the vulnerability to cyber manipulation [15] greatly exacerbate the situation.

As an exemplar, the Iridium satellite constellation provides L-band voice and data coverage to integrated receivers, satellite phones, and pagers. Originally, the Iridium satellite owners had asserted that "the complexity of the Iridium air interface makes the challenge of developing an Iridium L-Band monitoring device very difficult and probably beyond the reach of all but the most determined adversaries." However, at the Chaos Communication Camp, held in Zehdenick, Germany during August 2015, the conference organizers distributed 4,500 software-defined rad1o badges (a.k.a. HackRF), which were sensitive enough to intercept satellite traffic from the Iridium communications network (Iridium pager traffic is, by default, sent in cleartext, and most pager traffic remains unencrypted). Other vulnerabilities, such as in the firmware (digital "backdoors" embedded within the computer code as well as "hardcoded credentials") have been cited in reports related to satellite communications (SATCOM) security.

However, similar to other industries (e.g. automotive industry, ICS industry), space technology designers, manufacturers, and industry providers have progressed slowly in their efforts toward enhancing cyber security. Perhaps, it is due to the distributed responsibility. By way of example, as is delineated in Figure 3 below, A may commission the development of a satellite with B, which then assumes the cybersecurity responsibility of the satellite. B then outsources the satellite development to (and/or sources components from) to C and D, who each maintain their own cybersecurity responsibility for their respective components. When B completes the development of the satellite and delivers it to A, E is contracted to manage the operations of the satellite; at this point, E assumes cybersecurity responsibility for the satellite. Then, E commissions F to launch the satellite into space; at this point, F assumes cybersecurity responsibility during the launch process. The liability for this cybersecurity responsibility is often displaced to G, an insurance underwriter. Once the satellite is in orbit and is operational, E resumes cybersecurity responsibility for the operations of the satellite. Oftentimes, A will want to maximize profitability and will proceed to lease bandwidth and/or the processing capability of the satellite to other companies, such as H and I. Depending upon the usage (e.g. ICS), H and I will now have cyber liability as well. Due to the complex ecosystem of owner, developer, operator, and user cybersecurity responsibilities, there are a myriad of attack vectors along the cyber-physical supply chain.

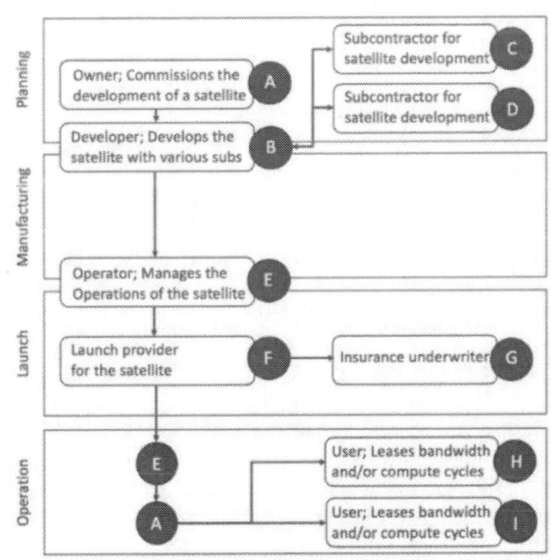

Figure 3. Cybersecurity Responsibilities for an Exemplar Satellite Project [16]

From a certain vantage point, the cyber rationale might seem quite robust given the seemingly "logical" delineation of responsibilities, but given the lesson learned from the NASA Space Shuttle Challenger (Orbiter Vehicle or OV-99) explosion in 1986, metaphorically, all it takes is one "O-Ring" (the primary and secondary O-rings, which were designed to prevent a leakage of hot gases were incapable of properly sealing the gaps between the Solid Rocket Booster (SRB) joints in extremely cold weather) for catastrophic (in this case, cyber) failure of the system as a whole.

A. Cyber-Physical Supply Chain Issues at Boeing and Elsewhere

As demonstrated by the July 2007 unveiling of Boeing's Dreamliner or Boeing 787 (a.k.a. "B787"), supply chain structures are becoming increasingly multi-layered and complex. Along this vein, for the first time in its history, Boeing (the world's largest aerospace company) outsourced its engineering of — and integration for — its aircraft parts. In it of itself, this particular fact may not raise any eyebrows until it is realized that more than 90% of the Dreamliner program was outsourced to a variety of supply chain partners across the globe [17]. Interestingly, for these partners to participate in the Dreamliner program, they were obligated to finance and oversee the development of — and assimilation for — the assigned outsourced specific part based upon very granular technical specifications provided by Boeing.

While Boeing did indeed reduce its own upfront developmental costs, and its Vice President for Global Supply Partners, Steven Schaffer, was feted as the "Supply Chain Manager of the Year" in 2007 by *Purchasing Magazine*, the back-story, according to Stan Sorscher, Legislative Director at the Society for Professional Engineering Employees in Aerospace (SPEEA) (a union representing over 20,000 scientists, engineers, technical and professional employees within the aerospace industry), was that Boeing was shocked when it was confronted by a rather opaque supply chain and realized that it no longer had a crystal-clear vantage point as to what went into the detailed designs of its own aircraft sections. After all, since the suppliers spent their own funds to design and develop the various assigned parts, they also, naturally, retained these precious designs as intellectual property. Also, because Boeing had selected, principally, those suppliers, who had the financial wherewithal to both proffer the initial capital expenditure (for the specialized research and development of the specific part), as well as instantiate the cash flow necessary to accommodate the need for Boeing to sell an aircraft before the supplier received any payment, it turned out that the performance metric of technical capability of the supplier came, for the most part, second to the performance metric of financial capacity. Therefore, from a product development vantage point, numerous Boeing suppliers may have been sub-optimally selected, and in turn, these financially minded subcontractors outsourced a myriad of tasks to a further network of, potentially, lowest bid sub-suppliers. Suffice it to say, not all the actors within this intricate sub-supplier fabric were commensurate with Boeing's high standards for excellence, and an exemplar of a quality assurance/quality control (QA/QC) issue includes the Federal Aviation Administration (FAA) asserting, in January 2011, that the code written by an Indian software company, HCL Technologies, for the Dreamliner's electrical systems, was so low in quality that it had to be redone [18]. Other commensurate situations include aircraft parts — being delivered to Boeing — that were simply unfinished. These shocking citations merely depict the proverbial tip of the iceberg as to what can go awry when transparency in the cyber-physical supply chain does not run deep; this further begets the question of how the cybersecurity protocols fared, if even the contracted core competencies were in disarray.

In a similar fashion, the re-use, modification of open-source software (OSS) code published by the National Aeronautics and Space Administration (NASA) and other space agencies have, over time, segued to "commercial offerings," via wrappers around the OSS; this has muddied the waters of the cyber-physical supply chain with regards to its provenance and overall transparency. By way of example, sometimes, commercial solutions may quickly advance to the forefront, but in some cases, many are overtaken by various OSS projects. Among various reasons, innovation, particularly as pertains to the commercial offerings, may decrease after the product reaches a certain level of maturity. In several other cases, the more successful commercial solutions are comprised of either the original or variants of OSS projects. Accordingly, it is becoming increasingly complex to distinguish what was originally "proprietary" and what is a derivative work product. In either case, cybersecurity vulnerabilities abound and need to be addressed.

B. Cyber Issues at NASA and Elsewhere

In Fiscal Year (FY) 2015, an audit at NASA revealed the need for a revamping of cybersecurity standards and protocols. The audit cited several attacks on NASA space assets, which were not publicly disclosed [19]. Previously, the Office of the Chief Information Officer (OCIO) was responsible for cybersecurity across all of NASA. However, OCIO teams could not fully contend with both the infrastructural security of NASA's various laboratories as well as the various attack vectors of its complex mission systems (let alone the emergent threats of the cyber electromagnetic spectrum). To contend with these issues, NASA's Jet Propulsion Laboratory (JPL) instantiated the Cyber Defense Engineering and Research Group (CDER), whose goal is to specifically to address mission systems, which may have unique cybersecurity requirements; in June 2019, a report published by the NASA Office of the Inspector General (OIG) revealed that in April 2018, attackers had breached NASA's network and exfiltrated approximately 500MB of data related to its Mars missions [20].

IV. Robust Decision Engineering Framework for Cyber Security

One mitigating cyber framework centers upon a [Big Compute] approach, as it is a blend of complexity science, cyber-physical supply chain science, network science, and decision engineering — "Cyber Discernment." Cyber Discernment shows promise, as it works for a fairly straightforward reason: it embodies the characteristics of how the world actually works. To analyze complex real-world relationships, the utilized methodological framework — "karassian netchain analysis" (KNA) — is utilized [21]. This framework differs from traditional netchain analysis (network and supply chain analysis) in three critical ways: (1) it adequately considers the network of dotted-line relationships that are not codified elsewhere; (2) it expands the observational space to include the interactions among heterogeneous actors within a given "horizontal" layer of a supply chain; and (3) it captures the latent potential for actors within the horizontal and/or vertical layers to deviate significantly from the average behavior, which may have ensuing dramatic effects. Furthermore, through KNA, it is possible to identify specific local community structures within the cyber-physical supply chain, via discernible "shapes" (i.e. morphology) that correspond to specific conditions and/or adaptations amidst various pressure sensitivities. The identification of these morphological motifs are crucial for mitigating against exfiltration, such as of the Mars mission data previously delineated.

While the social and physical sciences have traditionally tackled problems by breaking them into constituent parts and simplifying interactions between them, it is now clear within the context of the Challenger explosion that for the arena of space systems, the emergent patterns that beget predictions will appear only when problems are considered in their full complexity and local context. This approach vector will better illuminate cyber-physical supply chains and pertinent local community structures that must be: (1) orchestrated to achieve *annealed cyber resiliency*, (2) leveraged to secure pathways for *enhanced cyber security*, and (3) amalgamated to serve as the backbone of *latent cyber stability*.

The concept of "islands of stability," such as for KNA, is exemplified by the "sandpile effect" (more formally, the Bak-Tang-Wiesenfield sandpile model of non-equilibrium systems [22]) in which sand is dropped, one grain at a time, onto the same spot on a flat surface, until the addition of one more grain of sand causes an avalanche to slide down the slopes of the growing sandpile. In 1987, physicists Per Bak, Chao Tang, and Kurt Wiesenfield investigated the "sandpile effect" by using a computer to color the sandpile according to steepness—the steepest regions of the pile were colored in red, and the flattest, green; they discovered that a single grain of sand falling onto a red region would instigate an avalanche, which not only caused certain green regions to become red, but also compounded into a cascading series of avalanches that grew in size and intensity as it disturbed other red regions (i.e. cascading failure). Restated in terms of KNA, instability (e.g. a compromised component, such as an "O-ring") can spread throughout the entire network, via islands of potentially unstable nodes; these small sets of nodes with the power to influence the entire network are known as *Influence Dominating Sets (IDS)*. Just as a sandpile avalanche can create instability in previously stable areas, real-world phenomena (e.g. a compromised sub-system) can originate at just a few nodes (an occurrence of IDS) and eventually permeate an entire large-scale system. Identifying Negative Influence Dominating Sets (NIDS) in a given network requires a detailed knowledge and sophisticated analysis of the involved network so as to uncover the harbingers of instability and "perfect storm" crises lurking within a network, and, on the positive side, to identify opportunities to infuse *latent cyber stability, enhanced cyber security,* and *cyber resiliency* throughout the network by cultivating and/or influencing PIDS. One goal is to understand fundamental patterns and constraints that arise from those interactions, based upon the preliminary hypothesis that successful, sustainable coordination arises most readily out of PIDS, which can anneal a system and reduce brittleness.

A. Utilization of Artificial Intelligence for Cyber Diagnosis within a System

Without having conducted an interview or on-site investigation, it is difficult to assert what cyber paradigm should be implemented. However, the utilization of an apropos Artificial Intelligence (AI) paradigm, such as via a Convolutional Neural Network (CANN), for a preliminary diagnosis within a system has been successfully utilized, within a cyber context, to provide certain insights (particularly those at machine speed). An exemplar CANN is shown in Figure 4 below.

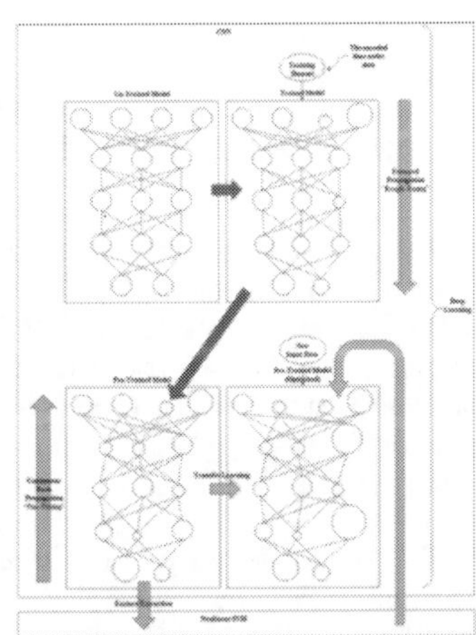

Figure 4. Hybrid Model involving various CNNs and a Nonlinear SVM, which segue to a [Deep Learning] Convolutional [Generative] Adversarial Neural Network (CANN) Paradigm to provide certain cyber insights (particularly those at machine speed) [23].

B. Exemplar Posited Hybridized Solution Stack for Cyber

Generally speaking, variants of an apropos AI CANN operating atop a hybridized solution stack to address cyber in a defense-in-depth fashion have successfully provided certain insights into the degree of cyber uncertainty and/or ambiguity in the system. An exemplar hybridized solution stack in shown in Figure 5 below.

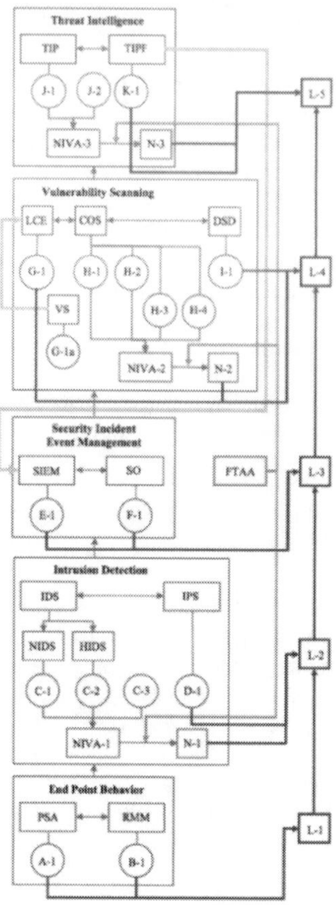

Figure 5. Hybridized Cyber Stability/Security/Resiliency Solution Stack to provide certain insights into the degree of cyber uncertainty and/or ambiguity in the ecosystem [24].

As can be seen in Fig. 5, there are groupings at different levels: (1) End Point Behavior Monitoring (EPBM) (comprised of Professional Services Automation [PSA] and Remote Monitoring and Management [RMM] tools); (2) Intrusion Detection Systems (IDS) (comprised of Network Intrusion Detection Systems [NIDS] and Host Intrusion Detection Systems [HIDs]), as well as Intrusion Prevention Systems (IPSs); (3) Security Information and Event Management (SIEM) and Security Orchestration (SO); (4) Vulnerability Scanning (VS) (comprised of a Log [Analysis] and Correlation Engine [LCE] as a Monitoring Strategy, Container-Orchestration System [COS], and Dynamic Service Discovery [DSD]); and (5) Threat Intelligence (TI) (comprised of Threat Intelligence Platforms [TIPs] and a Threat Intelligence Processing Framework [TIPF]). Each set of groupings pass their outputs to a N-Input Voting Algorithm (NIVA), which acts in concert with a Fault Tolerant Averaging Algorithm (FTAA), via ensemble method Machine Learning (ML). For Intrusion Detection, C-1, C-2, and C-3 passed their outputs to NIVA-1, whose output was refined by FTAA and the resultant was N-1 (red pathway). For VS, H-1, H-2, H-3, and H-4 passed their outputs to NIVA-2, whose output was refined by FTAA and the resultant was N-2 (red pathway). For TI, J-1 and J-2 passed their outputs to NIVA-3, whose output was refined by FTAA and the resultant was N-3 (red pathway). The FTAA refinement pathways are illuminated (green pathway). The various interim steps were as follows: (A-1)&(B-1)->(L-1), (N-1)&(D-1)->(L-2), (E-1)&(F-1)->(L-3), (G-1)&(N-2)&(I-1)->(L-4), and (K-1)&(N-3)->(L-5). Each layer of the solution stack passed its output to the layer above; hence, EPBM (L-1) -> IDS (L-2) -> SIEM (L-3) -> VS (L-4) -> TI (L-5) (purple pathway). Of course, the TIPF fed its output back to the SIEM, and the VS repertoire fed its output to the LCE (orange pathway).

C. *Assessment Methodology*

The learnings behind Figure 4 were that certain cyber insights (particularly those at machine speed) are necessary to understand the IDS described for KNA. The learnings behind Figure 5 were that certain cyber insights (particularly to identify the degree of uncertainty and/or ambiguity at each level in the ecosystem) are also necessary to contextualize the PIDS and NIDS as part of KNA.

The various tools and techniques are somewhat important within the ecosystem, but an assessment methodology that embodies diligence, persistence, and learning over time can be even more vital than the various tools and techniques. Figure 6 shows a common motif to intentional skewing of timestamping so as to adversely impact the timestamping (in this case, GPS-based timestamping paradigm for the Phasor Measurement Units [PMUs] of an ICS ecosystem was affected) paradigm for pertinent logs. It is emblematic of the outside-the-wire and out-of-the-box thinking required to identify sophisticated synthetic aberrations, which would bypass prototypical cyber defense systems.

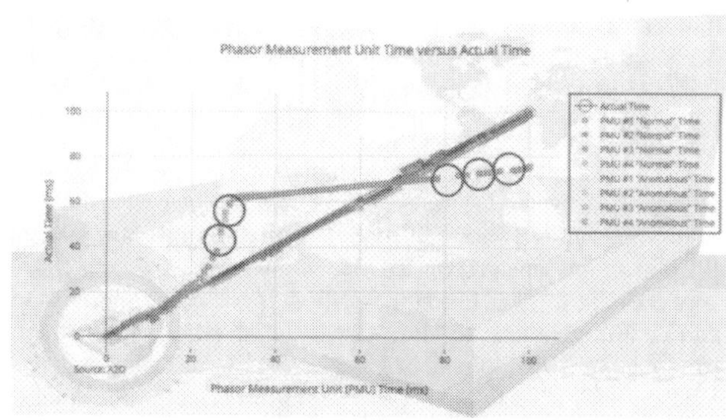

Figure 6. The Diligence and Persistence of Baselining Data over Time so as to identify Aberrations within the Timestamping Paradigm.

V. Conclusion

The public has already raised the specter of cybersecurity to space technology designers, manufacturers, and providers, such as SpaceX [25]. The dialectic is growing with intensity. As can be gleaned from the Boeing case study, there is a dilemma with regards to driving down production costs amidst the ever-increasing complexity of the cyber-physical supply chain; global supply chains exacerbate this dilemma. From our longitudinal research within this arena, we posit that the depth and breadth of any cyber investigation foray can well be achieved by employing an approach that we term Cyber Discernment. In Cyber Discernment, a methodological robust decision engineering framework, karassian netchain analysis (KNA), among others, is utilized to understand Negative Influence Dominating Sets (NIDS) or areas of instability and Positive Influence Dominating Sets (PIDS) or islands of stability. By understanding both heuristics and algorithmics for cyber at machine speed and ascertaining PIDS as well as understanding how best to mitigate NIDS, a form of *annealed cyber resiliency, enhanced cyber security,* and *latent cyber stability* can be achieved, thereby mitigating against unintended consequences, undesired elements of instability, and "perfect storm" crises lurking within the system. Future work will provide further anonymized case studies beyond those presented thus far.

ACKNOWLEDGMENT

The authors would like to thank I. Oktavianti and O. Prafito for their invaluable assistance with completing this paper. Without their ongoing assistance, the production of this paper would have been delayed. The authors would also like to thank the Decision Engineering Analysis Laboratory for the support in completing the requirements for this paper.

REFERENCES

[1] S. Chan, Chapter 5, "Measuring the Information Society, 150th Anniversary Edition" United Nations International Telecommunication Union (ITU), pp. 147-185, 2015.

[2] R. Spousta and S. Chan "Milk or Wine: Are Critical Infrastructure Protection Architectures Improving with Age?" Journal of Challenges, vol. 2, no. 1, pp. 1-13, 2015.

[3] S. Chan, "Prototype Orchestration Framework as a High Exposure Dimension Cyber Defense Accelerant Amidst Ever-Increasing Cycles of Adaptation by Attackers: A Modified Deep Belief Network Accelerated by a Stacked Generative Adversarial Network for Enhanced Event Correlation," The Third International Conference on Cyber-Technologies and Cyber-Systems, pp. 28-38, 2018.

[4] "U.S. Army Cyber Warfare Field Manual (FM) 3-38," *Department of the Army*, February 2014.

[5] "UT Austin Researchers Successfully Spoof an $80 million Yacht at Sea," UT News, The University of Texas at Austin, July 2013.

[6] Maritime Administration (MARAD), "2017-005A-GPS Interference-Black Sea," U.S. Department of Transportation. 2017.

[7] S. Chan, "Quality Assurance/Quality Control Engine for Power Outage Mitigation: The Challenge of Event Correlation for a Smart Grid Architecture Amidst Data Quality Issues," Advances in Intelligent Systems and Computing.

[8] S. Chan, "A Potential Cascading Succession of Cyber Electromagnetic Achilles' Heels in the Power Grid: The Challenge of Time Synchronization for Power System Disturbance Monitoring Equipment in a Smart Grid Amidst Cyber Electromagnetic Vulnerabilities," Advances in Information and Communication: Proceedings of the 2019 Future of Information and Communication Conference (FICC), vol. 2, pp. 912-935, 2019.

[9] R. Spousta and S. Chan, "Electrical Islanding Detection based on the Integration of Synchronized Phasor Measurements," IEEE Future Technologies Conference (FTC) 2016, pp. 68–73, December 2016.

[10] S. Chan, "Methods and Apparatus for Detecting and Correcting Instabilities within a Power Distribution System," U.S. Patent Trademark Office (PTO), August 2016.

[11] Kaspersky's Global Research and Analysis Team (GReAT), "The Epic Turla Operation," SecureList, August 2014.

[12] S. Sala, et al., "Mitigation of Rain-Induced Ka-Band Attenuation and Enhancement of Communications Resiliency in Sub-Saharan Africa," Proceedings Annual Workshop of the AIS Special Interest Group for ICT in Global Development, December 2013.

[13] R. Spousta, S. Chan, and B. Griffin, "Space 2.0: Expanding Global Internet Accessibility," The Fourth International Conference on Data Analytics, pp. 17-24, 2015.

[14] S. Chan and S. Sala, "Sensemaking and Robust Decision Engineering: Synchrophasors and their Application for a Secure Smart Grid," 7th IEEE International Conference on Digital Ecosystems and Technologies (DEST), pp. 102-107, July 2013.

[15] R. Spousta and S. Chan, "Ocean Data Vulnerability to Cyber Manipulation and Consequences for Infrastructural Resilience," IEEE Future Technologies Conference (FTC), pp. 672-680, December 2016.

[16] "Insuring Space Activities," Aon Risk Solutions, October 16.

[17] R. Preston, "Sorry, But Outsourcing Isn't Evil," InformationWeek, 3 August 2012.

[18] P. Cohan, "Is the Boeing 787's electrical system working?" Daily Finance, 20 August 2009.

[19] P. Martin, "NASA's Management of the Deep Space Network," NASA Office of Audits, pp. 1-42, March 2015.

[20] P. Martin, "NASA Cybersecurity: An Examination of the Agency's Information Security," Testimony before the Subcommittee on Investigations and Oversight, House Committee on Science, Space, and Technology, pp. 1-9, February 2012.

[21] S. Chan, "Robust Decision Engineering: Collaborative Big Data and its Application to International Development/Aid," 8th International Conference on Collaborative Computing: Networking, Applications and Worksharing (CollaborateCom), pp. 597-604, December 2011.

[22] P. Bak, C. Tang, and K. Wiesenfeld, "Self-Organized Criticality," Physical Review, vol. 38, no. 1, pp. 364-375, July 1988.

[23] S. Chan, I. Oktavianti,1 V. Puspita, and P. Nopphawan, "Convolutional Adversarial Neural Network (CANN) for Fault Diagnosis within a Power System: Addressing the Challenge of Event Correlation for Diagnosis by Power Disturbance Monitoring Equipment in a Smart Grid," The 2nd IEEE International Conference on Information and Communications Technology (2nd ICOIACT 2019), July 2019.

[24] S. Chan, "Prototype Open-Source Software Stack for the Reduction of False Positives and Negatives in the Detection of Cyber Indicators of Compromise and Attack: Hybridized Log Analysis Correlation Engine and Container-Orchestration System Supplemented by Ensemble Method Voting Algorithms for Enhanced Event Correlation," The Third International Conference on Cyber-Technologies and Cyber-Systems, pp. 39-48, 2018.

[25] Z. Abbany, "SpaceX's Starlink satellite internet: It's time for tough talk on cyber security in space," Deutsche Welle, 2018, [Online]. Available from: https://www.dw.com/en/spacexs-starlink-satellite-internet-its-time-for-tough-talk-on-cyber-security-in-space/a-42678704/ 2019.05.27

Surveying and Enhancing Grid Resilience Sensor Communications:
An Amalgam of Narrowband, Broadband, and Hybridizing Spread Spectrum

Steve Chan, Ika Oktavianti Najib*, Verlly Puspita
Center for Research on IOT, Data Science, and Resiliency (CRIDR)
San Diego, CA 92192, USA
*Email: inajib@cridr.org

Abstract—**Distribution utilities engaged in the operationalization of more "resilient, adaptable architectures" have begun to instantiate amalgams of broadband, narrowband, and hybridizing techniques (e.g., spread spectrum, among others) to bridge the gap between broadband and narrowband (e.g., by enhancing the resiliency of narrowband signals) by lowering power requirements while extending coverage so as to develop a more robust communication network; this more resilient communications paradigm better facilitates "expeditious outage response capabilities." This paper presents such an architectural instantiation.**

Keywords—Grid resilience; broadband; narrowband; hybridizing techniques; spread spectrum; communication network; expeditious outage response capabilities.

I. Introduction

Various splinter lines of efforts (e.g., weather sensors) related to the grid resiliency efforts in the Indo-Asia-Pacific have led to successful instantiations of amalgams of broadband, narrowband, and hybridizing techniques (e.g., spread spectrum, among others) to bridge the gap between broadband and narrowband (e.g., by enhancing the resiliency of narrowband signals) by lowering power requirements while extending coverage. Hyper-locale weather sensors have served as a common thematic for Oceania and Southeast Asia and associated working sessions have increased in cadence. These hyper-locale weather sensors, as just one exemplar, are emblematic of the need for honed communications techniques, so as to fully enable the reliability and economic potential, for ecozones (e.g., Oceania, [Brunei [Darussalam]-Indonesia-Malaysia-Philippines East [Association of Southeast Asian Nations] ASEAN Growth Area] BIMP-EAGA, etc.) that are comprised of geographically disparate and varied characteristics.

Hyper-locale weather information (without resorting to the need for reach-back processing) has served as a fundamental requirement for local fisherman and remote businessmen, alike; accordingly, hyper-locale weather sensors (which only the locals would have) provide incredible insight into the pattern of life for upcoming days and weeks (e.g., it is a good day for fisherman to put out to see, it is a good day for businessfolk to trade/travel, etc.). Contextual awareness is a common thematic (in terms of need) for Oceania and Southeast Asia. As regional cohesion between Oceania and Southeast Asia Increases (e.g., 2022 Asian Games to includes athletes from Oceania), the investment potential in Oceania is at an inflection point; the correct amalgam of Broadband, Narrowband, and Hybridizing Techniques (a.k.a. BNHT) can help facilitate this potential. The purpose of this paper is not to choose singularly among the various IoT devices, but to utilize an appropriate amalgam of existing IoT devices according to the situation and conditions, so that the stability and quality of the involved communications network closely approximates what is desired.

Section I provided an introduction. The remainder of this paper is organized as follows. Section II describes related works regarding narrowband, broadband, and spread spectrum. Section III provides details regarding the Internet of Things (IoT) and non-IoT, and Section IV discusses the Long Power Wide Area (LPWA) technologies such as Narrowband-IoT (NB-IoT), Long Range Wide Area Network (LoRaWAN), LoRaWAN Extended, and SigFox. Section V is explained about smart switch and finally, interim conclusions are summarized in Section VI.

II. Narrowband, Broadband, and Spread Spectrum

Communication sensors that are built according to the theme in this study consist of 3 types, namely narrowband, broadband, and hybridizing techniques (e.g., spread spectrum).

A. Narrowband

Transmission technologies differ according to how much of the wireless spectrum the associated signal utilizes (e.g., whether a wireless service uses narrowband or broadband signalling). For narrowband, a transmitter concentrates the signal energy at a single frequency or in a very small range of frequencies [1]. For a communication system utilizing narrowband transmission technology, the system will keep the bandwidth as narrow as possible to transmit the signal. The disadvantages of narrowband transmission are that it is highly susceptible to jamming and interference. This is due to the limited bandwidth utilized. Jamming relates to network interference caused by a very large power that transports signals that are not needed through the same bandwidth as the signal needed. Consequently, a signal with lower power will be marginalized/blocked. Examples of narrowband technology are the IEEE-802.15.4g standard utilizing a 12.5 kHz, T-1 at 1.54 Mbps via fibre optic, infrared, microwave, or two pairs of cables.

B. Broadband

Broadband has been central community networks around the world for over a decade and can be regarded as one of the mainstay technologies amidst the evolution of the internet network. Both the technologies and products of broadband internet networks are developed by Internet Service Providers (ISP). The trending of broadband makes internet access relatively inexpensive and easy (but quality is another issue). Historically, broadband technology has influenced the widespread use of the Internet [2]. There are two kind of broadband technologies: fixed broadband technology and mobile broadband technology. Fixed broadband is a technology wherein the end user must be at the same location to utilize the broadband service, while the mobile broadband technology (e.g., third generation or 3G, fourth generation or 4G, and fifth generation or 5G) can utilize the broadband service from any physical location.

Fixed broadband technology has several ways, namely Digital Subscriber Line (DSL) Fixed Wireline Broadband, Cable Fixed Wireline Broadband, and Fiber Fixed Wireline Broadband. Figure 1 describes the traditional DSL services (e.g., Asymmetric Digital Subscriber Line (ADSL), Very High Bit Rate Digital Subscriber Line (VDSL), etc.) is one way to have fixed wireline broadband services [1]. In DSL access, the traditional copper lines of the telephone network are equipped with digital subscriber line technology. Currently, in many countries in the world, DSL is the most common access network technology and is most commonly used by the public.

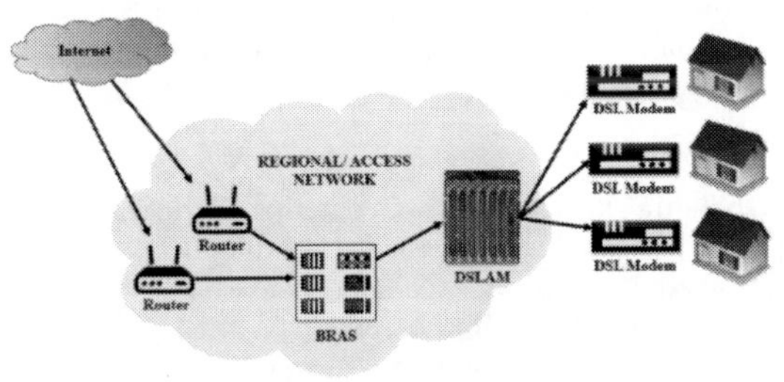

Figure 1. DSL Deployment and the Component [3]

Broadband utilizes wider frequency bands of the wireless spectrum and offers higher throughputs compared to narrowband technologies. A narrowband frequency is 3-500 kHz and a broadband frequency is 1.8-86 MHz.

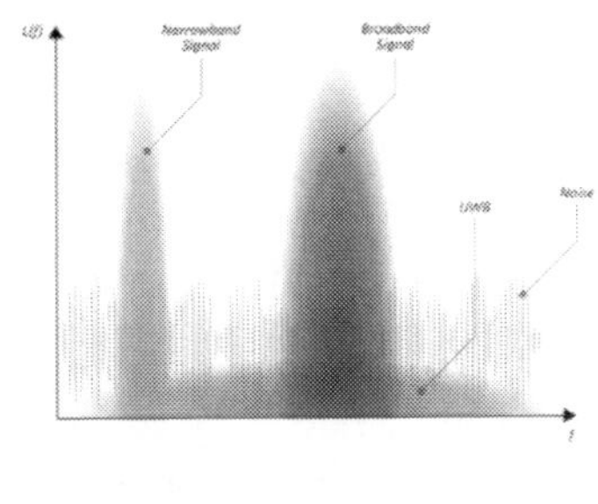

Figure 2. Narrowband and Broadband Signal [4]

Narrowband communication channels have long been used in many applications that depend on achieving reliable links in different operating environments, such as military tactical radios and industrial monitoring requirements. But because more information has to be conveyed between the two points by wireless means, such as for video streaming and sophisticated surveillance systems, broadband communication channels with greater data capacity are becoming more attractive.

Figure 2 explains that narrow band signals occupy much less frequency spectrum and require less transmit power for a given application than wide band signals, while Ultra-Wideband (UWB) signals are short pulses that send information while briefly occupying a large part of the traditional communication frequency spectrum. This is done to send and receive more voice, video, and data over a wider bandwidth frequency channel, which means it costs money, because a wider part of the frequency spectrum also contains more noise sources and higher noise levels [4].

C. Spread Spectrum

Spread spectrum is a form of wireless communication that utilizes multiple frequencies to transmit a signal. Spread spectrum technologies provide robustness to a variety of unintentional forms of interference that are found to impact a communications system, such as interception of signals, jamming, and multipath. One of the advantages of spreading a signal over a wide frequency band is that is requires less power per frequency than narrowband signalling [5].

Spread spectrum techniques were originally utilized by military communications system during World War II. Spread spectrum is more secure than narrowband and broadband signalling because, by way of example, the frequency hopping channel numbers are only known to the authorized receiver and transmitter of the information. The receiver must utilize the exact same hopping sequence to receive information from the transmitter. Consequently, it is extremely difficult for unauthorized receivers to decode and access the information. The two most common forms of spread spectrum are Frequency Hopping Spread Spectrum (FHSS) and Direct Sequence Spread Spectrum (DSSS).

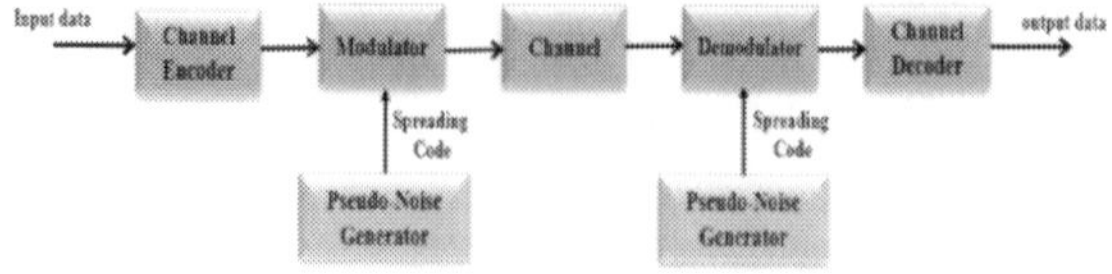

Figure 3. Model of Spread Spectrum Digital Communication System [6]

In FHSS transmission, the existing frequency is divided into multiple parts and then sent across the air in a random pattern of radio frequencies, hopping from frequencies to frequencies at fixed intervals. During that interval, some number of bits is transmitted utilizing some encoding scheme. Both transmitter and receiver channel utilize the same code to tune into a sequence of channels in synchronization.

In DSSS, the original data signal is multiplied with a pseudo random noise spreading code. The spreading code spreads the signal across a wider frequency band in direct proportion to the number of bits used. This spreading code has a higher chip rate, which results in a wideband time continuous scrambled signal. Different variants of spread spectrum techniques are used. Long Rang (LoRa) utilizes Chirp Spread Spectrum (CSS) while IEEE-802.15.4g (a standard for Smart Utility Network or SUN communications, which are an essential part of the smart grid), Ingenu (Low Power Wide Area network or LPWAN implementation), and Weightless-P (ultra-high performance LPWAN) utilize Direct Sequence Spread Spectrum (DSSS).

Figure 3 explains the general model of spread spectrum digital communication system. First, Spread Spectrum input the data into a channel encoder. Then, the data produces analog signal with Narrow Band width. Signal is further modulated using sequence of digits, spreading code, and spreading sequence. Spreading code generated by pseudo-noise or pseudorandom number generator. The effect of this process is demodulation which is used to increase the bandwidth of the signal to be sent and recovered data [6].

III. IoT AND NON-IoT

An Internet of Things (IoT) platform is a set of technology-enabled entities including physical smart objects, as well as systems and software services that are connected together [7]. There are four main components of an IoT system, namely the "thing" or object (e.g., sensors, actuators, etc.), the local network (e.g., gateway), the Internet, and back-end services (e.g., personal computer [PC] or mobile devices). The communication network for IoT can be construed in two parts: cellular and non-cellular. Cellular IoT hardware is typically equipped with Subscriber Identity Module (SIM) cards and connected to networks via 2G, 3G, and 4G, while non-cellular IoT are connected via wireless network.

The "things" in IoT need Internet Protocol (IP) address, as the "things" are mostly servers, switches, firewalls and routers, laptops, phones, and tablets with IP to IP connectivity. An IP address is an address or numeric identity that is given to a device so that the device is identified and can communicate with other devices. IP addresses can be further sub-divided in two, namely IP static and IP dynamic. IP Static is an IP address that is set or manually set by a network admin so that this IP address will not change automatically, unless it is manually changed by the network admin. The advantages of utilizing IP Static on communication network are that it is easy to remember a host, it is suitable for small-scale networks, and the router is set up with a static IP as well. IP Dynamic is an IP address that is set or set through a router that has been set up as a Dynamic Host Configuration Protocol (DHCP) Server, where the DHCP Server functions to provide an IP address automatically to each host connected to the network so that a computer connected to the network does not need to set the IP address again because it has been given one by the router. The advantages of utilizing IP Dynamic on communication networks are that it is suitable for large-scale networks, it facilitates the networks admin setting IP addresses, and no IP address collision will likely occur.

IV. LOW POWER WIDE AREA (LPWA) TECHNOLOGIES

LPWA technologies are a generic term for a group of technologies, which enable wide area communications at lower cost point and improved power consumption. LPWA has become one of the fastest growing area within IoT. Many LPWA technologies have developed in both the licensed and unlicensed bands, such as Narrow Band (NB-IoT), Long Range (LoRa), SigFox, etc. Solutions based upon the LP-WAN paradigm have a long coverage range of about 10 km and high-power efficiency that facilitates lifetimes for end-devices to about 10 years [8].These achievements are attained by making use of the following strategies: transmitting data at very low bitrates, making use of low frequency bands (sub-GHz bands), and limiting the communication capabilities of the end-devices (number of messages per day) [9].

A. *Narrowband Internet of Things (NB-IoT)*

NB-IoT is a new 3rd Generation Partnership Project (3GPP) technology released in June 2016. NB-IoT is designed to achieve excellent co-existence performance with General Packet Radio Service (GPRS), Global System for Mobile (GSM), and Long-Term Evaluation (LTE). NB-IoT can provide 50-100 times access to the existing wireless technology. NB-IoT has a 200 kHz wide carrier, which contains 12 Orthogonal Frequency-Division Multiplexing (OFDM) (a method of digital signal modulation in which a single data stream is split across several separate narrowband channels at different frequencies to reduce interference and crosstalk) subcarriers and unlicensed frequencies in the 700, 800, or 900 Mhz bands to assist with signal penetration in-building. NB-IoT increases the gain of 20dB and expects to cover the inaccessible places, such as underground pipelines, basements, etc [10]. NB-IoT supports three different operational modes: stand-alone operation, guard-band operation, and in-band operation.

The NB-IoT communication protocol is considered to be a new air interface for LTE. NB-IoT reduces LTE protocol functionalities to the minimum and enhances them as required for IoT applications [11]. For example, the LTE backend system is used to broadcast information that is valid for all end devices within a cell. As the broadcasting back-end system obtains resources and consumes battery power from each end device, it is kept to a minimum in size, as well as in its occurrence. It was optimized to small and infrequent data messages and avoids the features not required for IoT purposes, e.g., measurements to monitor the channel quality, carrier aggregation, and dual connectivity. Therefore, the end devices require only a small amount of battery, thus making it cost-efficient [11].

B. LoRaWAN

LoRa is a network technology solution for wireless battery-operated devices. LoRa uses unlicensed Industrial, Scientific, and Medical (ISM) bands, i.e., 868 MHz in Europe, 915 MHz in North America, and 433 MHz in Asia. LoRa allows long range communication (between 2-8 km in urban areas and 15-20 km in rural areas) with low power consumption. LoRa has the goal of providing secure bidirectional communication [12]. LoRa utilizes a chirp spread spectrum spreading modulation technology (can use one or more channels), which enables low energy consumption, end-to-end secure communication with low data rates [13]. The spread spectrum provides orthogonal separation between signals by using unique spreading factor individual signal. This method provided an advantage in managing data rate [14]. The resulting signal has low noise levels, enabling high interference resilience, and is difficult to detect or jam [15]. LoRa does not deploy a LBT (Listen-Before-Talk) feature; instead, it utilizes the duty cycle restrictions required by regulation and the maximum dwell time [16].

The technology is presented in two parts: Lora (the physical layer) and LoRaWAN (the communication layer), which an open source communication protocol defined by the LoRa Alliance. One of the most interesting features of LoRaWAN is the possibility of configuring certain transmission configuration parameters, enabling longer coverage ranges, greater transmission bit rates, and enhanced communication robustness [17]. LoRaWAN defines three classes for end point devices to address the different needs reflected in the wide range of possible application: Bi-directional end devices (Class A), Bi-directional end devices with scheduled receive slots (Class B), and Bi-directional end devices with maximal receive slots (Class C). LoRa and LoRaWAN layers can be seen in Figure 4 below.

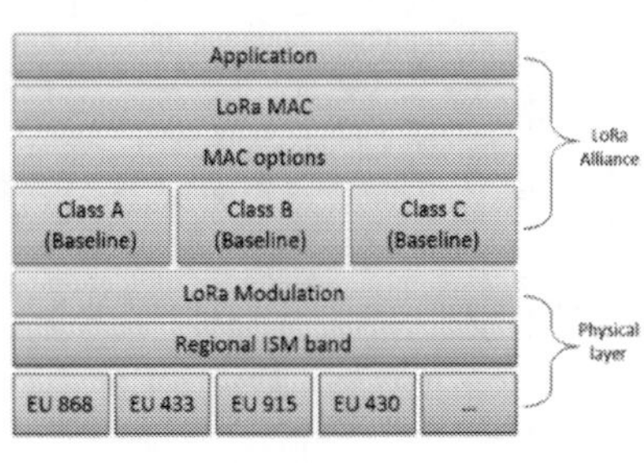

Figure 4. LoRa and LoRaWAN layer [18]

The system architecture comprises end devices, gateways, and a network server. End devices transmit directly to all the gateways within range utilizing LoRaWAN. LoRaWAN gateways correspond to base station in a cellular network, as well as communications between the end devices and the network server based upon Internet Protocol (IP). The end devices typically have sensors, LoRa transponders to transmit signal, and a micro-controller. Figure 5 presents the LoRaWAN architecture.

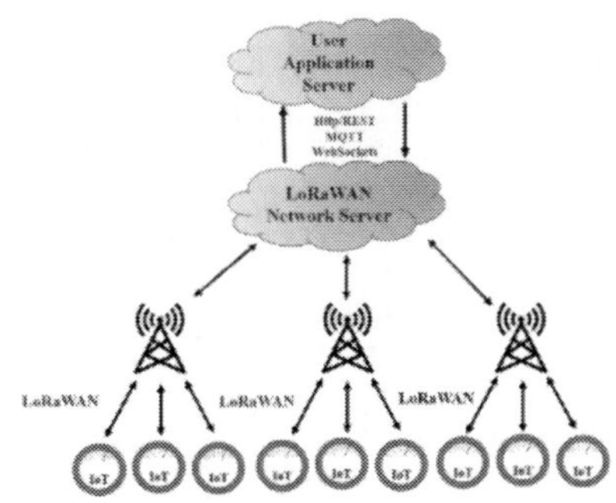

Figure 5. LoRaWAN Architecture [19]

C. LoRaWAN Extended

Low-power wireless networks are a key enabler for the Internet of things (IoT), but familiar options such as Bluetooth, Zigbee, Wireless Fidelity (WiFi), or cellular, lack an acceptable combination of extended range and battery life. To address this, new sub-GHz specifications are being offered, one of which is LoRaWAN.

LoRaWAN can achieve a 15 km range at power consumption levels low enough to enable 10-year battery life. Further, the availability of an off-the-shelf development kit lets designers quickly bring up the complete LoRaWAN network application with minimal effort. All seven layers of the OSI stack have a scope of LoRaWAN certification services with new LoRa Radio Frequency (RF) antenna performance requirements. In order to improve the range in a network with LoRaWAN technologies, the following aspects should be considered [20]:

- Gateway location: utilize outdoor antennas and increase the height of the antennas.
- Antenna selection
- High-quality connectors (N-connectors) and cables (LMR 400 or equivalent)
- Co-localization: avoid strong interference, for example from surrounding Global System for Mobile Communications (GSM) or Universal Mobile Telecommunications System (UMTS) stations.
- Installation of a LoRaWAN gateway should also ensure sufficient surge and lightning protection

D. SigFox

SigFox is a LPWAN network that utilized Binary Phase-Shift Keying (BPSK) modulation in a 100 Hz Ultra-narrow Bandwidth (UNB) sub-GHz band carrier to send small messages. SigFox utilizes unlicensed ISM bands, namely

868 MHz bands in Europe, 915 MHz bands in United States, and 433 MHz in Asia. SigFox utilizes the frequency bandwidth efficiently and experiences very low noise levels, high receiver sensitivity, very low power consumption, and has a low-cost antenna [21]. Initially, SigFox only utilized uplink communications, but eventually advanced by utilizing the bidirectional technology. The Ultra Mobile Broadband (UMB) modulation has limited data rates (100 bits per second), the maximum payload length for every uplink message is 12 bytes, and the maximum payload length for every downlink message is 8 bytes with a protocol overhead of 26 bytes. Despite the limitation, SigFox is suitable for IoT applications that are not time-crucial (e.g., monitoring water meters, air quality sensing, etc.).

Similar to LoRaWAN, the UNB modulation does not utilize LBT but applies duty cycle limitations per transmitter. The SigFox network architecture comprises devices and SigFox servers for an execution process in a cloud schema. Hence, the SigFox system is a cloud-based network system where data is passed to the backend server and customer portal directly [22]. The SigFox cloud system can automatically forward the messages utilizing a callback system. As the base stations can receive messages simultaneously over all the channels and observe the entire system bandwidth to detect and decode uplink data. The end device can randomly choose a frequency channel to transmit their messages. This simplifies the end device design and reduces its cost. Figure 6 presents the architecture of a SigFox network.

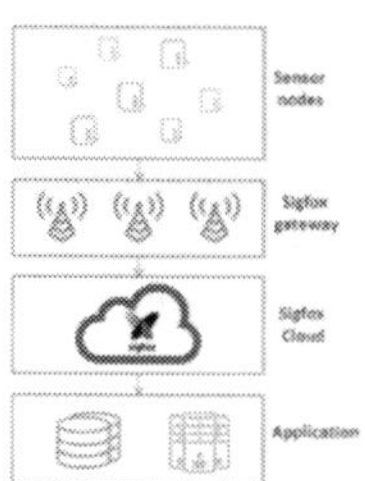

Figure 6. SigFox Architecture

Figure 7 explains the differences in NB-IoT, LoRaWAN, and SigFox technologies from several IoT requirements. Some IoT requirements consist of modulation, standardization, bandwidth, date rate, frequency, typical range, battery life, cost, and bidirectional. In the bandwidth category, LoRaWAN is better than NB-IoT and SigFox, which is 125 kHz and 250 kHz. Another advantage is that the battery life of LoRaWAN is much longer, i.e., up to 18 years and the cost is cheap. Behind the advantages of LoRaWAN, the weakness is in the data rate, which is only 50kbps, less than the NB-IoT 200 kbps and SigFox100 kbps.

Sensor communication can be broken down into 3 types, namely narrowband, broadband, and spread spectrum (hybridized technologies). For narrowband, wideband audio is one of the derivatives that show the development of narrowband technology. While broadband consists of 2 types, namely Fixed Broadband Technology (FBT) and Mobile Broadband Technology (MBT). Spread spectrum is hybridized techniques which can be categorized into IoT (IP address) and Non-IoT (Non-IP address). Figure 8 shows Architectural Instantiation of Sensor Communications, where in the spread spectrum derivative graph, LoRaWAN belongs to the category of IoT non-cellular.

IoT Requirements	NB-IoT	LoRaWAN	SigFox
Modulation	DBPSK	CSS	BPSK
Standardization	3GPP	LoRa-Alliance	SigFox company and ETSI
Bandwidth	200 kHz	125 kHz and 250 kHz	100 Hz
Data rate	200 kbps	50 kbps	100 kbps
Frequency	Licensed	Unlicensed ISM bands	Unlicensed ISM bands
Typical Range	1 km (urban), 10 km (rural)	5 km (urban), 20 km (rural)	10 km (urban), 40 km (rural)
Battery life	Up to 6 years	Up to 18 years	Up to 7 years
Cost	Expensive network	Cheap	High subscription cost to pay per devices
Bidirectional	Yes	Yes	No

Figure7. Comparison of NB-IoT, LoRaWAN, and SigFox Technologies

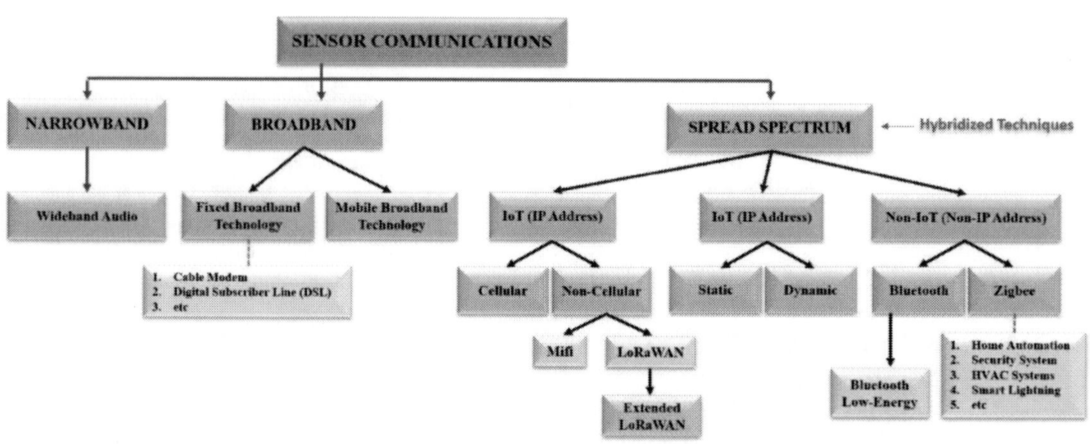

Figure 8. Architectural Instantiation of Sensor Communications

V. SMART SWITCH

Power utility companies utilize communication network so as to conduct real-time monitoring, protection, and optimization of the involved grid components including generation, transmission, and distribution. The planning and implementation of a communications network require the same attention as the installation of the power grid system itself. The communications infrastructure of power grid can be wired (e.g., fiber optic) or wireless. The advantages of the wireless infrastructure compared to the wired infrastructure are low costs and simple connection to distant and unreachable areas [23], whereas fiber optic can be expensive especially when deployed at the distribution level in large scale. Communication standards, such as Bluetooth, ZigBee, Z-wave, IPv6, wired Ethernet, cellular network, and wireless Ethernet (e.g., Wi-Fi) are a few of the standards that can be considered for adding connectivity to a power grid system.

The main challenges for a communications network system are loss of communication, data loss or latency, denial of service, as well as jamming of the Radio Frequency (RF) signal [24]. A smart network switch can be utilized with regards to loss of communications or latency problems. Smart network switching enables the system to automatically switch from an unstable Wi-Fi network (non-cellular) to cellular data or mobile network. This allows the system to preserve a consistent network connection and maintain a high level of connectivity.

The smart network switch is capable of transmitting and receiving signals to and from other devices (modules). Smart network switch utilizes requirements to support the system, such as multiple transceiver types or speeds including control, flexible low latency data inspection and data path manipulation capabilities, comprehensive and fast configuration and diagnostic interface (e.g., modes, queues), fast start-up including configuration, and powerful switch core. Additional requirements required by a smart network switch are time synchronization, Quality of Service (QoS), and security [25]. Smart switch consists of smart routing controller, open flow hybrid switch, and protocol convert module (see Figure 9) [26]. Smart routing controller executes the packet decision, open flow hybrid switch receive the decision command from open flow controller, and protocol converter module is a device utilized to convert standard or protocol.

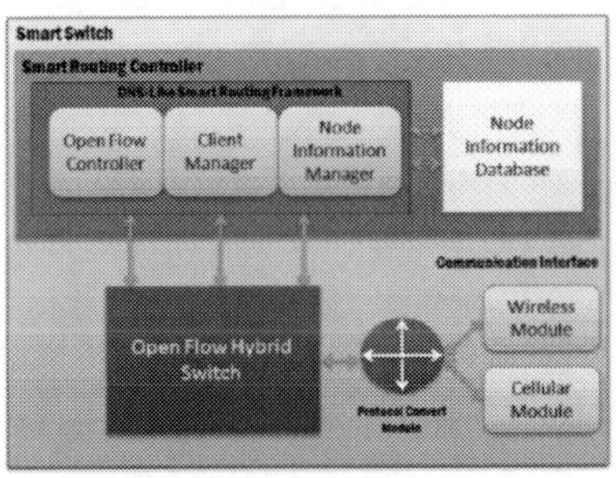

Figure 9. Smart switch architecture

Figure 10 below presents a general communication network and smart switch network embedded into a power grid system.

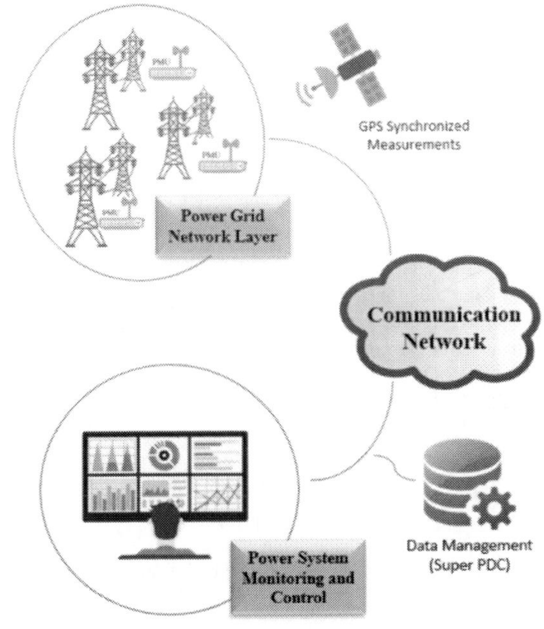

Figure 10. Communication network in power grid system

In Figure 9, the power grid system consists of power transmission infrastructures, communication networks, data management systems, and power grid monitoring and control center [27]. The information collection network is essentially a compound network consisting of satellite communications, Wi-Fi, cellular network, and internet. Smart network switches are embedded into the communication network system. Phasor Measurement Units (PMUs) are deployed over the power grid to monitor the state of the system. PMUs receive a common time reference from the Global Positioning System (GPS) satellites. The measurements from several PMUs are reported to a Phasor Data Concentrator (PDC). All collected data from the PDC are analyzed at a data management center for utilized for decision support. The power grid monitoring and control system receives instructions from the data management center and actuates the power system in real-time.

VI. CONCLUSION

In this paper, we presented a study on communications network technologies and recent trends of network technologies (e.g., Internet of Things [IoT] and Low Power Wide Area [LPWA] technologies, such as LoRaWAN, NB-IoT, and Sigfox) to develop a more robust communications system within a power grid. This paper discusses amalgams of narrowband, broadband, and hybridizing techniques (e.g., spread spectrum) for enhancing grid resilience sensor communications and provides an architectural instantiation for more robust sensor communications. In addition, the smart network switch has also been discussed, so as to resolve the loss of communications and/or latency problems within a power grid system. Overall, this paper presented an amalgam of broadband, narrowband, and hybridizing technique (e.g., spread spectrum) to bridge the gap between broadband and narrowband (e.g., by enhancing the resiliency of narrowband signals) by lowering power requirements while extending coverage so as to develop a more robust communication network; this more resilient communications paradigm better facilitates "expeditious outage response capabilities" for distribution utilities constitutes a more "resilient, adaptable architectures."

ACKNOWLEDGMENT

This research is supported by the Center for Research on IoT, Data Science, and Resiliency (CRIDR), an initiative of Decision Engineering Analysis Laboratory (DEAL) and The International Center for Theoretical Physics (ICTP), a United Nations Educational, Scientific, and Cultural Organization (UNESCO) Category 1 Institution.

REFERENCES

[1] T. Dean, Network+ Guide to Networks, 5thed., USA: Course Technology, pp. 369, 2010.

[2] Bobby. *Introduction to Broadband Internet and Types of Connections.* [Online]. Available from: https://bobbyfiles.wordpress.com/2008/12/03/pengenalan-internet-broadband-dan-jenis-jenis-koneksi/. 2008.12.03. [retrieved: June, 2019]

[3] O. Ergun,*Broadband Network Architecture-Access Network Models.* [Online]. Available from: https://orhanergun.net/2017/03/broadband-network-architecture-access-network-models/. 2017.03.29. [retrieved: June, 2019]

[4] Microwaves&RF. *What's the Difference Between Broadband and Narrowband RF communications?* [Online]. Available from: https://www.mwrf.com/systems/what-s-difference-between-broadband-and-narrowband-rf-communications. 2014.11.15. [retrieved: June, 2019]

[5] T. Dean, Network+ Guide to Networks, 5thed., USA: Course Technology, pp. 370, 2010.

[6] W. Stallings, Advanced Data Communications and Networking Data and Computer Communications, USA: Pearson Higher Ed, pp. 276, 2013.

[7] M. Fahmideh and D. Zowghi, "An Exploration of IoT Platform Development," Information Systems Elsevier, vol. 87, pp. 1-25, 2019.

[8] O. Georgiou and U. Raza, "Low Power Wide Area Network Analysis: can LoRascale?" IEEE Wireless Communication, vol.6, no. 2, pp. 162-165, 2017.

[9] R. S. Iborra, J. S. Gomez, and A. Skarmeta, "Evolving IoT Networks by the Confluence of MEC and LP-WAN Paradigms," Future Generation Computer System, vol. 88, pp. 199-208,2018.

[10] G. Zhang, C. Yao, and X. Li, "Research on Joint Planning Method of NB-IoT and LTE," 8th International Congress of Information and Communication Technology, pp. 985-991, 2018.

[11] K. Mekki, E. Bajic, F. Chaxel, and F. Meyer, "A Comparative Study of LPWAN Technologies for Large-Scale IoT Deployment," ICT Express, vol. 5, issue 1, pp. 1-7, 2019.

[12] O. Liberg, et al., Cellular Internet of Things, 2nd ed., London: Academic Press, pp. 219, 2019.

[13] M. Loriot, A. Aljer, and I. Shahrour, "Analysis of the Use of LoRaWAN Technology in a Large-Scale Smart City Demonstrator," in 2017 Sensor Networks Smart and Emerging Technologies (SENSET) conf. Beirut, Lebanon, September 2017, pp. 1-4, ISBN: 978-1-5090-6011-5.

[14] R. S. Sinha, Y. Wei, and S. H. Hwang, "A Survey on LPWA Technology: LoRa and NB-IoT," ICT Express, vol. 3, issue 1, pp. 14-21, 2017.

[15] B. Reynders, W. Meert, and S. Pollin, "Range and Coexistence Analysis of Long-Range Unlicensed Communication," in 2016 International Conference on Telecommunications (ICT), Thessaloniki, Greece, June 2016, pp. 1-6, ISBN: 978-1-5090-1990-8..

[16] O. Liberg, et al., Cellular Internet of Things, 2nd ed., London: Academic Press, pp. 342, 2018.

[17] R. S. Iborra, J. S. Gomez, and A. Skarmeta, "Evolving IoT Networks by the Confluence of MEC and LP-WAN Paradigms," Future Generation Computer System, vol. 88, pp. 199-208, 2018.

[18] P. Ram, *LPWAN, LoRa, LoRaWAN and the Internet of Things*, [Online]. Available from: https://medium.com/coinmonks/lpwan-lora-lorawan-and-the-internet-of-things-aed7d5975d5d. 2018.08.07 [retrieved: July, 2019]

[19] SimpleSoft, *Using Simple IoT Simulator to Simulate LoRaWAN Networks*, [Online]. Available from: https://www.simplesoft.com/SimpleIoTSimulatorForLoraWan.html. [retrieved: July, 2019].

[20] Smartmakers, "LoRaWAN range, part 1: The Most Important Factors for a Good LoRaWAN Signal Range," [Online]. Available from: https://smartmakers.io/en/lorawan-range-part-1-the-most-important-factors-for-a-good-lorawan-signal-range/. 2019.03.10 [retrieved: July,2019].

[21] N. I. Osman and E. B. Abbas, "Simulation and Modeling of LoRa and Sigfox Low Power Wide Area Network Technologies," in 2018 International Conference on Computer, Control, Electrical, and Electronic Engineering (ICCCEEE), Khartoum, Sudan, August 2018, pp. 1-5, ISBN:978-1-5386-4123-1.

[22] Y. Chung, J. Y. Ahn, and J. D. Huh, "Experiments of a LPWAN Tracking (TR) Platform Based on SigFox Test Network," in 2018 International Conference on Information and Communication Technology Convergence (ICTC), Jeju, South Korea, October 2018, pp. 1373-1376, ISBN:978-1-5386-5041-7..

[23] D. Baimel, S. Tapuchi, and N. Baimel, "Smart Grid Communication Technologies, " *Journal of Power and Energy Engineering*, vol.4, pp.1-8, 2016.

[24] G. Bag, L. Thrybom, and P. Hovila, "Challenges and Opportunities of 5G in Power Grids," In 24thInternational Conference and Exhibition on Electricity Distribution (CIRED), IET, October 2017, pp. 2145-2148, ISSN: 2515-0855.

[25] M. Ziehensack and M. Kunz, *Smart Ethernet Switch Architecture*, IEEE-SA Ethernet-IP @ Automotive Technology Day, San Jose, 2017. Available from: hhtps://standards,ieee.org

[26] J. Chiu, A. Liu, and C. Liao, "Design the DNS-Like Smart Switch for Heterogeneous Network Base on SDN Architecture," International Computer Symposium (ICS), Chiayi, 2016, pp. 187-191, ISBN: 978-1-5090-3438-3.

[27] M. Qiu, H. Su, M. Chen, Z. Ming, and L. T. Yang, "Balance of Security Strength and Energy for a PMU Monitoring System in Smart Grid," IEEE Communication Magazine, pp. 142-143, 2012.

Fast Training of Support Vector Machine for Forest Fire Prediction

Steve Chan, Ika Oktavianti Najib*, Verlly Puspita
Center for Research on IOT, Data Science, and Resiliency (CRIDR)
San Diego, CA 92192, USA
*Email: inajib@cridr.org

***Abstract*—Support Vector Machine (SVM) is a binary classification model, which aims to find the optimal separating hyperplane with the maximum margin in order to classify the data. The maximum margin SVM is obtained by solving a convex Quadratic Programming Problem (QPP) and is termed as the hard-margin linear SVM. This optimization problem can solve using commercial Quadratic Programming (QP) code, i.e., Lagrange multipliers. However, the training process is time-consuming. Several decomposition methods have been proposed, which split the problem into a sequence of smaller sub-problems. The Sequential Minimal Optimization (SMO) algorithm is a widely utilized decomposition for SVM. In this paper, SMO algorithm for SVM for regression is utilized to forecast forest fires. Moreover, the Stochastic Gradient Descent (SGD) algorithm is employed for comparison purposes. The comparative results analysis shows that SVR-SMO model outperforms the SGDRegressor model in predicting forest fires.**

Keywords—Fast training of support vector machine; support vector regression; sequential minimal optimization; stochastic gradient descent; forest fire prediction.

I. INTRODUCTION

Support Vector Machine (SVM), as proposed by Vapnik [1] is a supervised learning model that is utilized for classification, regression, and outlier detection problems. SVM implements the structural risk minimization principle, which seeks to minimize the training error and construct confidence intervals for the accuracy. SVM is a robust methodology for solving several classes of problems with small samples, nonlinearity, high dimensionality, and local minimum [2]. SVM has been utilized within several fields, including a feature recognition process, which transforms data from the input space into higher dimensional space, and optimization is performed upon the new vector spaces. This distinguishes SVM from the pattern recognition solution in general, which optimizes the parameters in the transformation results space which is lower than the input space dimension.

SVM has two phases: training and testing, where the training process is the most time-consuming. Training in SVM requires solving a Quadratic Programming (QP) problem. This problem is transformed utilizing the Lagrange multipliers method, and the solution is obtained for finding the set of optimal Lagrange coefficients [3]. Many methods have been proposed to solve the QP problem in the context of faster training.

The majority of SVM training optimization problems are solved utilizing a decomposition algorithm. The proposed decomposition methods lead to faster training, whereby the problem is decomposed more quickly into sub-problems. These decomposition methods repeatedly select a subset of the free variables and optimizes over these variables. One of the utilized decomposition methods is Sequential Minimal Optimization (SMO) proposed by Platt [4]. SMO avoids numerical QP problems and solves the smallest optimization problem at each iteration. Another method for solving optimization problems, which has also been widely utilized for machine learning is that of the Stochastic Gradient Descent (SGD). SGD is an iterative method for optimizing formula use to achieve production goal. In this paper, the SMO algorithm for Support Vector Regression (SVR) is utilized to forecast the problem domain of peatland forest fires. The SGD algorithm is also employed for comparative study with the SVR-SMO model.

Section I provided an introduction. The remainder of this paper is organized as follows. Section II describes related works regarding research implementation of SVM, SMO, etc. Section III provides details regarding the SVM theory, Lagrange Multipliers, Krush-Kuhn-Tucker (KKT) Condition, SVR and Section IV discusses the SVM training method consist of SMO, SGD, and Section V discusses the experiment and results. Finally, interim conclusions are summarized in Section VI.

II. RELATED WORKS

Lin et al. [5] formulated the original SVM problem as the Minimum Enclosing Ball (MEB) approach and proposed SMO for attaining fewer support vectors as well as obtaining an acceptable accuracy compared to the original SVM. The SMO has been modified by the idea of the active set and second order information. The result shows that the proposed method improves the efficiency and reduces memory consumption.

Feng et al. [6] implemented the Modified SMO (MSMO) algorithm of SVM so as to enable and speed up the learning process of the hardware system, via the Integrated Circuit (IC). MSMO is applied with two threshold parameters instead of one. Experimental results show that the designed system has a high detection rate and fast learning process of SVM.

Qihua and Shuai [7] present a new fast SVM learning algorithm for large-scale training set under the condition of sample aliasing. The main idea of this proposed algorithm is that those aliasing training samples, which are not of the same class, are eliminated first, and then the Relative Boundary Vectors (RBVs) are calculated. According to Qihua and Shuai's algorithm, not only the RBVs sample itself, but a near RBVs sample, whose distance to the RBVs is smaller than a certain value, is also selected for SVM training in order to prevent the loss of some critical sample points for the optimal hyperplane. The simulation results demonstrate that this fast learning algorithm is very effective and can be utilized as a pragmatic approach for large-scale SVM training.

Wijnhoven and With [8] evaluated the performance of Stochastic Gradient Descent (SGD) when only a part of the training set is presented to the training algorithm. The SGD algorithm was implemented for learning a linear SVM classifier for object detection. The obtained classification performance of Wijnhoven and With's model is similar to that of state-of-the-art SVM implementations as they are able to obtain a speed up factor in computation time of two or three orders of magnitude.

Cao et al. [9], who solved the problem of fault prediction and failure prognosis for electro-mechanical actuators, utilized SVR. With the large size of sample data, the improved SMO algorithm was employed to solve the SVR model problems. The SMO algorithm is developed by improving stopping criteria as the SVR method can overcome drawbacks of slow convergence and local minimum. The simulation results demonstrate that the SMO-SVR method has characteristics of high prediction accuracy and time efficiency, as well as indicators for preventive measure actions before failure occurs.

Priyadarshini et al. [10] utilized SVR and SMO for link load prediction of a network. SMO was utilized for model training, while SVR was utilized for forecasting. SVR models are robust to parameter variation and can generalize against unseen data and is quite proficient at continuous and adaptive online learning. The result indicates that SVR-SMO performance is quite satisfactory and promising for applications, such as real-time traffic condition prediction.

III. SUPPORT VECTOR MACHINE THEORY

SVM is a binary classification model, which aims to find the optimal separating hyperplane with the maximum margin to separate the involved classes of data (please refer to Figure 1). SVM addresses generalization utilizing a theoretical framework and shows that the generalization error is related to the margin of a hyperplane classifier [11]. This hyperplane is represented by the following equation, where w is called the weight vector, x is the input data, and b is referred to as the bias:

$$H: w^T \cdot x_i + b = 0 \quad (1)$$

$$H_+: w^T \cdot x_i + b = +1 \quad (2)$$

$$H_-: w^T \cdot x_i + b = -1 \quad (3)$$

Since the labels are the same as the {-1, 1} sides of the plane, the constraints can be rewritten as $y(w^T \cdot x + b) \geq 1$ for all training points x with label $y \in \{-1,1\}$(will have one constraint for each training point) [12]. Though the principle of maximum margin is derived through certain inequalities, the larger the margin, the smaller is the probability that a hyperplane will determine the class of a test sample incorrectly [9]. Therefore, the maximum margin of SVM is obtained by solving the following optimization problem:

$$\min_{(w,b)} \frac{1}{2}\|w\|^2 \quad (4)$$

Equation 4 is a convex Quadratic Programming Problem (QPP) and is termed as the hard-margin linear SVM. The formulation may be more succinctly written as:

$$\min_{(w,b)} \frac{1}{2} w^T w \quad (5)$$

$$s.t\; y_i(w^T \cdot x + b) \geq 1, \;\; i = 1, \ldots, m$$

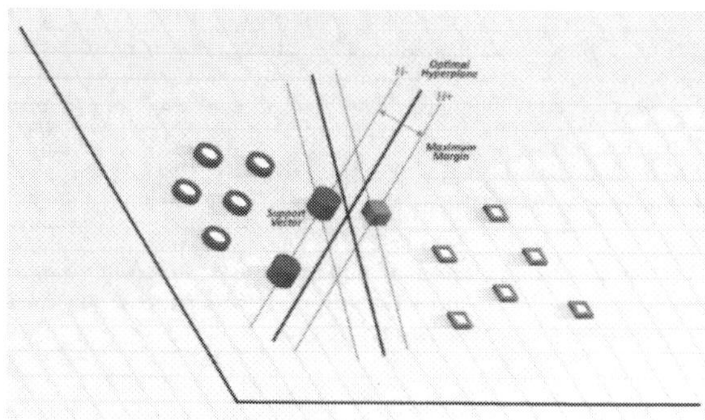

Figure 1. Optimal hyperplane within a two-dimensional space

Figure 1 show the data with two bordering parallel lines that form a margin around central separating line. As a consequence, the algorithm uncovers the elements in the data that touch the margins [13]. These are called the *support vector*. The other elements distanced from the border are not relevant to the solution. Support vectors are found after an optimization step involving a convex quadratic objective and a linear constraint. This optimization problem can then be solved utilizing commercial QP code, i.e., Lagrange multipliers. The method of Lagrange multipliers can handle the inequality constraints and posit the necessary and sufficient conditions for minimizing the primal form of the SVM [14]. With this condition, the primal form turns into an equivalent dual form.

A. Lagrange Multipliers

Lagrange multipliers constitute a mathematical method utilized to solve constrained optimization problems of differentiable functions [15]. One Lagrange multiplier α_i is defined for each constraint, and the constraints $y_i f(x_i) \geq 1$ are re-written as $y_i f(x_i) - 1 \geq 0$. The Langrangian is:

$$\mathcal{L}(w,b,\alpha) = \frac{1}{2}w^T w - \sum_{i=1}^{m} \alpha_i (y_i (w^T \cdot x + b) - 1) \quad (6)$$

Then, $\mathcal{L}$ is differentiated with respect to w, b, and the differential is set to zero:

$$\frac{\partial L}{\partial w} = 0 \rightarrow w = \sum_{i=1}^{m} \alpha_i y_i x_i, \quad (7)$$

$$\frac{\partial L}{\partial b} = 0 \rightarrow b = \sum_{i=1}^{m} \alpha_i y_i = 0 \quad (8)$$

and then the equation of w and b is placed back into the $\mathcal{L}(w,b,\alpha)$ equation in order to eliminate (w,b). Consequently, the Lagrange dual problem is obtained for the original SVM-primal problem.

$$\mathcal{L}(w,b,\alpha) = \max_{\alpha} \sum_{i=1}^{m} \alpha_i - \frac{1}{2}\sum_{i,j=1}^{m} y_i y_j \alpha_i \alpha_j {x_i}^T x_j \quad (9)$$

To train the SVM, the feasible region of the dual problem and the maximization of the objective function are necessary and sufficient to specify optimal solution. The optimal solution can then be checked utilizing the Krush-Kuhn-Tucker conditions.

B. *Krush-Kuhn-Tucker Condition*

Although the Lagrange multipliers provide an important optimization technique, it can only be employed under equality constraints, while the SVM minimization problem is restricted by inequalities [16]. In order to tackle the maximal-margin problem, Krush-Kuhn-Tucker (KKT) must be satisfied when performing Lagrange multipliers for inequality constraints. There are five KKT conditions that affect the dual problem [13]:

$$\frac{\partial L}{\partial w}\mathcal{L}(w,b,\alpha) = w - \sum_{i}^{m} \alpha_i y_i x_i = 0 \quad (10)$$

$$\frac{\partial L}{\partial b}\mathcal{L}(w,b,\alpha) = -\sum_{i}^{m} \alpha_i y_i = 0 \quad (11)$$

$$y_i(w^T \cdot x + b) - 1 \geq 0 \quad (12)$$

$$\alpha_i \geq 0 \quad (13)$$

$$\alpha_i(y_i(w^T \cdot x + b)) - 1 = 0 \quad (14)$$

C. *Support Vector Regression (SVR)*

The basic idea of SVR is to find a function $f(x)$ that has at most ϵ from the actualobtained target y_i for all training data [17]. Referring to Figure 2, the region bound by $y_i \pm \epsilon$ is called an ϵ-insensitive tube. The samples deviating from ϵ-insensitive tube can be integrated to the optimization problem by using slack variables (ξ). The error function for SVR can then be written as:

$$\min_{(w,b)} \frac{1}{2}\|w\|^2 + C\sum_{i=1}^{m}(\xi_i^+ + \xi_i^-) \quad (15)$$

Consequently, the dual optimization problem can be rewritten as follows:

$$\max_{\alpha^+,\alpha^-}\left[\sum_{i=1}^{m}(\alpha_i^* - \alpha_i)y_i - \epsilon\sum_{i=1}^{m}(\alpha_i^* - \alpha_i) - \frac{1}{2}\sum_{i,j}^{m}(\alpha_i^* - \alpha_i)(\alpha_j^* - \alpha_j)\mathbf{x}_i \cdot \mathbf{x}_j\right] \quad (16)$$

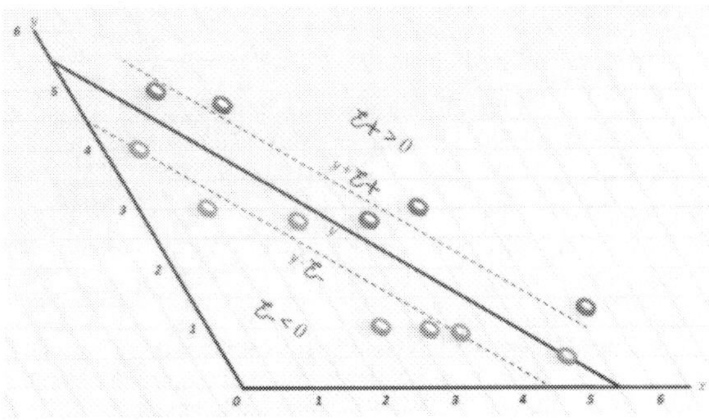

Figure 2. SVR with ϵ-tube

Accordingly, the standard SVR to solve the approximation problem is as follows:

$$f(x) = \sum_{i=1}^{m}(\alpha_i^* - \alpha_i)K(x_i, x) + b \quad (17)$$

where α_i^* and α_i are Lagrange multipliers and $K(x_i, x)$ is a kernel function.

IV. SVM Training Method

To reduce the computational complexity of SVM training, the basic and the most commonly used method is to select the most informative samples that have the most possibility to become the support vectors in the training sample set before training the SVM. In this paper, SMO and SGD algorithm are utilized for fast training of SVM. The first review the training procedures of SMO algorithm, and then describe SGD algorithm simply.

A. *Sequential Minimal Optimization (SMO)*

The SMO approach minimizes memory storage for decomposing a large QP problem into a series of smaller QP sub-problems. Each sub-problem is solved analytically to avoid utilizing a time-consuming numerical QP optimization, via optimizing two elements of α_i (Lagrange multipliers).

$$\mathcal{L}(w,b,\alpha) = \sum_{i=1}^{m} \alpha_i - \frac{1}{2}\sum_{i,j=1}^{m} y_i y_j \alpha_i \alpha_j {x_i}^T x_j \quad (18)$$

$$s.t. 0 \leq \alpha_i \leq C \ and \ \sum_{i=1}^{m} \alpha_i y_i = 0$$

where C is a SVM hyper-parameter. Because of the linear equality constraint involving the Lagrange multipliers α_i, the smallest possible problem involves two such multipliers. Then, for any two multipliers $\alpha_1$and α_2, the constraints are reduced to:

$$0 \leq \alpha_1, \alpha_2 \leq C, \quad (19)$$

$$y_1\alpha_1 + y_2\alpha_2 = k \quad (20)$$

where k is the negative of the sum over the rest of terms within the equality constraint, which is fixed at each iteration.

B. Stochastic Gradient Descent (SGD)

The SGD algorithm is able to minimize the objective functions that depend upon an integral [18]. SGD has two major steps: individual gradient computation and weight update. SGD continuously fluctuates to converge, where the weight update jumps to a better local minimum for the non-convex error function [19].

Algorithm 1. Stochastic Gradient Descent (SGD)

Input: Training data S, regularization parameters λ, learning rate η, initialization σ
Output: Model parameters $\Theta = (w_0, \mathbf{w}, \mathbf{V})$
$w_0 \leftarrow 0; w \leftarrow (0,...,0); V \sim N(0,\sigma);$
repeat
  for $(x, y) \in S$ **do**
    $w_0 \leftarrow w_0 - \eta\left(\frac{\partial}{\partial w_0} l(y(x|\Theta, y) + 2\lambda^0 w_0\right);$
    for $i \in \{1,....p\} \wedge x_i \neq 0$ **do**
      $w_i \leftarrow w_i - \eta\left(\frac{\partial}{\partial w_i} l(y(x|\Theta, y) + 2\lambda_\pi^w w_i\right);$
      for $f \in \{1,...,k\}$ do
        $v_{i,f} \leftarrow v_{i,f} - \eta\left(\frac{\partial}{\partial v_{i,f}} l(y(x|\Theta, y) + 2\lambda_f^v v_{i,f}\right);$
      end
    end
  end
Until stopping criterion is not met;

Figure 3. Algorithm Stochastic Gradient Descent

Figure 3 provides a Stochastic Gradient Descent (SGD) algorithm. SGD algorithm tries to find the right weights (w_0 , $\mathbf{w}$) by iteratively updating the values of w_0 and $\mathbf{w}$ by utilizing the value of gradient **V.** The value of the gradient V depends upon the inputs (S), the current values of the model parameter (λ, η, σ) and the cost function **f.** η is the learning rate which determines the size of the steps to reach a minimum, λ is the regularization parameter to reduces overfitting, and σ is standard deviation of sigma. Loss function $l\ (\hat{y}(x|\Theta, y)$ that measures the cost of prediction $\hat{y}$ when the actual answer is y. The model target is to get the best fit line to predict the value of y based upon the input value x, where x and y is training data sample.

V. Experiment and Result

In order to testify the effectiveness of the algorithms in this paper, the fast training algorithm, SVR-SMO and SGDRegressor, was applied to the peatland forest fire dataset. Further, the performance of SVR-SMO and SGDRegressor (accuracy and the CPU times) will be compared. All reported results are implemented by Python code. Dataset description and experiment results are shown on Section V-A and B respectively.

A. Data Description

The peatland forest fire dataset was obtained from the UCI Machine Learning Repository website [20] and was created by Paulo Cortez and Anibal Morais, University of Minho, Portugal. The meteorological dataset was collected from January 2000 to December 2003. This dataset contains 517 fire observations found in the Montesinho Natural Park in Portugal, 12 attributes of input features, and one output feature representing the total burnt area. This peatland forest fire dataset has multivariate time series features and for regression tasks. The attribute descriptions are given in Table I:

TABLE I. Attribute Description

No	*Attribute*	*Description*
1	X	x-axis coordinate
2	Y	y-axis coordinate
3	Month	Month of the year (a.k.a. month)
4	Day	Day of the week (a.k.a. day)
5	FFMC	Fine Fuel Moisture Code (FFMC) denotes the moisture content surface litter and influences ignition and fire spread
6	DMC	Duff Moisture Code (DMC) represent the moisture content of shallow and deep organic layers, which affect fire intensity
7	DC	Drought Code (DC) for fire intensity
8	ISI	Initial Spread Index (ISI) is a score that correlates with fire velocity spread
9	Temp	Temperature (in Celsius)
10	RH	Relative Humidity (RH) (in %)
11	Wind	Wind Speed (a.k.a. wind) (in km/h)
12	Rain	Rain (in mm/mm^2)
13	area	Total burned area (a.k.a. area) (in ha)

The first four rows denote the spatial and temporal attributes. FFMC, DMC, DC, ISI are the indexes for the Fire Weather Index (FWI) of the Canadian system for rating the fire danger. Temperature, RH, Wind, and Rain constitute meteorological information. Only two geographic features were included, the X and Y axis values, where the fire occurred [21]. Variables of the Total burned area has many 0 values (see the density plot in Figure 4). Consequently, Paulo Cortez and Anibal Morais transformed the variable utilizing the log transformation (log(x+1), where 1 will first be added to the area (to account for the 0 values)).

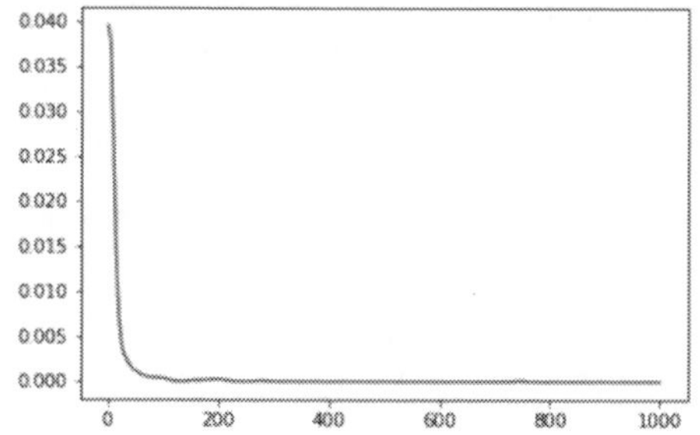

Figure 4. Area burned density

B. Experimental Results

SVR-SMO and SGDRegressor were implemented on a Jupyter Notebook utilizing the Python 3 kernel and run atop a machine with Intel(R) Pentium(R) Dual CPU T3400 @2.17 GHz and 2 GB of RAM. 70% and 30% of the employed dataset (517 instances) were selected as the training set and testing set, respectively. Then, both training and test sets were standardized with the StandardScaler function (mean = 0 and standard deviation = 1).

The SVR based upon SMO utilized grid search to optimize the parameters (C and epsilon) and carried out fivefold cross validation for selecting the C value from {0.01, 0.1, 1, 10} and the epsilon value from {10, 1, 0.1, 0.01, 0.001, 0.0001}. As the kernel function, we utilized the Radial Basis Function (RBF) kernel for the SVR kernel defined by $K(x_i, x) = \exp(-||x-y||^2/(2\sigma^2))$. Best parameters obtained by Grid Search are C = 0.01, epsilon = 1, and kernel = RBF.

Parameters of the SGDRegressor include alpha set defaults to 0.0001 to compute the learning rate. The L1 ratio is 0.1, iteration maximum is 1000, epsilon in the epsilon-insensitive loss function is 0.0001, the learning rate schedule is eta 0 = 0.01, the exponent for inverse scaling learning rate is power_t = 0.25, the validation fraction set defaults to 0.1, and the number of iterations with no improvement defaults to 5.

In this study, Root Mean Squared Error (RMSE) are implemented for evaluating prediction performance. RMSE is the square root of the ratio of the quadratic sum of deviations between predicted values and actual values to the times n of prediction. Moreover, the information refers to simulation result comparisons between SVR-SMO and SGDRegressor, as shown in Table 2.

TABLE III. PERFORMANCE COMPARISON OF SVR-SMO AND SGDREGRESSOR

Parameter	Method	
	SVR-SMO	***SGDRegressor***
ε	1	0.001
Max Iteration	1000	1000
CPU Times (s)	0.01639	0.02161
Accurasy (RMSE)	0.66698	3.80567

In Table 2, the results indicate that SVR-SMO exhibits better prediction ability for the UCI forest fire dataset when compared to the SGDRegressor method, while the training speeds for SVR-SMO and SGDRegressor were almost the same.

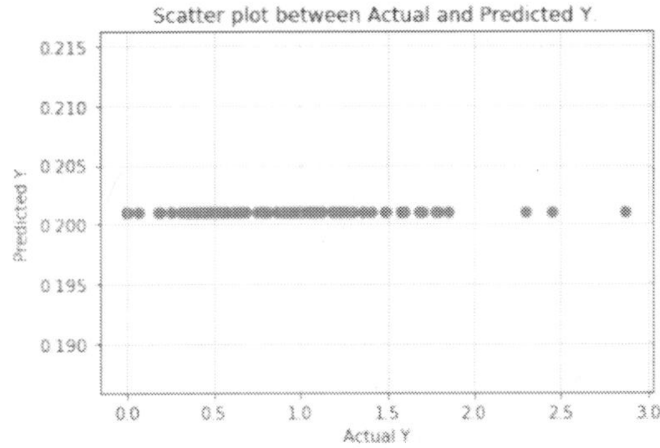

Figure 5. SVR with ϵ-tube

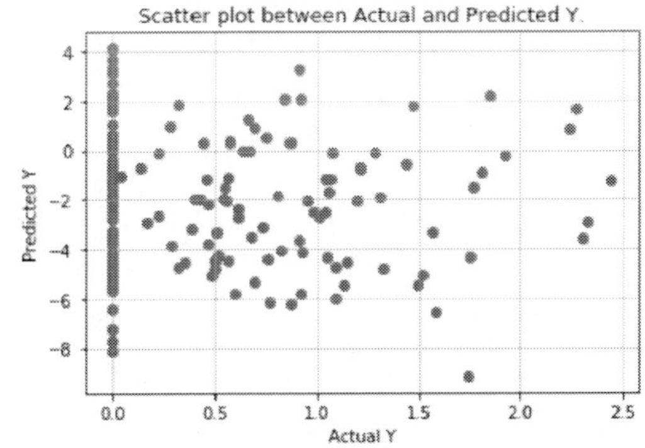

Figure 6. SVR with ϵ-tube

Figure 5 show the scatter plot between actual and predicted value of the burn area part of forest fire dataset utilizing SVR-SMO algorithm. Predicted Y is the estimated outcome or prediction made by the trained model for the given input data and the residual error is describe by e (epsilon). As can be seen in Figure 5, the resulting points form a line that represents the learned relationship between actual and predicted value. In other words, SVR-SMO algorithm reach the goal of regression analysis to fit a line to set of data points. Figure 6 presents scatter plot between actual and predicted value of the burn area part of forest fire dataset utilizing SGDRegressor algorithm. The graph shown that the data points is not linear because the plot of the residual possesses a random distribution. In this case, a line drawn through the data points is horizontal with slop equal to zero.

VI. CONCLUSION AND FUTURE WORK

In this paper, SVR based upon the SMO algorithm is utilized to predict the Total burned area as pertains to a forest fire and compared with the SGDRegressor algorithm. The comparatively small RMSE obtained from the experimental results shows that SVR based upon SMO algorithm has better performance than SGDRegressor, while the training speed for SVR-SMO and SGDRegressor were comparable. Future work will involve studying global convergence of more general decomposition algorithms for multi-objective optimization problems.

ACKNOWLEDGMENT

This research is supported by the Center for Research on IoT, Data Science, and Resiliency (CRIDR), an initiative of Decision Engineering Analysis Laboratory (DEAL) and The International Center for Theoretical Physics (ICTP), a United Nations Educational, Scientific, and Cultural Organization (UNESCO) Category 1 Institution. Sources of data for this research includes the Department of Information Systems, University of Minho, Portugal.

REFERENCES

[1] C. Cortes and V. Vapnik, "Support-Vector Networks," Machine Learning Journal, vol. 20, Issue 3, pp. 273–297, 1995.

[2] X. Jian-Hua, Z. Xue-gong, and L. Yan-da, "Advance in Support Vector Machine," *Chinese Control and Decision*, vol. 19, no. 5, pp. 481-484, 2004.

[3] R. A. Hernandez, M. Strum, W. J. Chau, and J. A. Q. Gonzalez, "The Multiple Pairs SMO: A Modified SMO Algorithm for the Acceleration of the SVM Training," *Proc. of International Joint Conference on Neural Networks*, USA, pp. 1221-1228, 2009.

[4] J. Platt, "Fast training of Support Vector Machines using Sequential Minimal Optimization," in Advances in Kernel Method-Support Vector Learning, pp. 185-208, 1999.

[5] B. Schdlkopi, C. I. C Burges and A. J. Smala, Editors, MIT Press, Cambridge, MA, pp. 185-208, 1999.

[6] J. Lin, M. Song, and J. Hu, "A SMO approach to Fast SVM for Classification of Large-Scale Data," *2014 International Conference on IT Convergence and Security (ICITCS)*, Beijing, pp. 1-4, 2014.

[7] L. Feng, Z. Li, Y. Wang, C. Zheng, and Y. Guan, "VLSI Design of Modified Sequential Minimal Optimization Algorithm for Fast SVM Training," *IEEE 2016 13th IEEE International Conference on Solid-State and Integrated Circuit Technology (ICSICT)*, Hangzhou, pp. 627-629, 2016.

[8] X. Qihua and G. Shuai, "A Fast SVM Classification Learning Algorithm Used to Large Training Set," *2012 Second International Conference on Intelligent System Design and Engineering Application*, Sanya, Hainan, pp. 15-19, 2012.

[9] R. G. J. Wijnhoven and P. H. N. With, "Fast Training of Object Detection using Stochastic Gradient Descent," *International Conference on Pattern Recognition*, Istanbul, pp. 424-427, 2010.

[10] Y. Cao, J. Wang, Y. Yu, and R. Xie, "Failure Prognosis for Electro-Mechanical Actuators Based on Improved SMO-SVR Method," *IEEE Chinese Guidance, Navigation and Control Conference (CGNCC)*, Nanjing, pp. 1180-1185, 2016.

[11] D. Priyadarshini, M. Acharya, and A. P. Mishra, "Link Load Prediction Using Support Vector Regression and Optimization," *International Journal of Computer Applications*, vol. 24, pp. 22-24, 2011.

[12] Jayadeva, R. Kemchandani, and S. Chandra, "Twin Support Vector Machines: Model, Extensions and Applications," Studies in Computational Intelligence, Springer International Publishing, vol. 659, pp. 1-211, 2017.

[13] B. Wang and V. Pavlu, "Support Vector Machine," *Based on Notes by Andrew Ng*, 2015.

[14] J. Unpingco, "Python for Probability, Statistic, and Machine Learning," 2nd edition, Springer International Publishing, pp. 1-384, 2016.

[15] J. Wu, Class Lecture, Topic: "Support Vector Machines," LAMDA Group, National Key Lab for Novel Software Technology, Nanjing University, China, 2019.

[16] B. T. Smith, Class Lecture, Topic: "Lagrange Multipliers Tutorial in the Context of Support Vector Machine," Memorial University of Newfoundland, Canada, 2004.

[17] R. F. d. Mello and M. A. Ponti, "Machine Learning: A Practical Approach on the Statistical Learning Theory," Springer International Publishing, pp. 1-362, 2018.

[18] A. I. Smola and B. Scholkopf, "A Tutorial on Support Vector Regression," *Statistics and Computing*, vol. 14, pp. 199-222, 2004.

[19] A. G. Carlon, R. H. Lopez, L. F. R. Espath, L. F. F. Miguel, and A. T. Beck, "A Stochastic Gradient Approach for the Reliability Maximization of Passively Controlled Structures," *Elsevier, Engineering Structures*, vol. 186, pp. 1-12, 2019.

[20] A. Sharma, "Guided Stochastic Gradient Descent Algorithm for Inconsistent Datasets," *Elsevier, Applied Soft Computing Journal*, vol. 73, pp. 1068-1080, 2018.

[21] Paulo Cortez and Anibal Morais, "Forest Fire Dataset," UCI Machine Learning Repository. February 2008. [Online]. Available from: https://archive.ics.uci.edu/ml/datasets/forest+fires/ 2019.05.23.

[22] Y. Wang, "What Influences Forest Fires Area?" 2016. [Online]. Available from: https://docplayer.net/63027297-What-influences-forest-fires-area-lab-5.html/ 2019.05.23.

Context-Referenced Telemetry Data for Distribution Utilities:
Quality Assurance/Quality Control by Lateral Sensors

Steve Chan, Ika Oktavianti Najib*, Verlly Puspita
Center for Research on IOT, Data Science, and Resiliency (CRIDR)
San Diego, CA 92192, USA
*Email: inajib@cridr.org

Abstract—**The notion of enhancing resiliency for electrical grids has become a priority for engineers and researchers within the past few years. Unforeseen natural disasters (e.g., lightning strikes, geomagnetic storms, floods, etc.) can cause devastating damage to electrical grid infrastructures. While disasters may strike with no warning, prototypical weather events can indeed be forecast. However, anticipating and quantifying the impact of weather events is a challenging task due to its stochasticity. In this paper, a weather monitoring system paradigm, as part of a lateral sensor system, is proposed. Lateral sensors for the électrical grid, such as by way of a hyper-locale set of weather sensors equipped with edge analytics and artificial intelligence, provide incredible insight, via various parameters, such as air temperature, barometric pressure, humidity, precipitation, solar radiation, and wind. These lateral sensor parameters can provide indicators regarding impending storms, which could impact power lines (e.g., via lightning strikes, downed trees, etc.) and cause communications interference. Spider radar plots concurrently reflecting both weather sensor data and grid sensor data have proven useful, as weather data can serve to provide contextual reference for the associated grid sensor telemetry data. Moreover, this involved lateral sensor utilizes a deep learning module, which is based upon a Generative Adversarial [Neural] Network (GAN). The results of this study demonstrate that the implementation of lateral sensors based upon a deep learning module can result in enhanced contextual awareness.**

Keywords—electrical grid; lateral sensor; weather monitoring system; hyper-locale sensors; 3D-printed technology; artificial intelligence; generative adversarial neural network.

I. INTRODUCTION

Resilience enhancements of electrical grids have become a priority for regulatory agencies around the world. Among other causes, extreme weather events, such as storms and lightning strikes, are considered to be some of the main causes of electrical disturbances worldwide [1]. In Indonesia, for example, the state utility company, Perusahaan Listrik Negara (PLN), has suffered major financial losses due to storms and downed trees [2]. These events are known as High-Impact Low-Probability (HILP) events, as the frequencies of occurrence are relatively low, but the impact is extremely high [3].

Over the past couple of years, critical infrastructure resilience initiatives have tended to focus upon power grid resilience efforts. Resilience, for these cases, is described as the ability of a power system to anticipate, adapt, and recover from disruption events. Resilience efforts are aimed at either preventing or mitigating the damage from outages and/or reducing outage durations.

The notion of electrical grid resilience has risen to become a critical issue for Indonesia. Millions of households (especially in remote area) suffer from unstable connections, unpredictable power surges, and frequent blackouts. To exacerbate these described problems, utilities have introduced heightened instability into the involved electrical systems by accelerating the usage of intermittent energy sources; while renewable energy does indeed create new opportunities as pertains to meeting demand, it is also accompanied by various technical challenges, as pertains to maintaining electrical grid stability. The adoption of renewable energy segues to a paradigm wherein the electrical grid network tends to become more decentralized. This complicates the "sense and respond" paradigm, as the "sensing" must now be more carefully synchronized, communicated, analyzed, and correlated.

A robust "sense and respond" paradigm is central for a reliable and stable electrical grid. First, with regards to "sensing" or monitoring, a variety of high-resolution telemetry sensor technologies play an important role in detecting, collecting, and providing that data for correlation. To complement these high resolution telemetry sensors, lateral sensors, which can ingest, process, and relay accurate information, such as key meteorological data, is of great import to electrical grid analysis.

The notion of a quality assurance/quality control function for lateral sensors to further contextualize and verify the telemetry data of high-resolution sensors at substations is proposed in this paper. Lateral sensors for the electrical grid, such as hyper-locale weather sensors, can provide incredible insight via parameters, such as air temperature, barometric pressure, humidity precipitation, solar radiation, and wind. These lateral sensor parameters can provide indicators and warnings as to impending storms, which could cause communications interference and impact power lines. Deployed lateral sensors, which include a weather monitoring system, have utilized a modified Generative Adversarial [Neural] Network (GAN) Deep Learning (DL) module. Spider radar plots reflecting both weather sensor data and grid sensor data concurrently have proven useful, as weather data can serve to provide contextual reference for the grid sensor telemetry data.

This Section I provides an overview of the paper. The remainder of this paper is organized as follows. Section II reviews state of art methods and techniques pertaining to the subject matter. Section III discusses the benefits of lateral sensor monitoring (e.g., weather monitoring) for the electrical grid. Section IV delineates the facilitating elements of a lateral sensor system. Section V presents a case study implementation and discusses the results from utilizing lateral sensors to complement the grid sensors at the terminal substation of an electrical grid. Finally, the conclusions are summarized in Section VI.

II. STATE OF ART METHODS AND TECHNIQUES

This section provides a review of different methods and techniques utilized for weather monitoring systems. Currently, Artificial Neural Network (ANN), Machine Learning (ML), and Internet of Things (IOT) are some state-of-the-art concepts as pertains to weather monitoring systems. Along this vein, Lone and Chavan proposed a design and implementation of a Wireless Smart Intelligent Network System (WSINS) utilizing Artificial Intelligence (AI) for monitoring various weather parameters [4]. They designed and implemented wind speed and directional sensors to provide real-time data; weather parameters, such as temperature, humidity, wind speed, and wind direction were monitored and visualized, via oa dashboard, which could readily pinpoint faulty nodes. In a similar vein, Mochida et al. constructed a weather monitoring system based upon Natural Language in Machine Learning (NLML) to analyze distributed meteorological data [5]. For Mochida's project, weather observation data was gathered with a 4K camera by Information Centric Networking (ICN) and utilized five weather-related parameters: temperature, wind speed, rainfall intensity, carbon dioxide concentration, and radiation dose. The experimental results demonstrated that the involved ML technique was able to classify meteorological data quite nicely, but it had difficulty in distinguishing whether the involved data had similar characteristics/features. Durrani et al. worked on a smart weather alert system for dwellers of distinct and disparate geographic areas utilizing a Non-linear Autoregressive Exogenous Neural Network (NARXNET) algorithm [6]. The solution presented was a smart weather station that not only monitored for weather-related data, but also predicted and generated instant alerts utilizing a combination of IOT and ML. The system deployed had a variety of monitoring sensors, such as temperature, humidity, rain, light intensity, pressure, wind speed, carbon monoxide, and air quality.

In addition to the aforementioned, numerous state-of-the-art techniques are presented within literature. In this paper, we present the notion of lateral sensors (that consist of 12 environmental monitoring sensors) conjoined with a deep learning module based upon a GAN so as to comprise an intelligent system. In this regard, we also leveraged 3D-printing for the production of these state-of-the-art sensors and utilized an IOT platform to collect, visualize, and analyze real-time data generated from these sensors. For this paper, we provide one such example of a lateral sensor — an intelligent weather monitoring system, which was implemented to complement the high-resolution telemetry sensor of an electric power grid system; it turns out that the intelligent weather system can provide quality assurance/quality control indicators to validate the various substation panel readings and continuous streaming telemetry data collected by the deployed grid sensors.

III. LATERAL SENSOR MONITORING FOR THE ELECTRIC POWER GRID

Automatic weather stations are commonly utilized as weather monitoring systems. The technology for manufacturing traditional automatic weather stations is very mature. Weather stations consist of various sensors to transmit an accurate stream of data related to weather variables. The automatic weather station acquires meteorological elements, such as air pressure, temperature, humidity, wind direction, wind velocity, rainfall, evaporation capacity, sunlight, radiation, and ground temperature [7]. The advantages are numerous; however, the relatively high production cost and long production period, which are the conspicuous characteristics of the traditional automatic weather station, limits the utilization of the traditional automatic weather station for the electrical grid ecosystem, particularly in developing countries. Consequently, the traditional automatic weather station may not be as ideally suited for the purposes of modern power system monitoring and analysis in many areas of the Indo-Asia Pacific [8].

The described limitations of the traditional automatic weather sensor can be overcome by a more scalable and extensible approach, such as offered, via 3D-printed weather sensors. The 3D-printed weather sensor has several advantages, such as inexpensive production costs, a size that is not too large, a relatively easy ongoing maintenance process, and the ability to update the sensor design so as to produce even better sensors as time progresses. Hence, 3D-printed sensors represent a solution set that can overcome the difficulty of providing a swarm of hyper-locale (detailed, accurate, and locally contextualized) weather sensors for an area.

For the case study put forth in this paper, the notion of 3D-printed weather sensors was demonstrated. The notion of a lateral sensor can be said to be very different from the prototypical weather sensor, which is currently widely used throughout the world. One of the things that distinguish the lateral sensor from the prototypical weather sensor is that the indicators captured by the lateral sensor are more complex and detailed; the concomitant technical challenge is that of processing as much of that data as possible at the edge (i.e., edge analytics) so as to minimize the amount of data being transmitted, via various Internet of Things (IOT) technologies. After all, there are limits to the amount of data that the available communications technologies can move.

Furthermore, the lateral sensor (whose further value-added proposition is that it is time synchronized) can be connected directly with other time-synchronized telemetry sensors, such as the Phasor Measurement Unit (PMU), which utilizes a Global Positioning System (GPS)-based clock to obtain real-time electrical grid data and leverages a GAN-based system for analysis. Overall, the lateral sensor has the ability to directly analyze data and send the analysis results, via a communications network, to be fused with other data, such as electrical grid data, at a reach-back concentrator located at an operations center or monitoring system center.

IV. Facilitating Elements of Lateral Sensor System

The lateral sensor system is specialized in that it leverages GPS-based timestamping and edge analytics; in this way it sends both extra data (the timestamp) and as well as reduces the data sent (due to the processing and filtering of data at the sensor), via the involved communications network. The notion of WSN, AI (e.g., deep learning module based upon GAN technique), and IOT as a system is well exemplified by the utilization of various components, which will be described below.

A. ThingSpeak IoT Platform

ThingSpeak is an open source Internet of Things (IoT) platform and Application Programming Interface (API), which enables the collection, visualization, and analysis of real-time data from sensors or actuators utilizing the HyperText Transfer Protocol (HTTP) protocol. The data collection utilizes the Representational State Transfer (REST) API or Message Queuing Telemetry Transport (MQTT). The involved data analysis and visualization component was MATrix LABoratory (MATLAB), a multi-paradigm numerical computing environment and programming language developed by MathWorks. ThingSpeak is the open IOT platform that accompanies MATLAB. The main component of ThingSpeak is its channel, which stores data sent from various devices. The ThingSpeak channel consists of data fields, location fields, and status fields. ThingSpeak enables user to analyze and visualize retrieved data using MATLAB. Figure 1 below delineates the ThingSpeak framework.

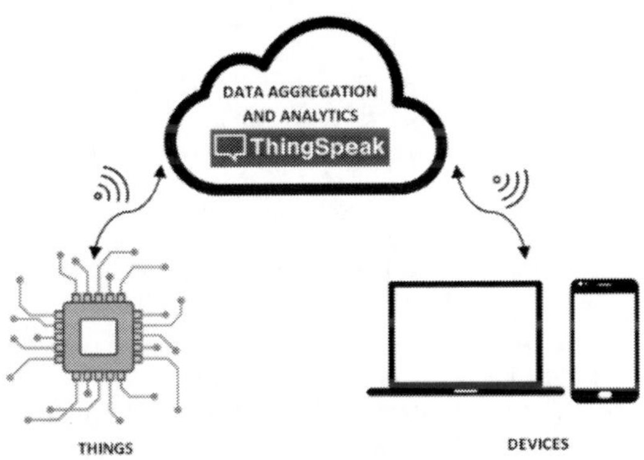

Figure 1. ThingSpeak Framework

For this particular case study, ThingSpeak was dependent upon each sensor being equipped with a cellular Subscriber Identity Module (SIM) card for the required internet connection related to the data collection piece; ideally, the sensor is connected to the internet, via wifi, but if there is no wifi in that area, then the choice of connectivity, via the sim card, is recommended.

Typically, a lateral sensor node is comprised of four basic components: (1) a sensing unit, (2) a processing unit, (3) a transceiver unit, and (4) a power unit. A lateral sensor node may also have application dependent additional constituent elements, such as location ascertainment, as in this case. Sensing units are further subdivided into two units: (1) sensors, and (2) analog to digital converters (ADCs). Similar to the entire system, of which the PMU is one constituent component, the analog signals produced by the sensors (based upon the observed phenomenon) are converted into digital signals by the ADC. For the described case of the lateral sensor, the processing unit at the sensor (i.e., edge analytics) processes the data. Data loggers, which are positioned in front of the processing unit, are electronic devices capable of recording data from sensors and constitute a major component of the telemetry system [9]. A data logger works with sensors to convert physical phenomena into electronic signals, and then convert these signals into binary data to be further analyzed by the processing unit [10].

Lateral sensors may have slighting more complex building components, but 3D printed lateral sensors are lighter and easier to assemble. One example of 3D printed lateral sensors, which have just been assembled, can be seen in Figure 2.

Figure 2. The 3D-Printed Lateral Sensor

The lateral sensor is capable of more robust sensor capture, and the resulting data is more accurate and precise. The overall system consists of a variety of sensors for weather monitoring as pertains to complementing grid monitoring sensors (see Table I).

TABLE I
REPRESENTATIVE SENSORS OF A LATERAL SENSOR SYSTEM

No.	Sensor	Description
1	Ozone sensor	O^3 detector that measures ozone concentration
2	Carbon Monoxide sensor	Detects the presence of CO gas
3	Hydrogen Sulfide sensor	Gas sensor for the measurement of H_2S
4	Volatile Organic Compounds sensor	Electrochemical sensor to monitor exhaust gases
5	Particulate Matter sensor	Monitors PM10 (particulate matter that has a diameter of less than 10 micrometers) and PM2.5 (particulate

No.	Sensor	Description
		matter that has a diameter of less than 2.5 micrometers) concentrations
6	Meteorological sensor	Measures climate and weather
7	Nitrogen Oxide sensor	NO_x sensor for smog and acid rain detection
8	Carbon Dioxide sensor	Measures CO_2 gas
9	Sulfur Dioxide sensor	Measure SO_2 gas
10	Non-Methane Hydrocarbons Compounds Gas Series Sensor	Measures NMHC GSS
11	Noise sensor	Sound sensor to analyze the surrounding ambient sounds within the audible frequency
12	Air Pressure sensor	Measures air pressure

B. *Wireless Sensor Network (WSN)*

The advantages of a Wireless Sensor Network (WS are that it is easy to maintain, utilizes less energy, and has high transmission distances [11]. The major elements of WSN are the sensor nodes and the base stations. Sensor nodes represent the sensing layer of a WSN and generate information (e.g., parameters) in the form of electrical signals. These signals are sent through the involved network system to base stations, which are the central processing and controlling units within the WSN [12].

Most of the sensor network routing techniques and sensing tasks require knowledge of location with high accuracy. It is common that a sensor node has a location ascertainment system [13].

C. *Deep learning module*

In this paper, the weather monitoring system of the lateral sensor utilized a deep learning module based upon a modified GAN technique. Deep learning techniques are well suited for handling large amounts of data and computationally intensive processes [14]. The word "deep" refers to the large number of hidden layers that comprise the neural network. One of deep learning techniques is GAN. GAN involves an unsupervised learning task in deep learning that automatically discovers and learns the patterns of input data. GAN frames the problem with two sub-models: the generator model $G(z)$ that creates random synthetic outputs and the discriminator model $D(x)$ that tries to determine whether information is true (generated from the domain) or false (generated). In other words, GAN learns to choose samples from a special distribution (i.e., "generative") by setting up a competition (i.e., "adversarial").

Formally, GAN is a structured probabilistic model with latent variables z and observed variables x. The generator $G(z)$ takes an input z from probability distribution $p(z)$, and the generated data is then fed back into the discriminator network $D(x)$. The discriminator network takes input from either the real data or from the generator's generated data and tries to predict whether the input is real or generated. It takes an input x from real data distribution $P_{data}(x)$ and then solves a binary classification problem giving an output in the scalar range 0 to 1 [15]. The function of the discriminator is optimized so as to assign the correct labels to both the training data as well as the data produced by the generator while the generator itself is trained to minimize and segue to the correct assignment of the discriminator [16]. For training, both generator and discriminator networks utilize the cost function. An exemplar GAN framework is shown in Figure 3 below, and the formulation of GAN is expressed in Equation (1) below.

$$min_G max_D V[D, G] = E_{x\sim P_{data}(x)}[\log D(x)] + E_{x\sim P_z(z)}[\log(1 - D(G(z))] \quad (1)$$

where x is the training data, z is the generated sample, p_{data} is the probability distribution of the training sample, and p_z is the probability distribution of generated sample.

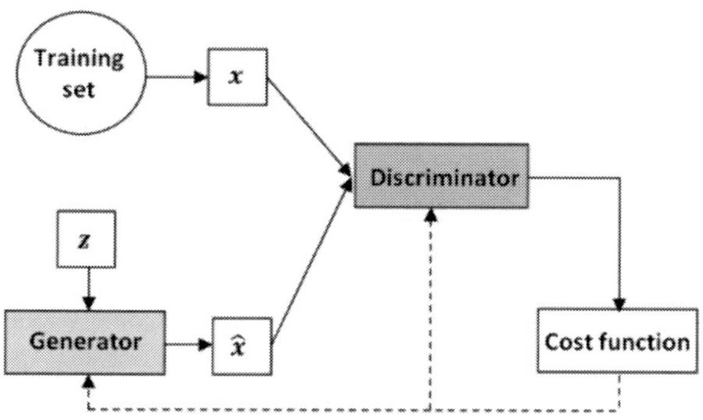

Figure 3. Generative Adversarial Network (GAN) Framework

V. WEATHER MONITORING SYSTEM BASED UPON A UNIQUE LATERAL SENSOR ARCHITECTURE

The discussed PMU real-time monitoring system was instantiated to help provide early warning to power engineers when a fault in the electrical grid is detected. The proposed system utilizes lateral sensors, which leverage a WSN architecture, GPS-based timestamping, ThingSpeak, a GAN deep learning system, and spider radar plots for data visualization analytics. The WSN is responsible for sending tsensor readings to the ThingSpeak cloud platform, via an IOT gateway, for real-time monitoring and analysis purposes. The parameters monitored include air temperature, barometric pressure, humidity precipitation, solar radiation, and wind. The lateral sensor connected directly to PMU and its GPS-based receiver for synchronized timestamping. In turn, the GAN system discerned pattern of the timestamped data so as to perform event correlation. The ensuing analysis was visualized, via Spider Radar Plots reflecting both weather sensor data and grid sensor data concurrently. This was invaluable, as weather data nicely serves to provide context reference for the grid sensor telemetry data. This is reflected in Figure 4 below.

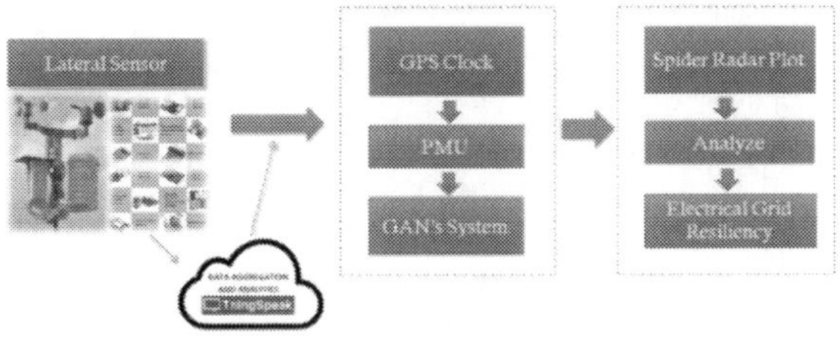

VI. IMPLEMENTATION OF LATERAL SENSORS

This study discusses the implementation of a lateral sensor predicated upon a weather monitoring system that utilizes a deep learning module, which is a modified GANN technique. The weather monitoring stations were installed at five distinct and disparate points within a sports complex, which supports international sporting events. The described lateral sensor utilized 3D-printing technology for the production of certain components of the overall sensor suite.

The 3D-printed lateral sensor was connected directly to a Global Positioning System (GPS)-based receiver so as to produce timestamps that could be correlated with the involved Phasor Measurement Unit (PMU) grid sensor that was utilized to detect disturbances within the electrical grid. The lateral sensor was equipped with a communications suite consisting of wifi and cellular capabilities.

The lateral sensor was found to exhibit a significant increase in performance over the sensor it replaced. The previous sensor was categorized as a "Automatic Waterlogger Telemetry" sensor. Basically, the sensor measured three main items: temperature, groundwater lever, and rainfall. Unlike the lateral sensor, the previous sensor system utilized telephone lines to collect the sensor data. Consequently, if the land-based communications network were interrupted, data could not be collected optimally. The other weakness of the previous sensor was the inability to find underlying data patterns within the data it collected and organized (please refer to Figure 5). This is caused by the absence of an interval that is set automatically according to the category (please refer to Figure 6).

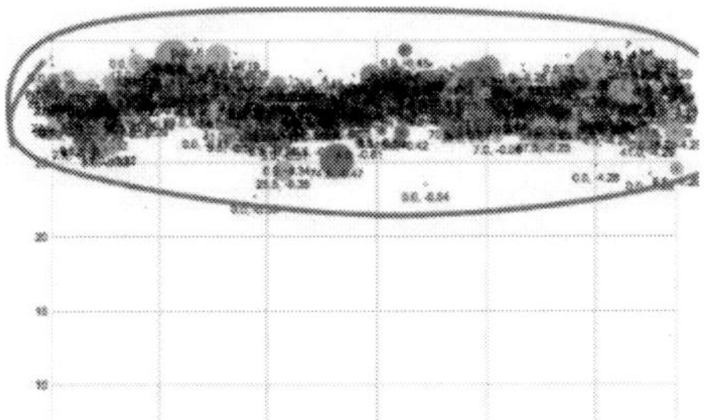

Figure 5. No Pattern is Ascertained from the Previous Sensor

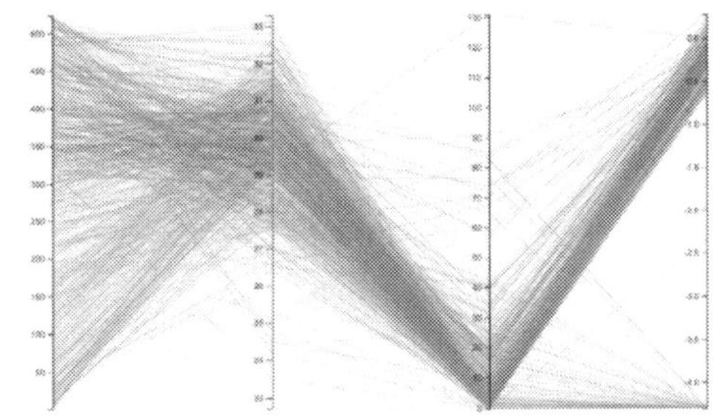

Figure 6. Parallel Coordinate System of Previous Sensor

After the installation of the lateral sensor, the data that was ultimately ingested, processed, analyzed, and correlated was much more accurate and had well-defined intervals as well as a deep learning module, which could readily analyze the data automatically and ascertain a specific pattern for each component (please refer to Figure 7). Overall, the lateral sensor detected more clusters than the previous sensor (please refer to Figure 8).

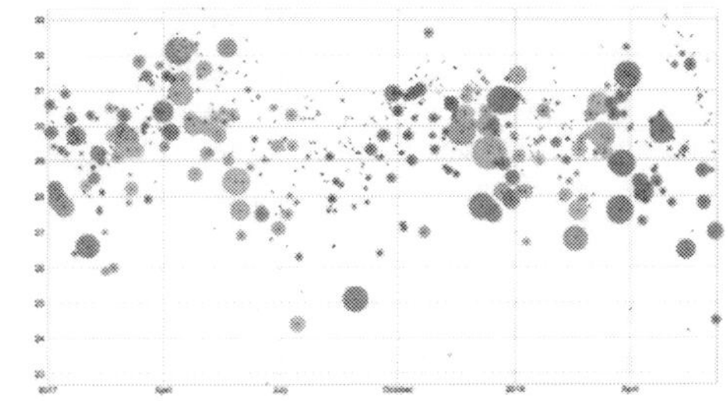

Figure 7. Data Analysis from the Deep Learning Module

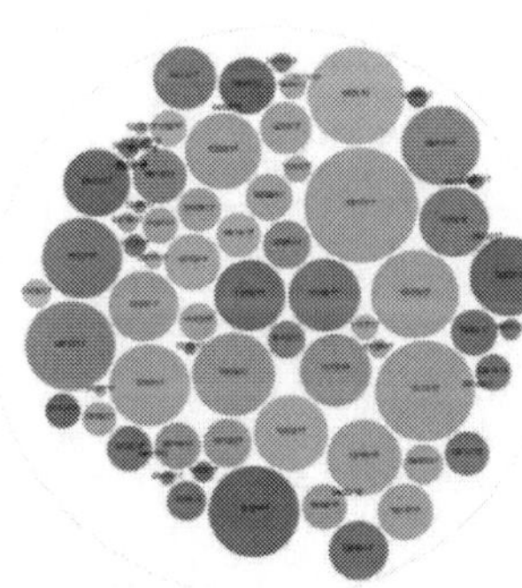

Figure 8. Data Analysis from the Deep Learning Module

VII. CONCLUSIONS AND FUTURE WORK

The results of this study demonstrated that the implementation of lateral sensors based upon a deep learning module, predicated upon a GAN, can be more robust in terms of leveraging operational data than previous monitoring paradigms. The deep learning module was able to discern underlying patterns within the ingested data as to indicators of an impending storm, which could cause communications interference, power surges, and power outages. Moreover, the deep learning module-based intelligent system was able to glean quite interesting trends for the particular locale where each particular sensor was located. It should be noted that the paucity of sensors in some areas and the far distances among the sensors posed some issues.

A number of future works are being planned to increase the application and suitability of this study. For the future works, we will examine techniques to facilitate the fine-tuning of lower resolution data. There is a wealth of algorithms for processing, among other things, remote sensing imagery. This can nicely complement and be correlated with the data from the lateral sensors described herein. In addition, to improve system performance, we can conduct a more comprehensive benchmarking of hybridizing techniques for processing IOT data and evaluate more advanced edge analytic paradigms for the lateral sensors. Moreover, Low Power Wide Area Network (LPWAN) technologies, such as ZigBee, Long Range Wide Area Network (LoRaWAN), and Narrow Band-Internet of Things (NB-IOT) can be utilized by the involved weather monitoring systems for a more robust communications network.

Acknowledgment

This research is supported by the Center for Research on IOT, Data Science, and Resiliency (CRIDR), an initiative of the Decision Engineering Analysis Laboratory (DEAL) and The International Center for Theoretical Physics (ICTP), a United Nations Educational, Scientific, and Cultural (UNESCO) Category 1 Institution.

References

[1] M. Panteli and P. Mancarella, "Influence of Extreme Weather and Climate Change on the Resilience of Power System: Impacts and Possible Mitigation Strategies," *Elsevier Electric Power System Research,* vol. 127, 2015, pp. 259-270.

[2] A. K. Prasetyo, "*Due to Bad Weather, the Network of PLN Kendal Had Been Disrupted,*" Radio Republik Indonesia, February 7, 2019. [Online]. Available from: http://rri.co.id/post/berita/633236/daerah/akibat_cuaca_buruk_jaringan_pln_kendal_sempat_terganggu.html/ [retrieved: June, 2019].

[3] A. Hussain, V. H. Bui, and H. M. Kim, "Microgrids as a Resilience and Strategies Used by Microgrids for Enhancing Resilience," *Elsevier Applied Energy,* vol. 240, 2019, pp. 56-72.

[4] K. S. Lone and S. D, Chavan, "Design and implementation of wireless smart intelligent network system using artificial intelligence for monitoring various weather parameters," 2018 Fourth International Conference on Computing Communication Control and Automation (ICCUBEA), Pune, India, 2018, pp. 1-4.

[5] T. Mochida et al., "Naming scheme using NLP machine learning method for network weather monitoring system based on ICN," 2017 20th International Symposium on Wireless Personal Multimedia Communications (WPMC), Bali, 2017, pp. 428-434.

[6] A, Durrani, M. Khurram, and H. R. Khan," Smart weather alert system for dwellers of different areas," 2019 16th International Bhurban Conference on Applied Sciences and Technology (IBCAST), Islamabad, Pakistan, 2019, pp. 333-339.

[7] I. Jamil, "Application and Composition Observing System of Automatic Weather Station and Power Grid," M. Eng. Thesis, Hohai University, 2013. [Online]. Available from: https://www.grin.com/document/266824/ June 17, 2019.

[8] H. Li, M. K. Ochani, H. Zhang, and L. Zhang, "Design of Micro-Automatic Weather Station for Modern Power Grid Based on STM32," *The Journal of Engineering,* vol. 2017, Iss. 13, November 2017, pp. 1629-1634.

[9] Z. W. Siew, C. H. Wong, S. E. Tan, H. P. Yoong, and K. T. K. Teo, "Design and Development of a Tablet Based Real Time Wireless Data Logger," in *2012 IEEE Global High-Tech Congress on Electronics,* 2012, pp. 111-116.

[10] S. S. Badhiye, P. N. Chatur, and B. V. Wakode, "Data Logger System: a Survey," *International Journal of Computer Technology and Electronics Engineering (IJCTEE),* 2011, pp. 24-26.

[11] C. Yawut and S. Kilaso, "A Wireless Sensor Network for Weather and Disaster Alarm Systems," in 2011 *International Conference on Information and Electronic Engineering IPCSIT Vol.6,* Singapore, pp. 155-159.

[12] D. Bandur, B. Jaksic, M. Bandur, and S. Jovic, "An Analysis of Energy Efficiency in Wireless Sensor Network Applied in Smart Agriculture," *Elsevier Computers and Electronic in Agriculture,* vol. 156, 2019, pp. 500-507.

[13] T. Kavitha and D. Sridharan, "Security Vulnerabilities in Wireless Sensor Network: a survey," *Journal of Information Assurance and Security,* vol. 5, 2010, pp. 031-044.

[14] F. Zantalis, G. Koulouras, S. Karabetsos, and D. Kandris, "A Review of Machine Learning and IoT in Smart Transportation," *MDPI Future Internet Journal,* vol. 11, 2019, pp. 1-23.

[15] K. Ganguly, "*Learning Generative Adversarial Networks: Next-Generation Deep Learning Simplified,*" Livery Place, UK: Packet Publishing Ltd., 2017.

[16] M. A. Ponti, L. S. F. Ribeiro, T. S. Nazare, T. Bui, and J. Collomosse, "Everything You Wanted to Know About Deep Learning for Computer Vision but Were Afraid to Ask," in 2017 *30th SIBGRAPI Conference on Graphics, Patterns, and Image Tutorials (SIBGRAPI-T),* Oct. 18, 2017, pp. 17-41.

Refinement Checker for Embedded Object Code Verification

Mohana Asha Latha Dubasi*, Sudarshan K. Srinivasan†, Sana Shuja‡, Zeyad A. Al-Odat†
*Configurable IP and Chassis Group, Intel Corporation, Hillsboro, OR, USA
†Electrical and Computer Engineering, North Dakota State University, Fargo, ND, USA
‡Department of Electrical Engineering, COMSATS University, Islamabad, Pakistan
Emails: *dubasi.asha@gmail.com, †sudarshan.srinivasan@ndsu.edu, ‡sanashuja@comsats.edu.pk, †zeyad.alodat@ndsu.edu

Abstract—**We present a formal verification methodology that automates the process to check for correctness of low-level real-time interrupt-driven object code programs. Automation helps in the verification of large-scale programs. Our methodology is based on the theory of Well-Founded Simulation (WFS) refinement, where both the formal specification and implementation are modeled as transition systems (TSs). WFS refinement is used as the notion of correctness and defines what it means for an implementation TS to satisfy its specification TS. WFS refinement has key features like stuttering and refinement maps. Stuttering aids in the abstraction of the state space of the implementation TS. Refinement map bridges the abstraction gap between the two systems. The efficiency and scalability of the approach is demonstrated on several device object code case studies.**

Keywords–embedded devices; formal verification; refinement-based verification; verification of object code, WFS refinement.

I. Introduction

Correctness of software used in safety-critical systems continues to be a critical challenge. For example, between the years 2005-2019, the U.S. Food and Drug Administration (FDA) [1] issued 52 medical device Class-1 recalls due to software issues. Class-1 recalls are applied when the use of the device is determined to cause serious adverse health consequences or death. It is now well-established that formal verification methods are a requirement to ensure software safety.

Our domain of interest is the verification of embedded software, which is largely what is used in control of medical devices, surgical robots, avionics equipment, etc. While many formal verification methods exist for reasoning about higher-level [2]–[4] software models and source code, there is currently a gap in the applicability of formal verification techniques that can efficiently scale and handle the low-level complexity of object code, which is the low-level code that is directly executed by the micro-controller embedded in the device used to perform control and other functions. It is definitely insufficient to apply formal verification only to source code as there are many sources of errors in the process of generating object code from source code that can compromise the safety of object code. The problem domain addressed in this work is the verification of embedded object code programs.

Typically, the objective of a formal verification methodology is to verify an implementation (the artifact to be verified, here, object code) against a specification (the artifact that captures the requirements to be satisfied by the implementation). Previously, we have developed a formal verification methodology for object code verification. The methodology is based on the theory of Well Founded Simulation (WFS) refinement [5]. In the context of WFS refinement, both the implementation and specification are modeled as Transition Systems (TSs: a mathematical modeling framework for code that is based on states of the program and transitions between states). WFS refinement essentially defines what it means for an implementation TS to correctly implement a specification TS. It has been explained in [5] how the low-level code is represented as an implementation TS and how it is the implementation of the high-level TS that acts as the specification.

The methodology was demonstrated by manually generating the required proof obligations for checking WFS refinement. However, this is insufficient for large programs. In this paper, we address this gap by proposing an algorithm for automatic WFS refinement checking optimized for object code verification. This algorithm checks for safety based on WFS refinement. Safety informally means that if the implementation makes progress, the result of that progress satisfies the specification requirements. The algorithm has been implemented and the automated tool flow has been applied to several object code control programs to demonstrate the effectiveness of the approach.

The rest of this paper is organized as follows. Related work is given in Section II. An overview of WFS refinement and related concepts is presented in Section III. The algorithm for safety verification is presented in Section IV. Results and conclusions are given in Sections V and VI, respectively.

II. Related Work

A large gap exists between high-level system models and the low-level actual code (*i.e.*, object-code), which is executed on the embedded device. The number of states and transitions in the high-level system models is typically less than 100, whereas, in the low-level models the number of states and transitions may be in the order of millions. Catching design bugs early in the design cycle of the system-level models is very useful. To bridge the gap between system-level models and actual code, model-driven approaches are adopted. Here, the high-level system models are represented as source code which is developed using platform-independent synthesis tools. The source code is then augmented with the device peripheral information and then compiled and assembled to generate the object code. During this process, numerous errors can creep into the object code compromising its safety. Our work is targeted at bridging the gap between the real-time high-level models and real-time object code and also ensuring that the object-code is safe.

There has been a lot of previous work in developing theory and optimized techniques for refinement based verification. A notion of refinement based on stuttering trace containment to verify the concurrent programs have been developed in [6]. A refinement-based testing method have been developed in [7], which checks for the functional correctness of hardware and low-level software. A characterization of stuttering bisimulation has been proposed in [8], here, stuttering bisimulation is a notion of correctness that defines what it means for two transition systems to be equivalent. Stuttering is accounted for in this work. An algorithm that checks equivalence between two transition systems which accounts for stuttering has been presented in [9]. Derrick *et al.* [10] have presented refinement checker for Z, which is a language that is used to express computer programs. These computer programs are system-level models. Gibson-Robinson *et al.* [11] have presented a refinement checker that check if one system is a refinement of the other, where both the systems are expressed as transition systems. This checker is used on software models like concurrent systems. However, these do not consider real-time interrupt-driven object code. In this work, we use WFS refinement which has a very nice property. The check is local, i.e., it is sufficient to reason about a single step of the implementation and specification. Since object code typically contains millions of transitions, this property can be exploited by reasoning about one transition at a time. This inturn reduces the verification burden. WFS refinement has two features: refinement-map and stuttering. Stuttering helps in abstraction techniques on the TS which reduces the state and path from exploding. Refinement-map bridges the gap between the system-level model and low-level object-code.

Etessami [12] and Dax *et al.* [13] have proposed specification languages for expressing stuttering-invariant properties, which are properties that do not distinguish behaviors of systems that differ only due to stuttering. The properties are verifiable using a model checker. Our work is complimentary to their approach, in that our goal is to exploit stuttering through abstractions to make verification more efficient and scalable.

Shaukat *et al.* [14] have presented an abstraction technique that helps to reduce the object code instructions statically. A number of tools exists [3] [4] [15] to verify real-time high-level models. UPPAAL-based tools like [16] [17] also exist. Al-Qtiemat *et al.* [18] have presented a methodology to generate the formal specification models from natural language requirements. The specification models, useful for refinement verification, are expressed as transition systems. These refinement approaches for real-time systems are targeted at high-level models and do not consider the use of refinement-map and stuttering. Since we incorporate refinement-map and stuttering, our approach is unique and applicable to the verification of low-level implementation such as object-code.

Jabeen *et al.* [19] have used the theory of refinement for the verification of FPGA-based stepper motor control using proof obligations. Manually developing proof obligations for real-time interrupt driven object code is time consuming because of the size of the instructions and may introduce human errors. In contrast, we address the automation of refinement-based verification.

The main goal of our work is verification of real-time object code against it's real-time high-level model. The real-time object code does not handle floating point numbers and C code. The goal is achieved by employing symbolic simulation on object code and this is a standard.

III. Background

WFS refinement is a notion of correctness which describes how an implementation system is correct with respect to its specification system. The specification is a mathematical model that describes the behavior of the system in high-level. Usually, the systems that are to be verified are represented as transition systems (TSs).

Definition 1. *[20] A transition system (TS) M is a 3-tuple $\langle S, R, L\rangle$, where S is the set of states, L is a labeling function that defines what is visible at each state and R is the transition relation that defines the state transitions. T is left-total.*

The formulation of the correctness properties and the completeness of the properties with respect to the input language is shown in [20].

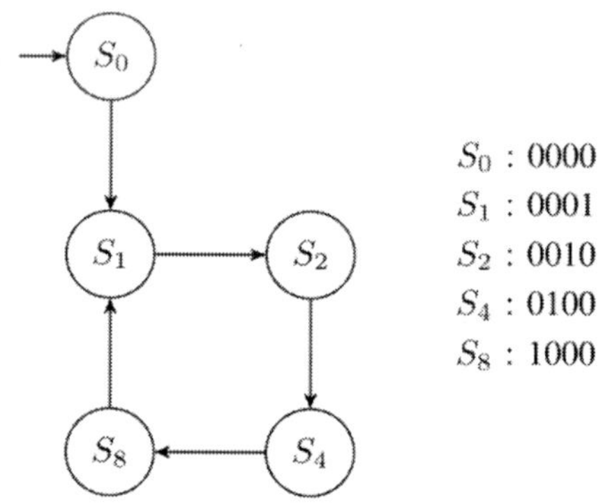

Figure 1. Stepper motor control specification TS

Stepper motor control is used as an example to describe object code verification using WFS refinement. Stepper motors are used in safety-critical applications which include medical devices like infusion pump, robotics like surgical robots, process control, etc. A stepper motor is a brushless DC electric motor, which contains 4 or 6 leads. Discrete rotation of the motor shaft is the result of current pulses that are applied to the motor. A repeating sequence of values such as 0001, 0010, 0100, 1000, 0001, etc, to the leads, cause the motor to spin. Software, that generates the above sequence, can be executed on the microcontroller which is interfaced to the motor. Figure 1 shows the specification TS (M_S) for 4-lead stepper motor control. The states are represented as S_0, S_1, S_2, S_4, S_8. The transition relation determines the direction of the shaft. The labeling function gives the values of the leads, which determine the state.

The implementation model for the stepper motor control would be the object code. This is obtained by generating a function for each instruction that describes the effect of the instruction on the state of the microcontroller. The state of the microcontroller is not as simple as the specification states (as shown in Figure 1), but consists of registers, flags, and memory of the microcontroller. The set of all such functions along with the initial state of the microcontroller defines the TS model of the implementation. The implementation model consists of millions of transitions because of the various possible values that the registers, flags, memory and special registers of the microcontroller can have during the execution of the object

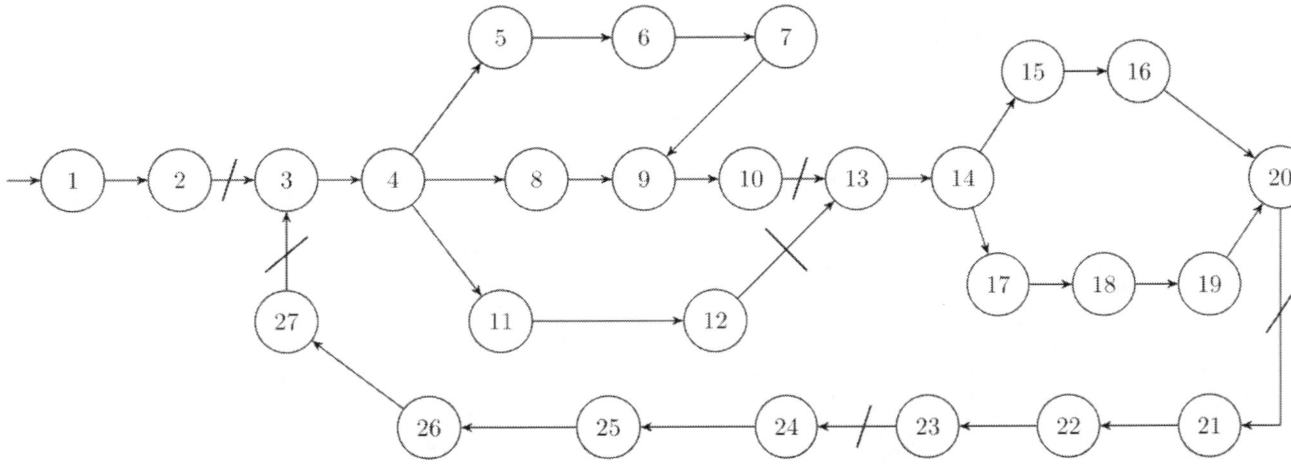

Figure 2. Stepper motor control implementation TS

code program. A details description about the implementation level can be found in [5]. An example of the implementation of the stepper motor control is shown in Figure 2 for the specification in Figure 1.

A detailed description of the WFS refinement is provided in [20]. Below is the definition of WFS

Definition 2. *[20] $B \subseteq S \times S$ is a WFS on TS $\mathcal{M} = \langle S, T, L \rangle$ iff:*

(1) $\langle \forall s, w \in S :: sBw \;\; :: \;\; L(s) = L(w) \rangle$; and

(2) There exists functions, $rankl : S \times S \times S \rightarrow \mathbb{N}$, $rankt : S \times S \rightarrow W$, such that $\langle W, \lessdot \rangle$ is well-founded, and $\langle \forall s, u, w \in S :: sBw \wedge sTu \;\; ::$
   - (a) $\langle \exists v :: wTv \wedge uBv \rangle \vee$
   - (b) $(uBw \wedge rankt(u, w) \lessdot rankt(s, w)) \vee$
   - (c) $\langle \exists v :: wTv :: sBv \wedge rankl(v, s, u) < rankl(w, s, u) \rangle \rangle$

Here, condition 1 states that for a WFS relation between s and w, they have to have the same labels. In condition 2, case (a) denotes the non-stuttering transition on the implementation side, case (b) denotes the stuttering on the specification side and case (c) denotes stuttering on the implementation side. Progress on the model is denoted by a non-stuttering transition where the states have different labels. Whereas in the case of stuttering transition the states have the same label. $rankt$ and $rankl$ are rank functions (discussed later).

When the specification and implementation systems are modeled as TSs, a step in the specification could correspond to multiple steps in the implementation. Hence, *stuttering is a phenomenon where multiple but finite transitions of implementation can match to the same specification transition.* WFS refinement has two key features: refinement-map and stuttering. Refinement-map, r, is a function that, given an implementation state, gives the corresponding specification state. A function like refinement-map is needed to bridge the abstraction gap between the implementation and specification systems.

The advantage of using WFS refinement is that it is sufficient to reason about single steps of the implementation and specification to check for correctness and find bugs. This makes WFS refinement applicable to deal with the complexity of object code. To avoid deadlock situations, in stuttering transitions, a witness function called rank is designed such that it decreases with each transition. In definition 2, two rank functions $rankt$ and $rankl$ corresponds to stuttering on specification and implementation side respectively.

Next is the definition of WFS refinement.

Definition 3. *[20] (WFS Refinement) Let $M = \langle S, T, L \rangle$, $M' = \langle S', T', L' \rangle$, and $r : S \rightarrow S'$. We say that M is a WFS refinement of M' with respect to refinement-map r, written $M \sqsubseteq_r M'$, if there exists a relation, B, such that $\langle \forall s \in S :: sBr(s) \rangle$ and B is a WFS on the TS $\langle S \uplus S', T \uplus T', \mathcal{L} \rangle$, where $\mathcal{L}(s) = L'(s)$ for s an S' state and $\mathcal{L}(s) = L'(r(s))$ otherwise.*

In the above definition, M and M' are the implementation and the specification TS respectively and r is the refinement-map function. If stuttering on the specification side is not considered, the definition can be interpreted as every implementation transition should either be a stuttering or a non-stuttering transition. If it can be proved that an implementation TS is a WFS refinement of a specification TS, then every behavior of the implementation is guaranteed to match a behavior of the specification. If the implementation TS has a label that does not match to its specification TS or a transition that does not match in the specification TS, then these situations correspond to a bug in the implementation model (here, $M \not\sqsubseteq_r M'$). If M is a WFS refinement of M' then, a state in M cannot be related to more than one state in M' (as the refinement-map is a function which is used to relate states of M to M').

From Figures 1 and 2, it is clear that the specification and the implementation do not have the same transition behavior. The refinement-map function for the stepper motor control program projects the 4-bits in a register in the microcontroller whose values controls the pins that are in turn connected to the leads of the stepper motor. The implementation TS (M_I) takes several steps (or transitions) to match a single transition of the specification TS. Here, once a refinement-map is constructed, in WFS refinement verification the idea is to look at each transition. For example, consider an implementation transition $\langle w, v\rangle$ where w, v belong to the set of implementation states. The transition should capture one of the following options. One option is that the implementation transition should match to the same specification state, i.e., $r(w) = r(v) = s$ where $r()$ is the refinement-map and s is a specification state. This option is called a stuttering implementation transition. The second option is that the implementation transition should match a specification transition, i.e., $r(w) = s$ and $r(v) = u$ where $\langle s, u\rangle$ is a transition in specification. This option is called a non-stuttering implementation transition. Using the refinement-map function on the implementation TS (Figure 2) gives that states 1 - 2 translate to state S_0 of the specification TS (Figure 1), states 3 -12 translate to S_1, states 13 - 20 to S_2, states 21 - 23 to S_4 and states 24 - 27 to S_8. The non-stuttering transition in implementation TS (M_I) (Figure 2) are shown with dashed arrows. For object code verification, stuttering rarely occurs on the specification side as the implementation typically has millions of transitions when compared to specification. Hence, case (b) of definition 2 is ignored.

In Figure 2, it can be noticed that many paths in the implementation lead to a specific non-stuttering step. All these finite paths are termed as stuttering segments. *Stuttering segment* π of $\langle w, v\rangle$ [5] where $\langle w, v\rangle$ is a non-stuttering transition can be described as a sequence of transitions in which $\langle w, v\rangle$ is preceded by zero to many stuttering transition(s) and another non-stuttering transition. The least length of a stuttering segment is one. This occurs when a non-stuttering step is preceded by another non-stuttering step. The stuttering segment then only consists of one transition, which is the non-stuttering step. Also, a non-stuttering step can have many stuttering segments. For the TS shown in Figure 2, the stuttering segments of $\langle 10, 13\rangle$ are:

1) $\{\langle 2,3\rangle, \langle 3,4\rangle, \langle 4,5\rangle, \langle 5,6\rangle, \langle 6,7\rangle, \langle 7,9\rangle, \langle 9,10\rangle, \langle 10,13\rangle\}$
2) $\{\langle 2,3\rangle, \langle 3,4\rangle, \langle 4,8\rangle, \langle 8,9\rangle, \langle 9,10\rangle, \langle 10,13\rangle\}$

Object code contains millions of transitions, hence, applying suitable abstraction techniques on the stuttering segments helps to deal with state explosion problem. This reduces the verification problem to analysis of stuttering segments.

IV. AUTOMATED WFS REFINEMENT FOR OBJECT-CODE

This section presents a procedure for automating WFS refinement for object code verification. According to definition 2, a TS satisfies WFS when either one of two conditions are satisfied by all transitions. Usually, in real-time object code verification, stuttering does not occur on the specification system. Hence, the refinement-based correctness formula can be reduced to,

$\langle \forall w \in$ object-code :: $v =$ object-code-step$(w) \wedge s = r(w)$
$\wedge\ u =$ SPEC-step(s) $\wedge\ \langle s, u\rangle \in$ SPEC then
(i) $r(v) = s$ (for stuttering transition) or
(ii) $r(v) = u$ (for a non-stuttering transition) $\rangle$ (1)

Here, once a refinement-map is constructed, in WFS refinement verification the idea is to look at each transition. Let $\langle w, v\rangle$ be an implementation transition where w, v belong to the set of implementation states. To satisfy the refinement-based correctness formula, the transition should capture one of the options of being either a stuttering transition or a non-stuttering transition. If the implementation transition shows a behavior that is neither stuttering nor non-stuttering then it indicates the presence of a bug in the implementation TS.

Typically object code (implementation TS (M_I)) consists of millions of transitions where a large portion of these transitions are of stuttering in nature. Hence, abstraction based on these stuttering transitions may be applied on the implementation TS (M_I). Applying stuttering abstractions on the TS makes the verification process faster and much more efficient.

1: **procedure** CHECKWFSREF(R_I, R_S, S_S, r)
2:   $R_U \leftarrow NULL$;
3:   **for** i $\leftarrow$ 1 **to** $|R_I|$ **do**
4:     $\langle w, v\rangle \leftarrow R_I[i]$;
5:     $s \leftarrow r(w)$;
6:     match $\leftarrow FALSE$;
7:     **if** $s \in S_S$ **then**
8:       **if** $r(v) = r(w)$ **then**
9:         match $\leftarrow TRUE$;
10:       **else**
11:         **for** j $\leftarrow$ 1 **to** $|R_S|$ **do**
12:           $\langle s, u\rangle \leftarrow R_S[j]$;
13:           **if** $r(v) = u$ **then**
14:             match $\leftarrow TRUE$;
15:             break;
16:     **if** match = $FALSE$ **then**
17:       $R_U \leftarrow R_U \cup \langle w, v\rangle$;
18:   return R_U;

Figure 3. Procedure for Checking WFS Refinement

The algorithm in Figure 3 presents a procedure that performs WFS refinement checking on the abstracted object code TS, which is the implementation TS. The inputs to the procedure include a list of transitions of R_I (implementation TS), a list of transitions of R_S (specification TS), a set of states of the specification (S_S) and the refinement-map r. R_U is the counterexample set, which the procedure will populate with implementation transitions that do not satisfy the WFS refinement correctness criteria (1). R_U is initially empty. The procedure iterates through each transition in R_I. The transitions of the implementation are of the form $\langle w, v\rangle$. Variable 's' is assigned to be the value refinement-map (w) (line 5). Predicate *match* is used to keep track of whether the implementation transition has found a matching specification transition, or is determined to be stuttering, or is neither.

A check is performed on 's' to see if it belongs to the set of states of specification (S_S). If 's' does not belong to S_S, then the w state has no corresponding specification state and therefore points to an error and the transition is added to R_U. When 's' exists in S_S, a check has to be performed on the implementation transition to see if it is a stuttering transition or a non-stuttering transition. In case the transition is a stuttering transition, the predicate *match* is set to true and the procedure proceeds to the next transition in the implementation.

If the transition is a non-stuttering transition, the procedure iterates through the specification transitions $\langle s, u \rangle$. If a u is found such that $r(v)$ is equal to u, then *match* is assigned true. Once a match is found, the procedure exits iterating through the specification transitions and moves on to the next implementation transition. If for a non-stuttering transition, $r(v)$ does not match with any u, then this points to an error in the implementation and the corresponding implementation transition is appended to R_U. When all the transitions of the implementation have been checked, the procedure ends by returning the list R_U (line 18).

The time complexity of this algorithm is $\mathcal{O}(|R_I||R_S|)$. The outer for loop has length of R_I passes. The if condition on line 7 has length of S_S passes. The inner for loop has length of R_S passes. The complexity of the algorithm is $|R_I| * (|S_S| + |R_S|)$. Usually, the number of transitions of the specification ($|R_S|$) is greater than equal to the number of states of specification ($|S_S|$) depending on the application. Hence, the overall time complexity is $\mathcal{O}(|R_I||R_S|)$.

V. RESULTS

Case Study - 1: The effectiveness of the algorithm presented in this paper were demonstrated on 22 different object code programs for stepper motor control. In this paper, three sequences of stepper motor control that uses 4 leads are used to develop the benchmarks. Double stepping sequence an be described as $\langle 0011 \rangle$, $\langle 0110 \rangle$, $\langle 1100 \rangle$, $\langle 1001 \rangle$, $\langle 0011 \rangle$, so on. Full stepping sequence an be described as $\langle 0001 \rangle$, $\langle 0010 \rangle$, $\langle 0100 \rangle$, $\langle 1000 \rangle$, $\langle 0001 \rangle$, so on. Half stepping sequence an be described as $\langle 0001 \rangle$, $\langle 0011 \rangle$, $\langle 0010 \rangle$, $\langle 0110 \rangle$, $\langle 0100 \rangle$, $\langle 1100 \rangle$, $\langle 1000 \rangle$, $\langle 1001 \rangle$, $\langle 0001 \rangle$, so on.

The programs were developed to run on an ARM Cortex-M3 based NXP LPC1768 [21] microcontroller. PORT 2 of the LPC1768 was used to connect the leads of the stepper motor using an electronic circuit. Repetitive Interrupt Timer (RIT) was used to generate interrupts at regular intervals of time in some of the benchmarks to implement the timing requirements for stepper motor control.

Table I shows the verification statistics for the benchmarks. The benchmark name indicates the type of control used. "Full", "Double", and "Half" indicate full stepping, double stepping, and half stepping were used, respectively. "RIT" indicates that the interrupts were generated by Repetitive Interrupt Timer (RIT) to implement the timing delays for the motor control. "noRIT" indicates that instead of the RIT timer, code was to implement timing delays. "clock" and "anti" indicate that the motor was controlled clockwise and anti-clockwise, respectively. The table gives statistics for both correct and buggy versions of the controllers. "FuncBug" indicate that the object code error was a functional error. Column 3 gives the number of transitions of the object code TS. Column 4 gives the number of transitions in the abstract TS (which is generated by applying suitable abstraction techniques). Column 5 gives the time taken to perform WFS refinement.

Case Study - 2: The effectiveness of the algorithm presented in this paper were also demonstrated on industrial example, an infusion pump. An infusion pump is a medical device that can give controlled dosage of medications, like opioids,

TABLE I. VERIFICATION STATISTICS

S.No	Object Code Benchmarks	# of Trans. of MM_I [million]	# of Trans. of of Abstract MM^a	WFS Verifi. Time [millisec]
1	Full-RIT-clock	2.5	10	3
2	Full-RIT-anti	2.5	10	3
3	Double-RIT-clock	2.5	10	4
4	Double-RIT-anti	2.5	10	3
5	Half-RIT-clock	4.5	18	4
6	Half-RIT-anti	4.5	18	3
7	Full-noRIT-clock	82.5	10	3
8	Full-noRIT-anti	82.5	10	4
9	Double-noRIT-clock	82.5	10	4
10	Double-noRIT-anti	82.5	10	6
11	Half-noRIT-clock	148.5	18	3
12	Half-noRIT-anti	148.5	18	5
13	FuncBug-Full -RIT-clock	2.5	10	5§
14	FuncBug-Full -RIT-anti	2.5	10	3§
15	FuncBug-Double -RIT-clock	2.5	10	4§
16	FuncBug-Double -RIT-anti	2.5	10	4§
17	FuncBug-Half -RIT-clock	4.5	18	5§
18	FuncBug-Half -RIT-anti	4.5	18	3§
19	FuncBug-Full -noRIT-clock	99	20	3§
20	FuncBug-Full -noRIT-anti	99	20	3§
21	FuncBug-Double -noRIT-clock	82.5	10	4§
22	FuncBug-Double -noRIT-anti	82.5	10	3§

§ indicates the time taken to generate counterexample

insulin, etc, or nutrients into the patients's circulatory system intravenously.

The program was developed for Alaris Medley 8100 LVP module infusion pump [22], [23] for our experiments. Pulse width modulation technique is used by this pump to control the dosage delivered. The pulse width modulation control code was implemented for the Alaris pump on an ARM Cortex M3 based LPC 1768 micro-controller. The pump was interfaced to the micro-controller so that our code can control the pump. The formal specifications for the pump control software was developed based on the requirements in [24].

TABLE II. VERIFICATION STATISTICS FOR INFUSION PUMP CONTROLLER

S.No	Object Code Benchmarks	# of Trans. of MM_I [million]	WFS Verifi. Time [millisec] of Abstract MM^a
1	IPC	24.3	3
2	IPC-FuncBug1	20.25	2§
3	IPC-FuncBug2	24.3	7§
4	IPC-FuncBug3	27	5§

§ indicates the time taken to generate counterexample

Table II shows the verification statistics for the infusion pump control case study. The transition system of the pump's control code had about 24.3 million transitions. The table gives statistics for both correct and buggy versions of the controller. "FuncBug" indicate that the object code error was a functional error. Column 3 gives the number of transitions of the object code TS. Column 4 gives the time taken to perform WFS refinement.

The code is not small snippets, but a working infusion pump setup where the code is used to run the infusion pump. It has been demonstrated that our method works with control code. In general, code can be arbitrarily large, we have not explored the scalability of our approach to problems in the order of 100K lines of code.

For case studies 1 and 2, the verification experiments were performed on an Intel Core i7 3.1 GHz processor with 8GB memory. Using suitable abstraction on the stuttering segments, the number of transitions in the implementation TS have been reduced from hundred of millions to less than 50 transitions. Because of this huge reduction in the size of the state space, it took less than a second to perform WFS refinement checking on the abstracted TS.

VI. Conclusion

The effectiveness of the refinement checker has been demonstrated from the verification results. Applying suitable abstraction on the stuttering segments reduces the number of transitions in the implementation TS for all the benchmarks. The reduced size of the implementation TS enables detecting and correcting the errors very easily since the verification tools are often used multiple times in practice.

This paper presents only the safety verification technique. It is intended to extend this work further by including techniques to detect deadlock errors. If the code is not making progress with respect to the specification, then such a behavior is known as deadlock.

Acknowledgment

This publication was funded by a grant from the United States Government and the generous support of the American people through the United States Department of State and the United States Agency for International Development (USAID) under the Pakistan - U.S. Science & Technology Cooperation Program. The contents do not necessarily reflect the views of the United States Government.

References

[1] US Food and Drug Administration (FDA), "Medical device recalls," https://www.accessdata.fda.gov/scripts/cdrh/cfdocs/cfRES/res.cfm, 2019, last accessed: April 2019.

[2] K. G. Larsen, P. Pettersson, and W. Yi, "Uppaal in a nutshell," STTT, vol. 1, no. 1-2, 1997, pp. 134–152.

[3] M. Bozga and et al., "Kronos: A model-checking tool for real-time systems (tool-presentation for ftrtft '98)," in Formal Techniques in Real-Time and Fault-Tolerant Systems, 5th International Symposium, FTRTFT'98, Lyngby, Denmark, September 14-18, 1998, Proceedings, ser. Lecture Notes in Computer Science, A. P. Ravn and H. Rischel, Eds., vol. 1486. Springer, 1998, pp. 298–302.

[4] J. C. Godskesen, K. G. Larsen, and A. Skou, "Automatic verification of real-time systems using epsilon," in Protocol Specification, Testing and Verification XIV, Proceedings of the Fourteenth IFIP WG6.1 International Symposium on Protocol Specification, Testing and Verification, Vancouver, BC, Canada, 1994, ser. IFIP Conference Proceedings, S. T. Vuong and S. T. Chanson, Eds., vol. 1. Chapman & Hall, 1994, pp. 323–330.

[5] M. A. L. Dubasi, S. K. Srinivasan, and V. Wijayasekara, "Timed refinement for verification of real-time object code programs," in Verified Software: Theories, Tools and Experiments - 6th International Conference, VSTTE 2014, Vienna, Austria, July 17-18, 2014, Revised Selected Papers, ser. Lecture Notes in Computer Science, D. Giannakopoulou and D. Kroening, Eds., vol. 8471. Springer, 2014, pp. 252–269.

[6] S. Ray and R. Sumners, "Specification and verification of concurrent programs through refinements," J. Autom. Reasoning, vol. 51, no. 3, 2013, pp. 241–280.

[7] M. Jain and P. Manolios, "An efficient runtime validation framework based on the theory of refinement," CoRR, vol. abs/1703.05317, 2017.

[8] K. S. Namjoshi, "A simple characterization of stuttering bisimulation," in Foundations of Software Technology and Theoretical Computer Science, 17th Conference, Kharagpur, India, December 18-20, 1997, Proceedings, 1997, pp. 284–296.

[9] J. F. Groote and A. Wijs, "An o(m\log n) algorithm for stuttering equivalence and branching bisimulation," in Tools and Algorithms for the Construction and Analysis of Systems - 22nd International Conference, TACAS 2016, Held as Part of the European Joint Conferences on Theory and Practice of Software, ETAPS 2016, Eindhoven, The Netherlands, April 2-8, 2016, Proceedings, ser. Lecture Notes in Computer Science, M. Chechik and J. Raskin, Eds., vol. 9636. Springer, 2016, pp. 607–624.

[10] J. Derrick, S. North, and A. J. H. Simons, "Building a refinement checker for Z," ser. EPTCS, J. Derrick, E. A. Boiten, and S. Reeves, Eds., vol. 55, 2011, pp. 37–52.

[11] T. Gibson-Robinson, P. J. Armstrong, A. Boulgakov, and A. W. Roscoe, "FDR3: a parallel refinement checker for CSP," STTT, vol. 18, no. 2, 2016, pp. 149–167.

[12] K. Etessami, "Stutter-invariant languages, omega-automata, and temporal logic," in Computer Aided Verification, 11th International Conference, CAV '99, Trento, Italy, July 6-10, 1999, Proceedings, 1999, pp. 236–248.

[13] C. Dax, F. Klaedtke, and S. Leue, "Specification languages for stutter-invariant regular properties," in Automated Technology for Verification and Analysis, 7th International Symposium, ATVA 2009, Macao, China, October 14-16, 2009. Proceedings, ser. Lecture Notes in Computer Science, Z. Liu and A. P. Ravn, Eds., vol. 5799. Springer, 2009, pp. 244–254.

[14] N. Shaukat, S. Shuja, S. K. Srinivasan, S. Jabeen, and M. A. L. Dubasi, "Static stuttering abstraction for object code verification," in CYBER 2018, The Third International Conference on Cyber-Technologies and Cyber-Systems, Athens, Greece. IARIA, Nov 2018, pp. 102–106.

[15] G. Behrmann, A. David, K. G. Larsen, P. Pettersson, and W. Yi, "Developing UPPAAL over 15 years," Softw., Pract. Exper., vol. 41, no. 2, 2011, pp. 133–142.

[16] A. David, K. G. Larsen, A. Legay, U. Nyman, and A. Wasowski, "Timed I/O automata: a complete specification theory for real-time systems," in Proceedings of the 13th ACM International Conference on Hybrid Systems: Computation and Control, HSCC 2010, Stockholm, Sweden, April 12-15, 2010, K. H. Johansson and W. Yi, Eds. ACM, 2010, pp. 91–100.

[17] A. Boudjadar, J. Bodeveix, and M. Filali, "Compositional refinement for real-time systems with priorities," in 19th International Symposium on Temporal Representation and Reasoning, TIME 2012, Leicester, United Kingdom, September 12-14, 2012, B. C. Moszkowski, M. Reynolds, and P. Terenziani, Eds. IEEE Computer Society, 2012, pp. 57–64.

[18] E. Al-Qtiemat, S. K. Srinivasan, M. A. L. Dubasi, and S. Shuja, "A methodology for synthesizing formal specification models from requirements for refinement-based object code verification," in CYBER 2018, The Third International Conference on Cyber-Technologies and Cyber-Systems, Athens, Greece. IARIA, Nov 2018, pp. 94–101.

[19] S. Jabeen, S. K. Srinivasan, S. Shuja, and M. A. L. Dubasi, "A formal verification methodology for fpga-based stepper motor control," Embedded Systems Letters, vol. 7, no. 3, 2015, pp. 85–88.

[20] P. Manolios, "Mechanical verification of reactive systems," Ph.D. dissertation, University of Texas at Austin, 2001.

[21] "Keil cortex-m evaluation board comparison," http://www.keil.com/arm/boards/cortexm.asp, last accessed: April 2019.

[22] CareFusion, Alaris PC Unit, Alaris Pump Module, Technical Service Manual, CareFusion, 2010.

[23] ALARIS Medical Systems, Inc., Directions for use. Pump Module, 8100 series, ALARIS Medical Systems, Inc., 2004.

[24] Y. Zhang, R. Jetley, P. L. Jones, and *et al.*, "Generic safety requirements for developing safe insulin pump software," Journal of Diabetes Science and Technology, vol. 5, no. 6, 11 2011, pp. 1403–1419.

Comparisons of Forensic Tools to Recover Ephemeral Data from iOS Apps Used for Cyberbullying

Aimee Chamberlain and M A Hannan Bin Azhar
School of Engineering, Technology and Design
Canterbury Christ Church University
Canterbury, United Kingdom
e-mail: aimee.chamberlain@yahoo.co.uk; hannan.azhar@canterbury.ac.uk

***Abstract*—Ephemeral applications are growing increasingly popular on the digital mobile market. However, they are not always used with good intentions. Criminals may see a gateway into private communication with each other through this transient application data. This could negatively impact criminal court cases for evidence, or civil matters, such as cyberbullying where evidence could be useful. To find out if messages from such applications can indeed be recovered or not, a forensic examination of the device would be required by the law enforcement authority. This paper reports forensically sound recovery of evidential data, in relation to cyberbullying, from three popular ephemeral applications using an iOS mobile device. Examinations were performed to evaluate two popular mobile forensic tools, Oxygen and MOBILedit, using parameters from the National Institute of Standards and Technology's (NIST) mobile tool test assertions and test plan. The results from the investigation recovered various artefacts from the mobile device as well as revealing some interesting forensic data related to cyberbullying.**

Keywords*— *Mobile forensics; NIST measurements; Oxygen Forensics; MOBILedit forensic; Ephemeral APPS; Cyberbullying.

I. INTRODUCTION

Mobile phones are an essential part of modern-day life. According to the Global System for Mobile Communications [1], there were 5 billion mobile users in the world by the second quarter of 2017, with a prediction that another 620 million people will become mobile phone users by 2020, together that would account for almost three quarters of the world population. Due to the increasing popularity in mobile phones, there is naturally an increasing concern over mobile security and how safe communication between individuals or groups is.

Criminals usually use mobile phones to communicate with each other. They may use regular chatting applications, but there is a growing opportunity within the mobile application market for criminals to use ephemeral applications, which allow users to send messages/multimedia, etc., to each other with the messages only lasting for a certain period of time [2]. Barker [3] reported that criminals are moving away from dark web interactions and on to ephemeral applications, such as WhatsApp, Snapchat, Telegram, etc. Data in these applications is known to delete itself which is prime for criminal communications. For example, Snapchat allows users to send 'Snaps' to each other containing pictures, which are deleted once the recipient user closes the message [4].

Since ephemeral applications only hold data for a certain period of time, an individual or group could easily send a hateful message to somebody and there would be no evidence of it. Moreover, more serious issues can be hidden through these types of applications, such as self-harm, and sexting. Charteris et al. [5] reported that out of 276 primary and secondary school professional staff that observed the application 'Snapchat' [6] being used at school, a total percentage of 26.9% of professionals reported Snapchat was used for bullying/harassment, sending inappropriate images/text, sexting, and self-harm. The results were from a viewpoint of teachers, counsellors, etc., which means there may have been a lot more students suffering from the same issues, but they did not come forward. According to Cook [6], 11% parents reported their children had been a victim of cyberbullying in 2011, an increase followed of 15% in 2016, and another increase followed of 18% in 2018. It appears that as the cyber world evolves and develops, the rate of cyberbullying increases.

With all the opportunities for new crimes to be committed through growing technology, it is crucial to ensure that the law enforcement agencies have the appropriate software and methods to deal with these crimes. There is a gap in literature in relation to comparisons of tools to recover evidential data, specifically focusing on ephemeral applications relating to cyberbullying. This paper will attempt to fill this gap by comparing two popular forensics tools, Oxygen [7] and MOBILedit [8] in recovering ephemeral data from popular mobile apps used for cyberbullying. Furthermore, this paper focuses on an iOS device, as there is already a large body of research on forensic investigations into Android devices [4][9][10].

The remainder of the paper will be organised as follows: Section 2 will discuss existing research in relation to mobile phone forensics, including forensic tools and ephemeral data. The methodology used during the analysis process will be discussed in Section 3, including logical acquisition and analysis of mobile forensic data and tool comparisons. Section 4 will cover the results of the analysis. Finally, Section 5 will conclude the paper and include possible future work.

II. LITERATURE REVIEW

There is already a vast amount of research on mobile forensics in general, which includes comparing forensic tools, performing different types of mobile acquisitions and focusing on particular pieces of data within the mobile device. There is also work completed on non-ephemeral applications, such as Ovens et al. [11] conducted a forensic analysis on Kik Messenger on iOS. While there has been similar studies in a wide range of apps, the focus of this review is to highlight the findings in extraction of artefacts from the apps which are specifically ephemeral.

Al-Hadadi et al. [12] forensically investigated a mobile device, an iPhone 4 running iOS 5.0.1 previously jailbroken by the mobile phone owner, as a part of a real legal case. The case was from the Sultanate of Oman, and the aim of the investigation was to forensically examine the iPhone to determine if the device had been hacked and sent messages over the application 'WhatsApp' out to the owner's contact list. In the investigation, the ISP report of the device was observed and examined, and two forensic tools were used to extract and examine mobile data, one tool being the Universal Forensic Extraction Device's (UFED) physical analyser Cellebrite, and the other being the Oxygen Forensic Suite. The credibility of both tools is highly regarded by computer forensic experts. Results showed that Cellebrite recovered more forensic evidence than Oxygen, including call log artefacts, SMS messages, web history, etc.

Azhar et al. [13] conducted a forensic experiment of two ephemeral messaging applications: Telegram and Wickr using Autopsy and logically acquiring a database file, as well as performing a RAM dump. Results showed that the application 'Wickr' stored received messages in encrypted ".wic" files. The RAM dump recovered username information from Wickr and artefacts from Telegram. This investigation compared ephemeral applications on Android platforms. The investigation more looked into packages and files within the application itself instead of using a mobile forensic tool. Performing similar investigatory analysis on an iOS platform would be an interesting study as a future work.

Umar et al. [14] tested three different forensic tools on a Samsung Galaxy S4 GT-I9500 using the application WhatsApp. The tools included WhatsApp DB/Key Extractor (open source), Belkasoft Evidence (trial version and proprietary) and Oxygen Forensic (proprietary). The forensic tools were tested against the NIST Mobile Device Tool Test Assertions and Test Plan ver. 2. Researchers in [14] forensically tested the mobile device using the tools, each either completed a logical or physical acquisition. WhatsApp DB/Key extractor performed a logical acquisition and Belkasoft Evidence was used alongside it to open the result from the acquisition. The results showed that the WhatsApp contact list was recovered, as well as a text message artefact including the sender and recipient of the message, as well as the time stamp. Belkasoft Evidence performed a logical acquisition, the acquisition was unable to recover the WhatsApp contact list but found multimedia and document artefacts. Oxygen forensic could perform both physical and logical acquisition. Oxygen forensic recovered the WhatsApp contact list as well as a text message artefact including the sender and recipient information, content of the message and a time stamp.

As can be seen from this brief review of the literature, there is a significant gap in extraction of ephemeral artefacts on iOS platforms and there has not been any research reported primarily focusses on artefacts related to cyberbullying. This paper will contribute to investigate in these aspects to fill the gap.

III. METHODOLOGY

The focus of the investigation was recovering data from ephemeral applications due to their uses by Internet "trolls" [15], also known as digital bullies. This paper is going to investigate how much data can be recovered from these types of applications from two different tools as listed in Table 1; the mobile device and applications are listed in Table 2.

TABLE I. FORENSIC TOOLS

Name	Forensic tools	
	Cost	*Version*
Oxygen Forensic Detective Enterprise	APPROX £1,100-£2000	10.3.0.100
MOBILedit Forensic Express	APPROX £76 for one mobile device, £1,150 for full license	6.1.0.15480

TABLE II. MOBILE DEVICE AND APPLICATIONS

Mobile used	Ephemeral Apps	
	App Name	*Version*
iPhone 6s NOT-JAILBROKEN	Snapchat	10.55.1
	Cyberdust	5.6.1.1049
	Confide	8.3.1

The investigation was carried out according to the four good practice guidelines of the Association of Chief Police Officers (ACPO) [16]. For example, the third principle of the guidelines state that an audit trail should be recorded throughout the investigation in a manner which a third party could recreate the steps taken in the investigation.

A. Ephemeral Apps for Cyberbullying

The three applications as listed in Table 2 were all chosen for different reasons. Snapchat is one of the most popular ephemeral applications. According to Omnicore [17], more than 25% of mobile phone users are on Snapchat, with 71% of the users being aged between 17 to 24. For this application, three contacts were added and two of those contacts had communication sending picture messages, as well as written messages back and forth. Ten picture messages were exchanged, three written messages were marked as 'saved', while one of other messages was not saved. The username for the mobile owner was 'aimee_test19'. For the Snapchat, the ephemeral artefacts were the picture messages for the investigation.

The next application, Cyberdust, was chosen due to the difference in its ephemeral features compared to other apps. The encrypted messages within the app delete themselves between users after 24 hours of it being sent [18]. The application also has other uses, such as a "watchdog" feature where users can check their email addresses to see if any data breaches have been completed. Another feature is known as "Stealth Search", where users can search the Internet privately, supposedly without any cookie trackers or trace remnants. This application was selected for the investigation as it creates ephemeral data, and it has many different functions, which allows the user to use the application for multi-purpose functions. For the investigation's purpose, only the secure messaging feature was used, where messages were encrypted and deleted after 24 hours. A total of eleven messages were exchanged. Two of the messages were picture messages. The username for the mobile owner was linked directly to the mobile number.

The final application, Confide [19], was chosen because of its end to end message encryption between users. Furthermore, the application does not allow screenshots to be taken from users. The messages between users are self-destructing once the recipient has read the message, and the user can only read the message by swiping down on the message on the screen to view it. Furthermore, the user can adjust the settings to change the ephemeral nature of the messages, if a message is not opened within 48 hours, the content of the message will delete itself regardless. All of these features would create an interesting investigation, as the application advertises very strong messaging security, so it would be intriguing to test the security through this forensic investigation. For the investigation purpose, this application was used to test the message encryption and data recovery from the application. A total of seven messages were exchanged. Like Cyberdust, here also the username for the mobile owner was linked directly to the mobile number.

B. *Forensic Tools*

Forensic tools used in the investigation were Oxygen Forensic Detective Enterprise [7] and MOBILedit Forensic Express [8]. Both tools have reputations to be able to forensically examine mobile devices and are widely used by professional investigators [20]. Oxygen is a more well used tool within Law enforcement, military operations and professional investigatory cases, with uses of the tool in over 100 countries [7]. MOBILedit Forensic is also popular, but it is used a little less, it is used in approximately 70 countries and is used in military investigations and law enforcement [8]. The mobile device was extracted on both tools using logical acquisition and then the analysis was conducted in forensic workstations. Oxygen Forensic Detective Enterprise was running on Windows 7 Enterprise version 6.1.7601. The MOBILedit was running on a Windows 10 Home version 10.0.17134. Both tools were tested against NIST test assertions from 'MDT-CA-01' to 'MDT-CA-09' as detailed in [21]. Throughout the investigation, nine NIST test assertions were closely followed and the forensic tools were tested according to the measurements.

Oxygen Forensic outputs a GUI home page which displays the kinds of information that has been extracted, allowing an investigator to navigate around the mobile contents easily. The 'Applications' tile was selected to investigate the three Ephemeral applications mentioned previously, including any data the applications held of the user, conversation data, etc. Once the 'Applications' tile was examined, the 'Passwords' tile was selected and examined. This was to see if any passwords were stored within the three ephemeral applications to test the general security of the applications.

The same extraction process was completed in MOBILedit Forensic Express [8]. Unlike Oxygen, MOBILedit outputs the mobile device extraction into a report. However, there was a contents page produced within the report. There was also a separate section for both 'Applications' and 'Passwords' similarly to Oxygen. Both of those sections were examined,.

In the next stage of the examination, a general keyword search was made within the Oxygen and MOBILedit in search for artefacts. The keywords searched included 'Snapchat', 'Dust' and 'Confide'. This was completed in case any other information relating to the applications was extracted and missed previously. The application names were used for the searches, as in a real-life scenario the digital forensic investigator may not know the contents of the messages, and may be left with no other search options other than the application names.

IV. RESULTS

The results analyse the key findings from the methodology. The results are presented with regards to the four categories: Oxygen Forensic Detective Enterprise; MOBILedit Forensic Express, Evaluation of findings and NIST measurements.

A. *Oxygen Forensic Detective Enterprise*

A list of applications on the mobile device was found in the 'Applications' tile using Oxygen. Snapchat was the first application to be investigated [4]. Figure 1 shows Snapchat data. Four areas were highlighted within the figure. This included the login user name 'aimee_test19', that was used to log into Snapchat and detection of an 'offensive words' used in messages. The next highlighted section was the evidence that there was messaging communication between a user 'aimee_test19' and another user. The final highlighted section shows a chat deletion message count with a value of one, which indicates that a message was deleted by the user, which was a true case. A general search of the extracted mobile device was conducted using the search feature on Oxygen Forensics. The findings included general application data within the file browser, such as the Snapchat library, stickers, etc.

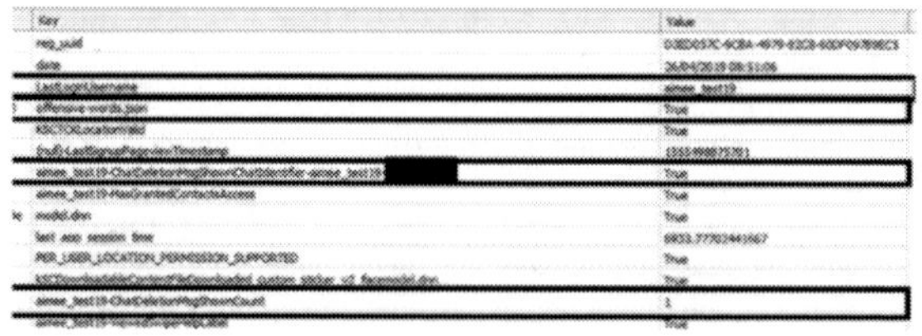

Figure 1. Snapchat artefacts in Oxygen.

The next application investigate was Cyberdust [18]. Previously, Snapchat appeared in the 'Applications' tile on Oxygen displaying itself as a normal application. However, with Cyberdust only the application folder was recognised, and Cyberdust was not acknowledged as a full application like Snapchat, however the folder proved there was evidence of an application called Cyberdust being present on the mobile device. This could be because the application did not require a username and password to log in, rather the user's mobile number instead, which therefore meant the phone did not identify it as an application in the same way as Snapchat, where it requires a username and password. Figure 2 shows results from a general search of the word 'dust'.

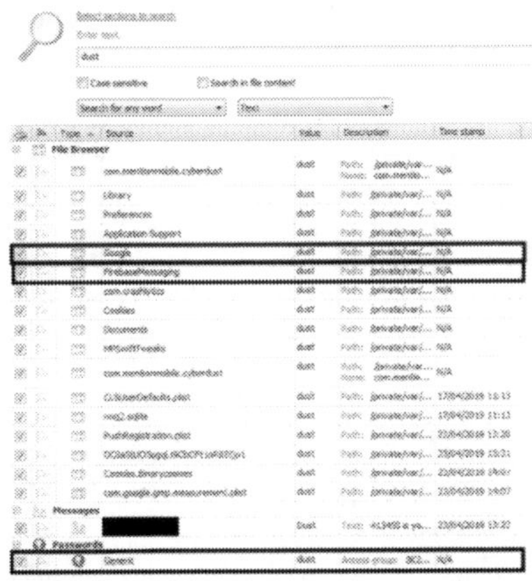

Figure 2. Cyberdust general search Oxygen

The results from the file browser show private folder pathway names. This acknowledges the existence of the application itself within the mobile device, but it does not have definitive messages between two users. However, as Figure 2 highlights, both 'Google' and 'FireBaseMessaging' were in the private folders. FireBase, formerly known as google cloud messaging, is a cross-platform cloud solution for messaging [22]. This means that the data from the application could be deleted on the mobile device itself, but data may be uploaded elsewhere in the cloud and therefore access could be granted through that, but this needs to be explored further. For this investigation however, it was proven that the application, Cyberdust, was a messaging application, but there was no evidence of messages between two users. Additionally, Figure 2 highlights a 'Generic' password in the search. This shows that the application has stored a password, most likely the user's password, but has encrypted it with a token.

Figure 3. Confide general search Oxygen.

The last application investigated was Confide [19]. Similarly, to Cyberdust, there was little evidence to prove the application Confide existed under the 'Applications' tile. Unlike Snapchat, the only data Confide showed within the Applications tile was a private pathway. Figure 3 shows results from a general search of the word 'Confide'. The results showed general application files in private folders within the file browser. The number '+17752040571' in Figure 3 is a verification text message from the application itself to verify the user's account. Even though there was evidence that the Confide was installed in the phone, no application specific communication between users or user log in details was recovered. There were however, four passwords that were linked to the application Confide. Three being generic and one being an Internet password. The passwords could have been the user login password, but the passwords were encrypted. Therefore, the passwords weren't visible and were secure for the user's account.

B. MOBILedit Forensic Express

The next part of the investigation was to examine the mobile device and the applications under examination using MOBILedit Forensic Express. Once the report generated from MOBILedit, the next step in the investigation was to navigate to the applications section of the report focusing on Snapchat, Cyberdust and Confide. The first application investigated was Snapchat [4]. Figure 4 shows the accounts used to log in to Snapchat and the list of contacts and the pathways to "plist", where the contact's information was stored.

Figure 4. Snapchat data in MOBILedit.

Figure 4 proves that the mobile device was linked to a Snapchat account with the username 'aimee_test19', and both victim and suspect were likely to had communication as the names (username blackened out) appeared on the contact log of the phone. This finding would let further interrogation to the suspect during the investigation. Similarly to Oxygen, MOBILedit also found general application artefacts under private folders, but nothing significant that contributed to the investigation.

The next application that was looked at within MOBILedit was Cyberdust [18]. Figure 5 shows Cyberdust pplication data and the account the mobile device linked to the application. As Figure 5 displays, one account was evidently linked from the mobile device to the application. This proves the mobile user did use the application and also had an account. However, there were no account details recovered from that section of the report and unlike Snapchat, no contacts were found either, when the user did in fact have one contact on the application. However, this may be because the user contact was directly through a mobile number, which was already in the mobile user's general phone contact list. Therefore, the contact may not have been stored on the application itself.

Figure 5. Cyberdust application in MOBILedit.

Some data was recovered from the 'Passwords' section within the generated report as shown in Figure 6. The "Password" had the label of "PhoneNumber". The data itself was the mobile user's unencrypted phone number. No other data was found in the passwords section of the report. Since the phone number was stored by the application, it shows evidence of a user account on the mobile device.

Figure 6. Phone number recovery in Cyberdust.

The last application MOBILedit investigated on the mobile device was Confide [19]. Figure 7 displays Confide within the application list generated by MOBILedit. Unlike Snapchat and Cyberdust, the generated report displayed no information on contacts or accounts within Confide. Similar to the finding by Oxygen, Figure 6 suggests that there was little evidence that the mobile device had an account with the application.

Figure 7. Confide application data MOBILedit.

Figure 8. Phone number and password artefacts in Confide.

Figure 8 displays the mobile number and the password artefact recovered from the application. The account was the mobile user's unencrypted phone number, and the password was the user password for the created account for the application. The password was also unencrypted. This suggested that the application have stored the user password unsafely.

C. *Evaluation of findings*

Both tools used in the mobile investigation output slightly different results. While neither recovered messages from the ephemeral applications tested, both of them recovered artefacts elsewhere. Oxygen and MOBILedit successfully recovered data on all applications: Snapchat, Cyberdust and Confide. While different artefacts and data were detected, the fact that no physical copies of messages were recovered in any application, using either of the forensic tools, proves how efficient ephemeral applications are at protecting user privacy. Oxygen detected offensive words being sent/received, this would be useful within a cyberbullying case, even though the message itself was not recovered. The evidence detected of communication between the mobile user and another contact would also prove useful as the application would be able to tell detectives who the mobile user had been in contact with. This would also be useful in a cyberbullying case, as there would be evidence the 'bully' had contact with the victim.

Furthermore, the detection of Cloud messaging within Cyberdust suggested that although physical messages were not recovered within the application, the messages could have been uploaded elsewhere to a Cloud network and access could be gained through the network. This would provide a chance for messages to perhaps be recovered in a cyberbullying case.

For Confide, Oxygen displays the password in encrypted format, while the MOBILedit shows it in unencrypted format. MOBILedit also recovered an unencrypted version of the registered mobile number, which Oxygen could not. For the Snapchat, MOBILedit detected account data, such as the mobile user's username and the contact list within the application. However, MOBILedit failed to detect other evidences, such as offensive words, evidence of communication between the mobile user and another contact, and the evidence of a message being deleted.

D. *NIST Measurements*

MOBILedit met all nine NIST measurement requirements tested in this research, while Oxygen did not, yet Oxygen did meet most of them. Comparisons of all nine test cases have been reported in Table 3.

TABLE III. NIST TEST RESULTS

Measurements tested	**NIST test assertions applications Were the requirements met? (Y = Yes N = No)**	
	Oxygen Forensic Detective Enterprise	***MOBILedit Forensic Express***
MDT-CA-01	Y	Y
MDT-CA-02	N	Y
MDT-CA-03	N	Y
MDT-CA-04	N	Y
MDT-CA-05	Y	Y
MDT-CA-06	Y	Y
MDT-CA-07	Y	Y
MDT-CA-08	Y	Y
MDT-CA-09	Y	Y

Oxygen provided the user with a "Select All" individual data objects (MDT-CA-02) while completing the logical/filesystem acquisition, it also provided the ability to "Select Individual" data objects (MDT-CA-03) for acquisition; in both of these cases MOBILedit failed. In another test case (MDT-CA-04), where Oxygen had a success over MBOILedit was during data acquisition, when connectivity between the mobile and tool was disrupted; a notification was given to alert the user. Both tools could successfully present all supported data elements in useable formats via preview pane or generated report, as required by NIST measurement test id MDT-CA-05. Both tools also reported other test cases, such as reporting equipment related information (MDT-CA-09) and hash values for the data objects (MDT-CA-09).

V. CONCLUSION

To conclude, this forensic investigation was successful in how it was carried out, it followed professional ACPO guidelines [16], the tools were tested against NIST measurements, and the whole investigation was forensically sound. However, no full ephemeral messages were recovered with either of the tools, but other significant artefacts were found which proved rather interesting to the investigation and to potential cyberbullying cases. One significant finding was that of the Snapchat's 'offensive words' detection, which may help aid evidence in cyberbullying cases to prove inappropriate language may have been used towards a victim. In forensic investigations, the investigators have to look very deep into the data and have a lot of patience, as one small piece of evidence could change the case, such as the offensive word. On reflection, a physical acquisition may have provided a much more thorough investigation to recover deleted data, but that can be tested in future work. Also, in the future more tools can be compared in recovering evidential data from a wide range of ephemeral applications.

REFERENCES

[1] GSMA, *Number of Mobile Subscribers Worldwide Hits 5 Billion*. [Online]. Available from: https://www.gsma.com/newsroom/press-release/number-mobile-subscribers-worldwide-hits-5-billion/ [Accessed: 07- Aug- 2019].

[2] C. Cotta, A.J. Fernandez-Lelva, F. Fernandez de Vega and F. Chavez, "Application Areas of Ephemeral Computing: A Survey" in 'Transactions on Computational Collective Intelligence': David Camacho, University of Malaga, pp. 155-157, 2016.

[3] I. Barker, *Cyber criminals turn to messaging apps following dark web crackdown*, Betanews, 2017. [Online]. Available from: https://betanews.com/2017/10/25/criminals-turn-to-messaging/ [Accessed: 07- Aug- 2019]

[4] T. Alyaha and F. Kausar, "Snapchat Analysis to Discover Digital Forensic Artefacts on Android Smartphone", 8th International Conference on Ambient Systems, Networks and Technologies, ANT-2017 and the 7th International Conference on Sustainable Energy Information Technology, SEIT 2017, 16-19 May 2017, Madeira, Portugal, pp. 1035-1040, 2017.

[5] J. Charteris, S. Gregory, Y. Masters and M. Maple, "Snapchat at school – 'Now you see it…': Networked affect – cyber bullying, harassment and sexting", Innovation, Practice and Research in the Use of Educational Technologies in Tertiary Education 33rd International Conference, University of South Australia, Adelaide, Australia, pp. 111-114, November 2016.

[6] S. Cook, *Cyberbullying facts and statistics for 2016-2018*, 2018. [Online]. Available from: https://www.comparitech.com/internet-providers/cyberbullying-statistics/ [Accessed: : 07- Aug-2019]

[7] Oxygen Forensics, *Oxygen Forensic Detective Enterprise*, [Online]. Available from: https://www.oxygen-forensic.com/en/products/oxygen-forensic-detective-enterprise [Accessed: : 07- Aug- 2019].

[8] MOBILedit Forensic, *MOBILedit Forensic Express*, [Online]. Available from: https://www.mobiledit.com/online-store/forensic-express [Accessed: : 07- Aug- 2019].

[9] D. Walnycky, I. Baggili, A. Marrington, J. Moore and F. Breitinger, "Network and device forensic analysis of Android social-messaging applications", The Proceedings of the Fifteenth Annual DFRWS Conference, USA, pp. S77-S84, August 2015.

[10] V. Vijayan, *Android Forensic Capability and Evaluation of Extraction Tools*, 2012. [Online]. Available from: https://www.academia.edu/1632597/Android_Forensic_Capability_and_Evaluation_of_Extraction_Tools [Accessed : 07- Aug- 2019]

[11] K. M. Ovens and G. Morison, Forensic analysis of kik messenger on ios devices. Digital Investigation, vol. 17, pp. 40-52, 2016.

[12] M. Al-Hadadi and A. AlShidhani, "Smartphone Forensics Analysis: A Case Study", International Journal of Computer and Electrical Engineering, vol. 5, pp. 577-579, 2013.

[13] M. A. H. B. Azhar and T. Barton, "Forensic Analysis of Secure Ephemeral Messaging Applications on Android Platforms", Jan. 2017, doi: 10.1007/978-3-319-51064-4.

[14] R. Umar, I. Riadi and G. Zamroni, "Mobile Forensic Tools Evaluation for Digital Crime Investigation", International Journal on Advanced Science, Engineering and Information Technology, vol. 8, pp. 949-955, 2018.

[15] Panda Security, *What is an online troll?*, 2017. [Online]. Available from: https://www.pandasecurity.com/mediacenter/security/what-is-an-online-troll/ [Accessed: 07- Aug- 2019].

[16] ACPO, *ACPO Good Practice Guide for Digital Evidence*, 2012. [Online]. Available from: https://www.digital-detective.net/digital-forensics-documents/ACPO_Good_Practice_Guide_for_Digital_Evidence_v5.pdf [Accessed: 07- Aug- 2019].

[17] Omnicore , *Snapchat by the Numbers: Stats, Demographics & Fun Facts*, [Online]. Available from: https://www.omnicoreagency.coma/snapchat-statistics/ [Accessed: 07- Aug- 2019].

[18] Dust, *The APP that protects your assests*, [Online]. Available from: https://usedust.com/ [Accessed: 07- Aug-2019].

[19] Confide, *Your Confidential Messenger*, [Online]. Available from: https://getconfide.com/ [Accessed: 07- Aug- 2019]

[20] Forensic Focus, *MOBILedit Forensic Express From Compelson*, 2018. [Online]. Available from: https://forensicfocus.com/c/aid=229/reviews/2018/mobiledit-forensic-express-from-compelson/ [Accessed: 07- Aug-2019]

[21] National Institute of Standards and Technology, *Mobile Device Tool Test Assertions and Test Plan, 2016*. [Online]. Available from: https://www.nist.gov/sites/default/files/documents/2017/05/09/mobile_device_tool_test_assertions_and_test_plan_v2.0.pdf [07- Aug- 2019].

[22] FireBase Messaging, *Firebase Cloud Messaging*, [Online]. Available from: https://firebase.google.com/docs/cloud-messaging [Accessed: 07- Aug- 2019]

Recovery of Forensic Artefacts from a Smart Home IoT Ecosystem

M A Hannan Bin Azhar and Samuel Benjamin Louis Bate
School of Engineering, Technology and Design
Canterbury Christ Church University
Canterbury, United Kingdom
Email: hannan.azhar@canterbury.ac.uk; sblbate@gmail.com

Abstract— **This paper reports an investigation into a modern smart-environment ecosystem comprising of multiple Internet of Things devices: Amazon Echo, Nest Indoor Camera and Philips Hue smart-bulb. As of yet, there is still little to no documentation, nor established methodology for the examination, acquisition and documentation of evidentiary artefacts from a smart-environment. Much of the research still remains individual to each device and does not incorporate the "melting pot" reality of most smart-environments. The methodology outlined in this paper was artefact-centric, and was purposely designed to facilitate the creation, discovery and documentation of network-native, cloud-native and device-native artefacts. Whilst not all aspects of the investigation were successful, a strong groundwork of documentation of the artefacts present on each of the smart-devices examined has been compiled, so as to inform and lay the foundations for future studies on this area of research.**

Keywords- Internet of Things Forensics; Internet of Things ecosystem forensics; Digital forensics; Smart Home; Internet of Things; Amazon Alexa; Nest Camera; Smart-Bulb.

I. INTRODUCTION

It has been forecasted that by 2022 smart-homes will number half a billion equating to 22.5% of households globally [1], with Internet connected devices numbering as many as 100 billion [2] by 2020. Increasingly these smart-devices have been used to automate our daily lives from scheduling of alarms that coincides with the level of lighting in the bedroom to become a hub for the social media or to order goods and services in a quick and convenient manner. However, with the ever-growing importance and reliance placed on these devices, the security and privacy concerns, widely reported [3][4] from these devices, cannot be ignored. Personal data, such as addresses, contact details and banking information are all stored in some manner by these devices, and can be recalled by the device at any given time to process a command contextually relevant to that information. The inherent weakness of these devices due to their lack of dedicated defense leaves them susceptible to outside unauthorised access by attackers, as seen by the rise of botnet Distributed Denial-of-Service (DDoS) attacks, most notably in the Mirai botnet, wherein devices were hijacked, enslaved and utilised to cause chaos and damage on a widespread scale [3]. Thus, criminals are targeting these devices to commit a new form of burglary, which necessitates the need for forensic investigation of home Internet of Things (IoT) devices with aim to recover potential wealth of evidence by the law enforcement agencies [4]. There are generally three areas of interest to a digital forensic investigator when examining a device for artefacts of evidentiary value, specifically how and when the device might have communicated or otherwise logged an event. These three categories of interest are communications or events specific to the device itself, known as device native artefacts; communications made across a shared network, known as network native artefacts and communications between the device and a service via the cloud, known as cloud-native artefacts [5]. Even though some authors reported extraction of artefacts from smart IoT devices [5][6][7], there is lack of research reporting investigation of a smart eco-system connecting a wide range of devices. Ecosystems created by a range of interconnected devices can be complex due to their heterogeneous nature [5]. The results presented in this paper will demonstrate retrieval and interpretation of numerous network, cloud native and device specific artefacts taken from a smart-environment consisting of a range of devices, specifically by including a smart bulb, Philips Hue smart-bulb [8], which was not explored before. Other IoT devices in the smart environment were Amazon Echo [9], a Nest Indoor Security Camera [10] and an Android smartphone [11].

The remainder of the paper will be organised as follows: Section 2 of this paper reviews existing work on forensic investigations of Smart IoT devices. A brief explanation on the methodology used will be discussed in Section 3. Results and analysis will be reported in Sections 4 and 5. Finally, Section 6 concludes the paper.

II. LITERATURE REVIEW

Apthorpe et al. [7] conducted their investigation upon a "melting pot" [12] smart-environment, utilising a Nest Camera, a Sense Sleep Monitor, and a WeMo Switch smart-plug. Their investigation was conducted from the perspective of a passive observer to a network, such as a system administrator or an Internet Service Provider (ISP). During the experiment, they found that using a packet sniffing software they were able to reliably obtain evidence of the presence and activity of these devices on the network, namely through communications between the devices and their respective companies' domains. They noted that the Sense Sleep Monitor, through its communications with those domains, left a tangible trail of artefacts that an observer to the system would easily be able to identify and subsequently discover the wearers activity [7]. Sleeping patterns were also able to be identified, such as times the wearer would go to bed and wake up in the morning, or during the night.

Chung et al. [5] were also able to identify cloud-native artefacts produced by the Amazon Echo during its usage due to its reliance on Internet services throughout its operation which they could access through unofficial Application Programming Interfaces (APIs) [13]. Another online source, Piette [14], has extensively documented the APIs for the Amazon Echo, which are integral to the daily operation of the device and could potentially hold valuable evidence to a digital forensic investigation. It is possible to view a user's data that is stored in the cloud through these APIs, and each piece of user data is assigned as a "card" by Amazon for storage. Organisation of user data by Amazon means it is easy to search through these artefacts to locate user data, and discern the time and date of actions performed by the user, as well as the type of actions performed. However, these cards do not last usually more than a few days [14] and this severely limits their evidentiary potential as there is only a matter of hours for an investigator to discover them before the artefacts are lost forever.

As with Chung et al. [5], Dorai et al. [6] similarly were able to find client-native artefacts present in their investigation of a Nest device smart-environment with a focus on Internet Protocol (IP) enabled security cameras. A vast number of artefacts were retrieved that provided evidence of the Nest companion app having been used on a device. As reported by Dorai et al. [6], whilst artefacts of evidentiary value could be retrieved, the detection algorithm employed by the IP camera devices, unless fine-tuned by the owner, produces a great number of false-positives as well as false-negatives through either reporting events. As such, the artefacts produced by the operation of the device should be examined in conjunction with other sources of evidence where possible, so as to validate that neither a false-positive, nor false-negative, occurred. Ji et al. [15] corroborated these findings in their own investigation into IP cameras and in developing a tool named HomeSpy, and were able to monitor the network and cloud-native artefacts produced by such devices, proving that monitoring of these artefacts bears a great evidentiary value to the investigators.

III. METHODOLOGY

The study detailed in this paper analyses a smart environment consisting of an Amazon Echo [9], a Philips Hue smart-bulb [8], a Nest Indoor Security Camera [10] and an Android smartphone [11]. The Android Operating System (OS) was selected for its market dominance [16], representing a higher likelihood of its involvement in a crime-scene. The environment in which the testing took place was designed to emulate a smart-home ecosystem, with the devices all set-up and connected to a home network, as shown in Figure 1. At the center of the ecosystem was the router and hub that connected the devices across the network and Internet, either through Wi-Fi or a wired connection. The Philips Hue system uses a hub, so there is no direct communication between the smart phone and the smart light bulbs, as the commands to the bulb goes through the hub via the Zigbee protocol. As all the traffic was broadcasted over the network, by connecting an observation machine via a wired ethernet to the hub allows capturing and analysis of packets for the examination.

The smartphone was used within the environment, as a controller for the devices, to simulate a user's interaction within the smart-home. In addition to controlling the devices via the smartphone, If This Then That (IFTTT) [17] application was used to create interactions between smart-devices, known as 'recipes', in which an action on one triggers another. Using the mobile to control the devices, and the IFTTT to link their interactions with one another, evidentiary artefacts were created on the smartphones, the devices, the network and cloud with the aim to be retrieved and examined. As shown in Figure 1, listed beneath the Cloud, Android mobile and Laptop are the tools, utilities, applications and other possible locations where evidence might be produced during the experiment. Due to the nature of the experiment, a private network was used to limit the amount of unwanted traffic occurring across it, which would otherwise potentially obscure the examination of artefacts transmitted.

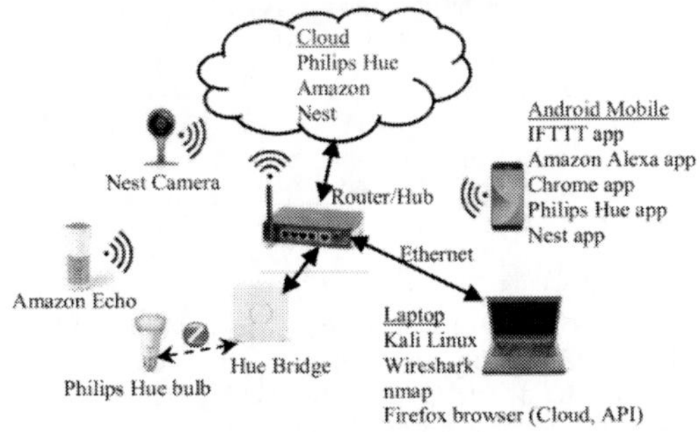

Figure 1. A Smart-Home ecosystem.

The examination of the devices was structured in several stages, each taking its own form and artefact-centric. The main objective of the investigation was not to apportion guilt for a crime committed within a smart-environment, but to provide an overview for what artefacts are generated by smart-devices during their daily usage. First and foremost was the passive observation of the devices whilst in use, as in Apthorpe et al. [7], to observe and record network-native artefacts, such as communications instigated by the devices to external services and IP addresses during their usage. This observation was conducted with the network traffic analysis software Wireshark [18] running on a laptop with Kali Linux [19], an OS used in forensic investigations, which comes with many useful utilities and tools pre-installed.

The next stage of the investigation was concerned with the discovery and documentation of cloud-based artefacts generated during the devices' usage. To investigate these artefacts, several methods were used. Firstly, unofficial APIs for the Amazon Echo [14] were used to allow access to the available data stored by the device in the cloud. Secondly, the user accounts of the smart-devices were accessed to investigate any cloud-native artefacts that might be discoverable through the user account portals of each of the device's respective websites.

The final stage of the investigation involved port-scanning of the devices used to see if any ports were open on them that might allow remote access to the onboard storage of the devices. For this, the 'nmap' utility (on Kali Linux) was used with the 'aggressive' flag, which offers a wider range of information about the device in addition to the visible ports. The aggressive scan allowed the probing of OS detection (-O), version scanning (-sV), script scanning (-sC) and traceroute (--traceroute) on the devices in addition to any open ports that might be exploited to gain access to the devices. The ACPO good practice guidelines [20] state in the first and second principles that in the recovery of data of evidentiary value, the data should not be altered in any way, and if it is, this must be explained and justified. These principles also extend to the physical modification of a device to gain access to data upon it, such as removing an exterior casing from an Amazon Echo to access the on-board storage device, that was otherwise inaccessible. This paper's research strictly adhered to these principles, and as such, no physical modification of the evidence took place.

IV. Results of Network-Native and Device Specific Artefacts

This section reports the artefacts discovered during the passive observation of the network and while using the port scanning to gain remote access to the devices. The results are presented for both network-native and device-specific artefacts.

A. *Amazon Echo*

Network-native artefacts were observed during the usage of the Amazon Echo device in the form of communications created by the device, directed to Internet Protocol version 4 (IPv4) addresses related to Amazon and official third-party advertisement organisations related to Amazon. Upon asking the Amazon Alexa "Alexa, what is the time?" a communication was observed with the Internet Protocol version 4 (IPv4) address "13.32.69.70" (Figure 2), which was identified as a UK based Amazon address using the 'whois' lookup tool included with Kali Linux's terminal. In addition to the UK address, contact was also made with a US address also associated with Amazon. As can be noted in Figure 2, IP addresses similar to "13.32.69.70" were communicated with during the operation; however, these are similarly registered to Amazon Technologies with a range of IP addresses having been reserved and registered for communications purposes.

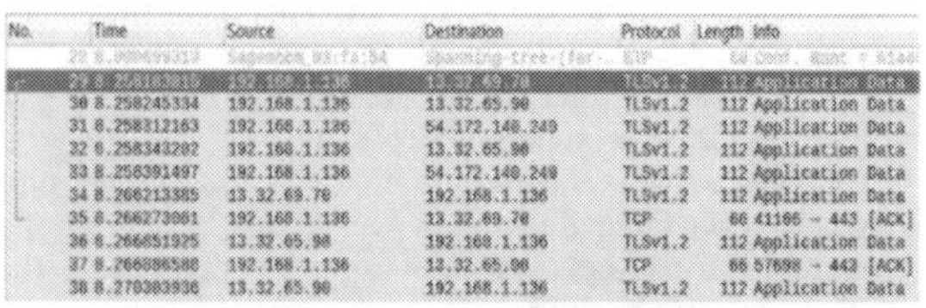

Figure 2. IPv4 address related to Amazon.

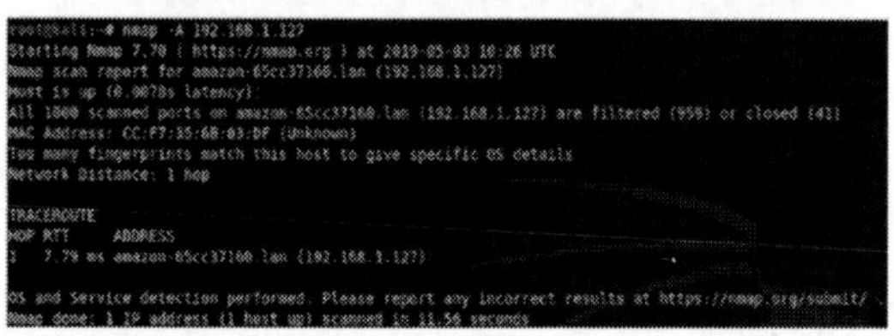

Figure 3. Port scan of the Amazon Alexa.

The aggressive port scanning of Amazon Alexa revealed that it was largely locked down (Figure 3). This is to be expected of Amazon Echo, which handles sensitive personal information, such as the user's full name and email address. Due to the closed ports, displayed during the scan in Figure 3, there were no access points to enter the device's on-board storage remotely.

B. *Nest Indoor Security Camera*

In order to create network-native artefacts from the Nest camera, live streaming of the camera's feed and its ability to play audio, recorded from the mobile controller's microphone, were used; however, no artefacts were visible across the network.

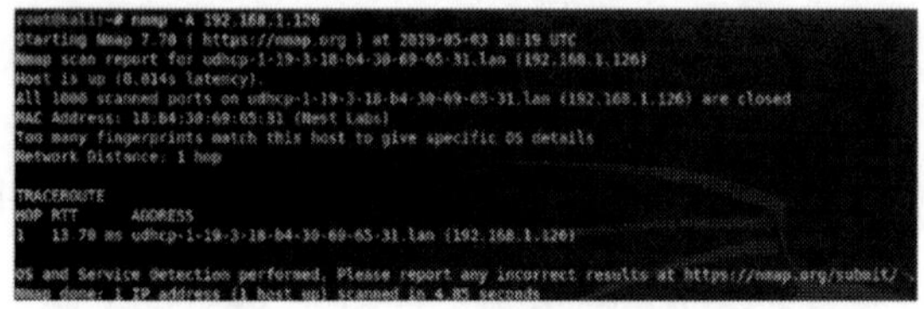

Figure 4. Port scan of the Nest camera.

Aggressive scanning of the camera revealed that all 1000 scanned ports were closed, as shown in Figure 4. This indicates that the device received the querying packets sent during the scan and responded with a packet, indicating there was no service active or listening on that port [21]. As with the Amazon Echo, the lack of discovered open ports meant that there was no way to remotely access the device's on-board storage.

C. *Philips Hue smart-bulbs and bridge*

With regards to the Philips Hue smart-bulb, using the 'nmap' utility, the Philips Hue smart-bulb bridge was identified, as evidenced by Figure 5.

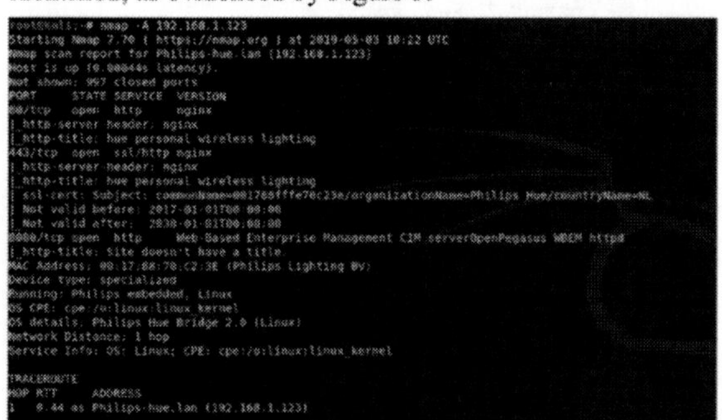

Figure 5. Port scan of Philips Hue smart-bulb bridge.

The aggressive scanning revealed that the Philips Hue smart-bulb bridge had three open ports, these ports were for "http" and "ssl/http" services. Moreover device-native artefacts were present in the scan of the Philips Hue smart-bulb bridge in Figure 5, specifically in the form of details of the Linux-based OS, Philips Hue Bridge 2.0, the device was operating on. The webserver listening on the port 80 of the bridge carry an inherently weak form of security due to the way it allows user to control the bulbs [22]. Given that a malware or an attacker can see the history of devices previously connected to the local area network using the 'arp' command, access to the bulb can be easily gained through the hashing of a whitelisted Media Access Control (MAC) address.

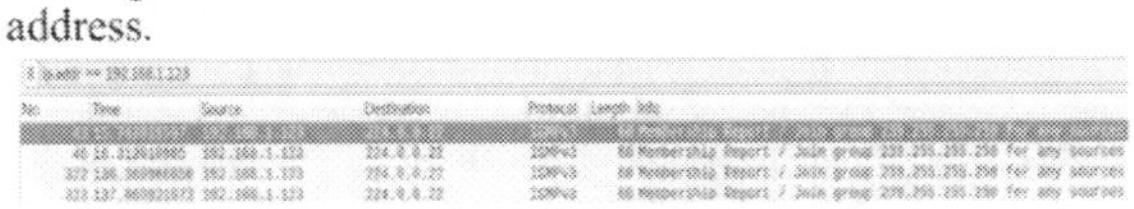

Figure 6. Wireshark observation of smart-bulb bridge.

Controlling the device using the Philips Hue smart-phone application, the bulbs were turned on and off several times in an attempt to simulate an attack of hacking and controlling of the smart bulbs, causing them to flash. It was observed via the Wireshark's report, as shown in Figure 6, that the device left traces of the activity on the network by making several "Membership Report/Join group" requests during the event. The significance of these artefacts would be that to an investigator, midway through such an attack there would be clear evidence of its occurrence upon the network.

D. Artefacts from Multiple Devices

IFTTT was used in the experiment to connect multiple devices to observe how they interact with one another on a network level. The application allows users to make 'recipes', which are essentially if/then statements. In the case of the experiment, the setup was that when the Amazon Echo's timer ended, the Philips Hue smart-bulbs would flash on and off.

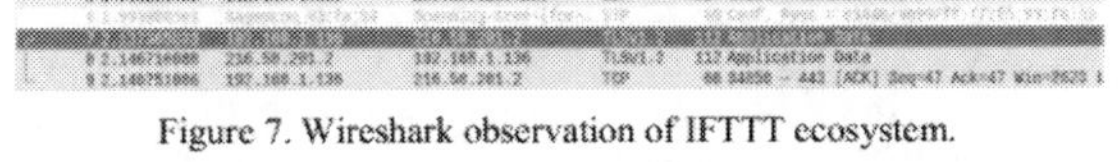

Figure 7. Wireshark observation of IFTTT ecosystem.

Figure 7 shows a Wireshark observation of the Echo's timer reaching zero, triggering the Philips Hue smart-bulbs to flash on and off. As can be seen in the final three events, application data is detected originating from the Philips Hue smart-bulb bridge, which contacts the IP address "216.58.201.2". A simple 'whois' lookup of this IP reveals this to be a Google registered IP address.

With regards to the network-native artefacts, it is worth noting that the Amazon Echo proved to be the 'loudest' device on the network, generating a mass of network-native artefacts, while communicating not only with servers owned by Amazon but with the third-parties for the purpose of advertisement. It appeared that a single command invoked on the Amazon Echo generated more traffic and network-native artefacts than that of when the rest of the devices were put together.

V. RESULTS OF CLOUD-NATIVE ARTEFACTS

This section reports the artefacts discovered in the cloud storage generated by each device while they were used in the smart environment. Results are categorised by each device type.

A. Amazon Echo

There were many recorded examples of cloud-native artefacts created in the usage of the Amazon Alexa device, of which seven separate categories of artefacts could be observed. The artefact categories were as follows: customer status, authentication, bluetooth, music account details, provider capabilities, third party consent and devices listed to the Amazon account. It primarily concerns the initial setup of the user's Amazon Account with that device with flags, such as "countryOfResidenceSet", "eulaAcceptance" and "preferredMarketplaceSet".


```
{"authenticated":true,"canAccessPrimeMusicContent":false,
,"customerEmail":"sbl082forensic@gmail.com","customerId":
"A1UPCFISGWVC05","customerName":"sbl082 forensic"}
```


Figure 8. Alexa Authentication Artefact.

Figure 8 displays the Authentication artefact. This artefact seems to concern whether or not the user's account is authenticated ("authenticated:true"), presumably via a confirmation email following sign-up as well as other information specific to the user's account, such as their email address, name and Amazon ID. Additionally, the status of the user is also listed (whether or not they have Amazon Prime membership) labelled as "canAccessPrimeMusicContent".


```
forensic","primeStatus":false,"service":"AUDIBLE"}
[{"associated":true,"customerId":"A1UPCFISGWVC05",
 "email":"sbl082forensic@gmail.com",
 "firstName":"sbl082forensic"
 "primeStatus":false,"service":"CLOUD_PLAYER"}]
 forensic","primeStatus":false,"service":"TUNE_IN"}]
```


Figure 9. Alexa Music account detail.

Figure 9 displays some of the artefacts from the registered account's music details. Information, such as the customer's identity, personal information and their prime membership status can be seen identified here. Moreover, associated services that can be accessed such as "AUDIBLE", "CLOUD_PLAYER", and "TUNE_IN" are listed here. Amongst other artefacts recovered were Alexa's Bluetooth, Provider Capabilities and Device artefacts. This concerns the Bluetooth connectivity of the Amazon Echo, and details the device's serial number and the software version operating on the device. Provider Capabilities detail what control applications, such as "AUDIBLE" can have over the Alexa device, such as "bookmarkSong" as well as the capability to use the search functions ("canSearchForStationByArtist") on the device. Device artefact lists the Alexa device associated with a user's Amazon account and contains information regarding the name of the device ("“accountName”") as well as services that might be run from the device including "TIMERS_AND_ALARMS", "VOLUME_SETTING" and "VOICE_TRAINING".

B. Nest Indoor Security Camera

Numerous cloud-native artefacts were observed during the experimentation period due to Nest's reliance on an always-online connection to the Internet to allow the device to communicate with the Nest's servers. Cloud-native artefacts for Nest Camera consisted of hours of raw video footage saved to the cloud storage, which is viewable both through the Nest companion application and website. In addition to the raw hours of footage from the camera, the device also flags when movement is detected within the frame and is able to recognise when a person enters the frame and bookmarks that footage (as 'Events') for viewing at a later time.

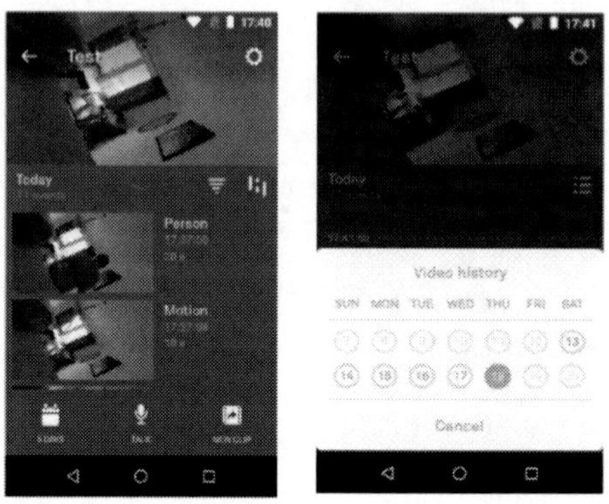

Figure 10. Nest Application on Android.

Figure 10 is a screenshot of the Nest application on Android, viewing the cloud-native 'events' artefacts. As can be seen, the service is able to distinguish between motion and people within a scene, which it stores for review by the owner. It also shows the wider number of cloud-native artefacts available to be viewed, which are raw footage recordings from previous days. It was also found that with the Nest Aware membership, up to 30 days of raw footage recorded from the user's Nest device can be saved to Nest's servers for viewing at a later time.

C. Philips Hue smart-bulb

Interestingly, it appears that the Philips Hue smart-bulb and its associated bridge remain permanently linked to any previous accounts and applications authorised upon them, by any previous owner. Therefore, the new owner of the bulb would have access to personal information, such as names and email addresses of the previous owner. These artefacts can be accessed by any account associated with the bridge, as evidenced by the screen-capture in Figure 11, where a previous owner's name and email address have been blackened out. Similarly, trace of one of the author's personal email address, sblbate@gmail.com, was also found, as it was used in a prior installation of the Hue Bridge.

Retrieval of personal data associated with previous owners would constitute a data breach under the General Data Protection Regulation (GDPR), as both names and email addresses are deemed personal data according to the GDPR guidelines [23]. Even though, finding a suspect's details, as a possible previous user of the device, can be of great interest to an investigator, it should be noted that removing an associated account with the bridge is relatively simple task; as such, anti-forensics measures could be employed by a suspect by deleting their account or unlinking their account from the bridge.

Figure 11. Philips Hue's Other users Artefacts.

Product ID	hb70c23eacb1b45a	Ethernet MAC Addr	00:17:88:70:c2:3e
Model	BSB002	Internal IP Address	192.168.1.123
Firmware version	1931140050	Netmask	255.255.255.0
ID	001788fffe70c23e	Gateway	192.168.1.254

Figure 12. Philips Device specific artefacts on Cloud.

Figure 12 demonstrates example artefacts unique to the Philips Hue Bridge device captured from the Philips Hue website. In this case, it is possible to view the device's MAC address, its firmware version and unique identity. In addition to this, it is also possible to view the IP address and Gateway currently associated with the bridge. Further investigation on artefacts revealed that naming of the application "hue_ios_app#A**********'s iPhone" demonstrate that the application includes the host device's name set by the user, which can provide further evidence of which device the application was used on.

VI. CONCLUSIONS AND FUTURE WORK

This paper reports a large number of artefacts from various devices, especially by using a smart bulb in the ecosystem, with the IFTTT application used in the experiment to connect multiple devices to observe how they interact with one another. Even though the recovery of the device-native artefacts were limited due to the closure of any port for the remote access, numerous artefacts were discovered and documented on a network and cloud level; which includes personal details, logged video footage, and details of previous owners. These artefacts, when applied to a real-world investigation, have significant importance to identifying the implied ownership of the devices through personal information tied to these devices and stored on cloud servers. It is interesting to note that they all contain a great degree of personal information that would provide strong evidence to an investigator seeking to prove the identity of the owner. In the case of the Amazon Echo, its extensive documentation of a wide range of personal information was documented, e.g. email addresses, full names and agreements made including End User License Agreements (EULAs), authorisations for third-party music and streaming services, etc.

Nest (like Amazon) had a wealth of cloud-native artefacts available for viewing to an investigator. Though, where it did not have much in the way of addresses and names, it did offer up to five days of recorded footage. This footage came complete with periods of interest, automatically flagged up for quick and convenient viewing, further categorised into alerts caused by a person in the frame and identified motion.

The Philips Hue smart-bulb and bridge continued the trend of storing large swathes of personal data in its cloud-native artefacts, tying accounts used in the past to the Philips Hue bridge and, in a sense, merging them together. As covered in the literature review, IoT devices typically are lacking when it comes to security, and the Philips Hue bridge seems to be no exception to this. It not only stores personal information but collates multiple users of a unique device into one shared hub, in which any user can view the information of others.

Whilst there was not a specific focus upon testing anti-forensics measures, anti-forensics must form a core component of any future research, building upon the foundation that this study provides. Moreover, to broaden the scope of the study, a wider range of mobile platforms including iOS should be explored to see what client-native artefacts can be recovered from Apple's Operating System and hardware, and to compare the differences, if any, between Android and iOS. Furthermore, future research should endeavour to develop an IoT specific forensic tool, so that majority of the investigation in this paper can be automated, enabling quicker retrieval of artefacts from the smart home ecosystem.

REFERENCES

[1] R. De Renesse, *Smart Home Devices Forecast Report: 2017-22 | Ovum Link, Ovum.informa.com*. [Online]. Available from: https://ovum.informa.com/resources/product-content/smart-home-devices-forecast-report-201722 (Accessed: 7-Aug-2019)

[2] C. Perera, A. Zaslavsky, P. Christen, and D. Georgakopoulos, "Context Aware Computing for The Internet of Things: A Survey", IEEE Communications Surveys & Tutorials, vol. 16(1), pp. 414-454, 2014, doi: 10.1109/surv.2013.042313.00197.

[3] Z. Whittaker, *Mirai botnet attackers are trying to knock an entire country offline, ZDNet*. [Online]. Available from: https://www.zdnet.com/article/mirai-botnet-attack-briefly-knocked-an-entire-country-offline/ (Accessed: 7-Aug-2019).

[4] E. Casey, "Smart home forensics", Digital Investigation, vol. 13, pp. A1-A2, 2015, doi: 10.1016/j.diin.2015.05.017.

[5] H. Chung, J. Park, and S. Lee, "Digital forensic approaches for Amazon Alexa ecosystem", Digital Investigation, vol. 22, pp. 15-25, 2017, doi: 10.1016/j.diin.2017.06.010.

[6] G. Dorai, S. Houshmand and I. Baggili, "I Know What You Did Last Summer: Your Smart Home Internet of Things and Your iPhone Forensically Ratting You Out", In Proc. of the 13th Int. Conf. on Availability, Reliability and Security, USA, Article 49, 10 pages, 2018, doi: https://doi.org/10.1145/3230833.3232814.

[7] N. Apthorpe, D. Reisman, and N. Feamster, "A Smart Home is No Castle: Privacy Vulnerabilities of Encrypted IoT Traffic", 2017, doi: arXiv:1705.06805.

[8] Philips Hue, *Hue White ambiance Starter kit E27*, [Online]. Available from: https://www.philips.co.uk/c-p/8718696728925/hue-white-ambiance-starter-kit-e27/specifications (Accessed: 7-Aug-2019).

[9] Amazon Echo, *Echo Plus (1st Gen) – With built-in smart home hub (White)*, [Online]. Available from: https://www.amazon.co.uk/Echo-Plus-With-Built-In-Smart-Home-Hub-Black/dp/B01J4IYBI0?th=1 (Accessed: 7-Aug-2019).

[10] Google Nest, *Google Nest Cam Indoor*. [Online]. Available from: https://store.google.com/gb/product/nest_cam_specs (Accessed: 7-Aug-2019).

[11] Android Phone, *Samsung Galaxy J3 (2016)*. [Online]. Available from: https://deviceguides.vodafone.co.uk/samsung/galaxy-j3-2016-android-5-1-1/specifications/ (Accessed: 7-Aug-2019).

[12] I. Vujačić, I. Ognjanović, and R. Šendelj, "SM@RT Home Personal Security and Digital Forensic Issues", The Eight Int. Conf. on Business Information Security, Serbia, October 2016.

[13] Analytic Physics, *Accessing Amazon Echo Data with JavaScript*, [Online]. Available from: http://analyticphysics.com/Diversions/Accessing%20Amazon%20Echo%20Data%20with%20JavaScript.htm (Accessed: 7-Aug-2019).

[14] O. Piette, *The Amazon Echo API*, [Online]. Available from: https://www.piettes.com/the-amazon-echo-api/ (Accessed: 7-Aug-2019).

[15] X. Ji, Y. Cheng, W. Xu and X. Zhou, "User Presence Inference via Encrypted Traffic of Wireless Camera in Smart Homes", Security and Communication Networks, pp. 1-10. 2018, doi: 10.1155/2018/3980371.

[16] Device Atlas, *Android v iOS market share 2019*, [Online]. Available from: https://deviceatlas.com/blog/android-v-ios-market-share (Accessed: 7-Aug-2019)

[17] IFTTT App, [Online]. Available from: https://ifttt.com/ (Accessed: 7-Aug-2019).

[18] Wireshark Website, [Online]. Available from: https://www.wireshark.org/ (Accessed: 7-Aug-2019).

[19] Kali Linux, [Online]. Available from: https://www.kali.org (Accessed: 7-Aug-2019)

[20] ACPO, *ACPO Good Practice Guide for Digital Evidence*, [Online]. Available from: https://www.digital-detective.net/digital-forensics-documents/ACPO_Good_Practice_Guide_for_Digital_Evidence_v5.pdf (Accessed: 7-Aug-2019)

[21] J. Williams, *Port Scanning 101: What It Is, What It Does, Why Hackers Love It, And Why You Will Too*, [Online]. Available from: https://blog.ipswitch.com/port-scanning-101-what-it-is-what-it-does (Accessed: 7-Aug-2019)

[22] N. Dhanjani, *Hacking Lightbulbs: Security evaluations of the Philips Hue Personal Wireless lighting system*, [Online]. Available from: https://www.dhanjani.com/docs/Hacking%20Lighbulbs%20Hue%20Dhanjani%202013.pdf (Accessed: 7-Aug-2019)

[23] GDPR, *GDPR Regulation*, [Online]. Available from: https://eur-lex.europa.eu/legal-content/EN/TXT/PDF/?uri=CELEX:32016R0679 (Accessed: 7-Aug-2019)

International Academy, Research, and Industry Association (IARIA)
412 Derby Way
Wilmington, DE 19810

ISBN 978-1-7138-0049-1

CURRAN ASSOCIATES INC.
proceedings.com

3rd International Conference on Design, Analysis, Manufacturing and Simulation (ICDAMS 2018)

MATEC Web of Conferences Volume 172 (2018)

Chennai, India
6-7 April 2018

edp sciences